PRA

THE USER-FRIEN
FINDING OURSELVES IN THE STORIES OF JESUS

"Reading Marilyn's book is like having a conversation with a dear friend—the kind of friend that is incredibly insightful, laugh-out-loud funny, empathetic; she just 'gets it.' She also has that wonderful quality of inspiring you to become your best self. Her raw, real approach to the scriptures makes them digestible and delightful to study. I especially loved her explanation of "spiritual proprioception" in the chapter about the Sermon on the Mount. So grateful the next installment in the User-Friendly series is here! It's great to pick up the conversation again!"   —Amy Turner

"Wonderful . . . The author has the uncanny ability to make ancient literature relevant to the problems and issues that face me and my family today. I enjoy a book that makes me both smile and think hard—this one did both! The section on needing a more diverse sacrament meeting was hilarious and the section on calling on angels to be dispatched made me reread the section several times and think of my wonderful mother who has been gone for some time but still a part of my life."   —Marc Francis

"*The User-Friendly New Testament* lets readers see Jesus Christ again, for the first time. Through candid storytelling and real-life applications, Faulkner takes readers from wherever they are on the faith spectrum to a deeper understanding of the Savior and His power to fill life with joy. This book brings the New Testament out of the meridian of time and into modern-day life as Faulkner mingles ancient and contemporary realities to show how strikingly relevant Jesus Christ's life and teachings are today. Her wit and candor make it a joy to read."   —Mindi Bullick

"When I read a book, I look for new insights or thoughts I had not considered previously. While the New Testament is very broad, Marilyn delivers in making it "User-Friendly" to the reader. She has selected salient teachings of Christ that we so desperately need today—the Master's principles have not changed or become outdated. I feel Jesus is more of a friend!"   —Michael Sessions

"I love reading Marilyn's perspective on the scriptures because it is practical, approachable, and rooted in a broad and deep knowledge of doctrinal context."   —Michael Potter

"Marilyn has a gift for making parallels between the centuries. Her ability to review scripture lessons Jesus and His disciples taught 2000 years ago and show how they are similar to my experiences, thoughts, shortcomings, and desires today is remarkable! This made me laugh, cry, contemplate, and feel inspired (in 'doable' little ways) to be more like my Savior." —Karen Martin

"Marilyn's User-Friendly scripture series beautifully fills the gap between understanding the deeper meaning of scriptures and figuring out how they apply to our modern lives. We are encouraged to 'liken all scriptures unto ourselves,' and Marilyn's wonderful and unique insights help tremendously in this endeavor. *The User-Friendly New Testament* is filled with deep doctrine, yet the reading is easy, more like a casual chat with a close friend. Her discussions always convey something new and original but the perspectives are so natural nad convincing that they seem like they were already known, just being brought back into view. This series has been the most impactful scripture study help I found in years and has provided practical, everyday helps in my life. I highly recommend them to all students of the gospel." —John Alexander

"If we are commanded to 'liken the scriptures unto ourselves,' there is no better resource than *The User-Friendly New Testament*. Marilyn Green Faulkner seamlessly blends ancient scripture with modern revelation, historical context with contemporary examples, and even peppers in insights from other religious traditions to round out our understanding of these sacred texts. But she doesn't stop there! Ms. Faulkner also draws from psychology, medicine, literature, and even advertising to further illuminate a personal application of the principles found in the Gospels." —Amy J.

"*The User-Friendly New Testament* is a thought-provoking, intellectually stimulating read, but it is so much more than that. It offers very real, practical advice as to how to apply the gospel of Jesus Christ in our daily lives. From making your Sabbath day more meaningful to dealing with loss or tragedy to strengthening your relationship with Jesus Christ, this book contains solutions to life's challenges and, perhaps even more importantly, asks questions to help us start to find answers for ourselves." —Kyle J.

NEW
TESTAMENT

Other books by

MARILYN GREEN FAULKNER

The User-Friendly Old Testament

The User-Friendly Book of Mormon

Back to the Best Books:
A Unique Guide to 36 Great Books
That Enlighten, Inform, and Inspire

NEW TESTAMENT

FINDING OURSELVES IN THE STORIES OF JESUS

MARILYN GREEN FAULKNER

CFI
An imprint of Cedar Fort, Inc.
Springville, Utah

ISBN 13: 978-1-4621-2305-6

Published by CFI, an imprint of Cedar Fort, Inc.
2373 W. 700 S., Springville, UT 84663
Distributed by Cedar Fort, Inc., www.cedarfort.com

Library of Congress Control Number: 2018953609

Cover design by Markie Riley
Cover design © 2018 Cedar Fort, Inc.
Edited and typeset by Allie Bowen and Kaitlin Barwick

Printed in the United States of America

10 9 8 7 6 5 4 3 2 1

Printed on acid-free paper

For our Grandchildren:
Ginger, Rad, Fiona, Beverly, Lucy,
Thomas, Josie, Walker, James,
and those we have yet to meet.
We love every one of you.

Contents

Chapter One:
Introduction: What Was Jesus Really Like? 1

Chapter Two:
The Nativity: Where the Atonement Begins 13

Chapter Three:
What Would Mary Do? 22

Chapter Four:
Matthew: Scaling the Sermon on the Mount 31

Chapter Five:
Mark: A Lesson in Celestial Branding 41

Chapter Six:
A Sabbath-Keeping Self-Help Session 52

Chapter Seven:
Luke: Jesus and the Hero's Journey 61

Chapter Eight:
Knocking on Heaven's Door: The Purpose,
Process, and Power of Prayer 78

Chapter Nine:
John: Jesus, the God of Miracles 93

Chapter Ten:
How to Be Born Again and Again 105

Chapter Eleven:
The Last Supper and Family Traditions 118

Chapter Twelve:
When We Survey the Wondrous Cross 132

Contents

Chapter Thirteen:

Life after Life: The Power of the Resurrection 142

Chapter Fourteen:

How to Act like an Apostle 154

Chapter Fifteen:

Cognitive Dissonance and the Day of Pentecost 165

Chapter Sixteen:

The Rooftop View: How God's Church Works 172

Chapter Seventeen:

Paul's Celestial Road Trip: Our Road to Damascus 183

Chapter Eighteen:

The Adjacent Possible: How Diversity
Enriches the Church 193

Chapter Nineteen:

Superpowers, Spiritual Gifts, and
the Parable of the Talents 207

Chapter Twenty:

Lessons from the Master Minister:
Christ among the Nephites 216

Chapter Twenty-One:

A Sacred Space: Finding Jesus in the Temple 234

Chapter Twenty-Two:

Conclusion: What Would Jesus Really Do? 260

Index 275

About the Author 277

Chapter One

INTRODUCTION: WHAT WAS JESUS REALLY LIKE?

Jesus said, "And this is life eternal, that they might know thee the only true God, and Jesus Christ whom thou hast sent" (John 17:3 KJV).

From a practical standpoint, what does it mean to know Jesus Christ? Our life experiences are far removed from His. Jesus was an Orthodox Jew who lived during the time that Israel was occupied by the Romans. Thus, His life was tightly circumscribed by government control, and He enjoyed few of the freedoms that we take for granted. He was raised in a very small village and probably never traveled more than fifty miles from home during His lifetime, and if He went anywhere, He had to walk. Many of us travel fifty miles or more every day! The earliest written records we have about Him begin decades after His death, and as a result the accounts of His life and travels are somewhat confusing; they do not always tally with each other. So it is difficult to get a day-to-day account of His

> Look for yourself, and you will find in the long run only hatred, loneliness, despair, rage, ruin, and decay. But look for Christ, and you will find Him, and with Him everything else thrown in.
> —C. S. Lewis

activities, as we can with other historical figures. How, then, can we know Jesus?

Though we are hampered in our search to know Jesus by time and circumstance, there are still ways that we can reach across the centuries to Him. For example, we can identify several roles that Jesus filled, and by examining those roles we can get a feel for what His daily routine would have been like. We know that Jesus was a master teacher, who was called "Rabbi" by both His followers and His enemies. We know that He was a miracle worker: accounts of His miraculous healings fill much of the gospel narrative. And we know that He claimed to be, and was acknowledged by many as the promised Messiah, the one anointed to bring God's kingdom to the earth. A closer look at these three facets of His identity may give us a better knowledge of Him.

JESUS THE RABBI

"Rabbi" comes from the Hebrew word *rav,* which in Jesus's day meant something like "master." It was a term of respect and did not necessarily connect the designee to a particular congregation.[1] In first-century Judaism there were many itinerant rabbis who traveled from town to town, teaching and gathering disciples. Commentator David Bivin posits that as a child prodigy, Jesus would early have drawn the attention of the best theological minds of His day and would have undoubtedly received formal rabbinical training toward such a vocation. A description of rabbinical training from around this time gives us a sense of the path that a bright young scholar like Jesus would have followed:

> At five years of age, one is ready for the study of the Scripture, at ten years of age one is fit for the study of the Mishnah, at the age of thirteen for bar mitzvah, at the age of fifteen for the study of Talmud, at the age of eighteen for marriage, at the age of twenty for pursuing

---

1. Roy Blizzard and David Bivin, "Study Shows Jesus as Rabbi," *Bible Scholars*, accessed August 24, 2018, http://www.biblescholars.org/2013/05/study-shows-jesus-as-rabbi.html.

a vocation, at the age of thirty for entering into one's full vigor . . .
(Avot 5:21).[2]

David Bivin explains that although the term "rabbi" is anach-
ronistic, it may be the most helpful in portraying Christ appropriately as a teacher of scripture prominent enough to attract His own
students.

> By the time Jesus began his public ministry, he had not only received
> the thorough religious training typical of the average Jew of his day,
> he had probably spent years studying with an outstanding sage (or
> sages) in the Galilee. Jesus thus appeared on the scene as a respected
> sage himself. He was recognized as such by his contemporaries, as
> passages in the New Testament illustrate.[3]

The Gospel narratives reinforce this picture of Jesus as an itinerant sage, or rabbi, traveling from place to place, depending on
the hospitality of others, and taking no monetary compensation for
His teaching. He was called "Rabbi" by Jewish leaders as well as by
the common people: they expected Him to offer commentary on
scripture, to have followers, and to organize informal meetings. We
can visualize the Savior in these settings, because many of them are
described for us. He was not just wandering around; He was following a pattern of rabbinical teaching that was very familiar to the
people of His day.

Love of God's word is paramount in the life of every Orthodox
Jew, and for Jesus, the study of scripture would have included study
of the Talmud, the compilations of rabbinical commentary on the
law. Jesus followed the traditional pattern of giving commentary
on the law, but His "midrashim" took a totally new direction. The
commentary in the Talmud was designed to ensure that no part of
the law would be violated, and to accomplish this objective many
new regulations were put in place. Jesus was not the first to describe
this as "putting a hedge around the law": such commentary was

---

2. Ibid.
3. David Bivin, *New Light on the Difficult Words of Jesus: Insights from His Jewish Context*
(Holland, Michigan: En-Gedi Resource Center, 2005), 9.

considered essential for an Orthodox Jew to study and obey. For example, the simple injunction to "not do any work" on the Sabbath had mushroomed into thirty-nine categories of activities that were prohibited, from using two hands to button a button to turning on a stove. But rather than enlarge on this, as most rabbis did, Jesus sharply criticized the Jewish leaders for the confusing concoction of regulations that had strangled the spirit in which the original law was given.

Teaching in the rabbinical style by making comments about the statements in the Torah, Jesus Himself can be described as putting a hedge around the law, but His version of a "hedge" was completely different and quite startling. Because He saw people as capable of rising above the rules and experiencing a complete change of heart, He suggested a reexamination of every commandment from that perspective. For example, rather than enumerating in detail what was "lawful" to do on the Sabbath, He insisted that it was "lawful" simply to do good on that Holy Day. Instead of a thorny hedge of rules and restrictions, He offered a living, growing tree of life, based on the ultimate law of love. Though it was a complete departure from the customary teachings of His day, in its format His teaching was rabbinical, and in substance it was actually in keeping with the original law of Moses. Jewish commentator Amy-Jill Levine writes: "Our responsibility is to love God and to love our neighbour which is what Jesus taught and it's also what Judaism taught—and that would make sense because Jesus was Jewish."[4]

This basic tenet of Judaism had become mired in a slavish devotion to details about when and where and how the law should be obeyed. This, instead of the law itself, had become the center of rabbinic commentary. A few examples of His radical approach suffice to show the difference between the traditional approach of avoiding evil by erecting barriers and Jesus's teaching, which was to change the mind and the heart and let the actions follow:

---

4. Amy-Jill Levine, *Short Stories by Jesus: The Enigmatic Parables of a Controversial Rabbi* (New York: Harper Collins, 2014).

Ye have heard that it was said of them of old time, Thou shalt not kill; and whosoever shall kill shall be in danger of the judgment: But I say unto you, That whosoever is angry with his brother without a cause shall be in danger of the judgment:

Ye have heard that it was said by them of old time, Thou shalt not commit adultery: But I say unto you, That whosoever looketh on a woman to lust after her hath committed adultery with her already in his heart.

Ye have heard that it hath been said, Thou shalt love thy neighbour, and hate thine enemy. But I say unto you, Love your enemies, bless them that curse you, do good to them that hate you, and pray for them which despitefully use you, and persecute you. (Matthew 5:21–22, 27–28, 43–44 KJV)

Though He might not have been assigned to a synagogue, a rabbi was viewed as a leader. People followed these rabbis from place to place to learn from them, and Jesus encouraged this. Not only did Jesus encourage disciples to "come and follow me," He challenged the authority of those members of the Jewish clergy who did have authority. When Jesus said, "Ye have heard," He referred to the formal teaching in the synagogue by the leaders of the Jews. By His challenge of these official statements, He not only taught a new doctrine, He placed Himself in the position of a leader, even a revolutionary. Many of the tense conflicts that took place between Jesus and the official leaders (both Jewish and Roman) arose from His natural authority over others. Even if He did not have jurisdiction over a particular synagogue, Jesus was a rabbi. When He led, people followed.

I am reminded of a humorous moment in the young life of a friend that occurred when he was serving as a missionary in Italy. Their district was meeting in a small rented building in the middle of nowhere, when suddenly the door opened and Thomas Monson, at that time one of the Twelve Apostles, strode into the room. They were, of course, completely surprised, and my friend told me he afterward congratulated himself on his presence of mind. When

Elder Monson demanded to know, "Who is in charge here?" this elder immediately responded, "Well, you are, Sir!"

And thus it was with Jesus. Wherever He went, He was in charge.

JESUS THE MIRACLE WORKER

Very early on in Jesus's ministry, He began to demonstrate control over the physical world. His first miracle was to change water into wine, and on other occasions He miraculously fed thousands of people. He healed people who were known to have suffered maladies for years; He cast the evil spirits out of others who were also well-known members of the community. In at least two cases, He raised someone from the dead in the presence of witnesses. His miracles addressed some of the greatest fears we have in life: fear of starvation, of disease, and of death. It is hard to imagine the impact this must have had on an impoverished populace that faced a daily struggle for survival. "When evening came, many who were demon-possessed were brought to him, and he drove out the spirits with a word *and healed all the sick*" (Matthew 8:16 NIV, italics added).

> *Jesus could have cured the leper with a word. There was no need he should touch him. No need did I say? There was every need. For no one else would touch him. The healthy human hand, always more or less healing, was never laid on him; he was despised and rejected. It was a poor thing for the Lord to cure his body; he must comfort and cure his sore heart. Of all men a leper, I say, needed to be touched with the hand of love.*
>
> —George MacDonald

That one word "all" gives us a sense of the magnitude of Jesus's impact. He wasn't a magician who did tricks; He was a miracle worker. Hundreds of people were healed by Him over the course of His ministry, and as His fame grew, the sick and the afflicted flocked to Him in droves. Jesus appeared to choose His healing moments carefully to demonstrate a higher principle, often choosing outcasts, the marginalized, and those for whom the institutionalized church had no place. Along with alleviating suffering, Jesus used His miracles to show how to live the law of Moses in a new way. A good example of the double impact of His miracles is shown in the episode where He healed the nameless woman with a feminine disorder that, because it involved bleeding, would have made her a permanent outcast.

"And a woman was there who had been subject to bleeding for twelve years, but no one could heal her" (Luke 8:43 NIV). Jesus (and those observing Him as He stopped to touch this woman and speak with her) would have been perfectly familiar with this injunction from Leviticus:

> When a woman has a discharge of her blood many days at a time other than her monthly period or has a discharge that continues beyond her period, she will be unclean as long as she has the discharge, just as in the days of her period. (Leviticus 15:25 NIV)

Jesus chooses this woman as the recipient of His healing power, not only because of her obvious need, but to make a point: A law that was designed to protect the health of the community had become a source of additional heartbreak and suffering. Then, layered on top of this lesson about individual worth is another lesson about social justice. Jesus is enroute to the home of Jairus, head of a family of stature. This woman He has stopped to help is nameless; she is no one. Yet it is for her, as much as for Jairus, that the law of Moses was created, to give each individual importance and value in the eyes of society. Jesus reinforced with His miracles what He taught in His sermons.

One cannot overestimate the importance of Jesus as a miracle worker. Contemporary scholars who attempt to discredit every supernatural event in His life and to portray the miracles as something symbolic or even hallucinatory completely miss the point of what caused people to believe in Jesus. Professor of Judaic Studies, Shaye I. D. Cohen, explains how Christ's miracles set Him apart:

> The core of the gospels is Jesus as the miracle worker, Jesus as a man who made a deep impression upon those who he came in contact

with, his ability to attract large crowds, his ability to attract a dedicated core group of followers or disciples. . . . After all, there presum-
ably were many Galilean teachers or preachers in the first century of
the Common Era. There will have been many who were executed
by Rome as trouble makers or people who are threats to the social
order. They will have been many wandering holy men around about
Judea or even the Roman Empire. But this man clearly was peculiar.
This man clearly made a mark, left an impression, somebody you
didn't forget. Somebody who had power in a social sense. Someone
who actually was able to somehow attract, enchant, and hold a large
group of followers already in his lifetime. [5]

Many readily accepted Jesus as someone with priestly authority, perhaps more because of His miraculous healings than because
of His words. Though Jesus was not a Levite, He was indeed a
priest. He officiated in higher ordinances, forgave sins, and did all
the things priests had basically ceased to do. His frustration as He
"cleansed" the temple can easily be understood when we realize that
He had been performing the blessings and ordinances that should
have been going on there.

The Apostle Paul also saw a direct correlation between the power
of Jesus and His priesthood authority:

> But when Christ came as a high priest of the good things that are
> now already here, he went through the greater and more perfect tab-
> ernacle that is not made with human hands, that is to say, is not a
> part of this creation. He did not enter by means of the blood of goats
> and calves but he entered the Most Holy Place once for all by means
> of his own blood, thus obtaining eternal redemption. The blood of
> goats and bulls and the ashes of a heifer sprinkled on those who are
> ceremonially unclean sanctify them so that they are outwardly clean.
> How much more, then, will the blood of Christ, who through the
> eternal Spirit offered himself unblemished to God, cleanse our con-
> sciences from acts that lead to death, so that we may serve the living
> God! (Hebrews 9:11–14 NIV)

---

5. Shaye I. D. Cohen in "What Can We Really Know about Jesus?: Evaluating the
Fragmentary Evidence," PBS, April 1998, accessed September 10, 2018, https://www
.pbs.org/wgbh/pages/frontline/shows/religion/jesus/reallyknow.html.

After the feeding of the five thousand, the crowd tried to con · Him into providing daily manna as a proof of His divinity. Jesus not only saw through that ruse, but testified of His higher status, not as a teacher of truth, but as the very source of truth.

> Jesus answered, "Very truly I tell you, you are looking for me, not because you saw the signs I performed but because you ate the loaves and had your fill. Do not work for food that spoils, but for food that endures to eternal life, which the Son of Man will give you. For on him God the Father has placed his seal of approval." (John 6:26–28 NIV)

> Jesus said to them, "Very truly I tell you, it is not Moses who has given you the bread from heaven, but it is my Father who gives you the true bread from heaven. For the bread of God is the bread that comes down from heaven and gives life to the world."
> "Sir," they said, "always give us this bread."
> Then Jesus declared, "I am the bread of life. Whoever comes to me will never go hungry, and whoever believes in me will never be thirsty." (John 6:32–35 NIV)

THE ANOINTED MESSIAH

And this leads us to the last role, that of the Anointed One, the Christ, the Promised Messiah. This is the category that separates Jesus from every other itinerant rabbi, great teacher, famed healer, or even miracle worker. Jesus claimed to be the Messiah. As His ministry progressed, He became more outspoken about this role and about being God's divine Son.

For the Jews, whether or not Jesus was the Messiah that was prophesied of was a matter of debate. But Jesus left no question that He saw Himself as that Anointed One. In the last week of His life, He rode into Jerusalem in a direct simulation of a Roman king's triumphal entry; it seems that He was determined to force this comparison. He embodied the triumvirate of prophet, priest, and king, and He knew it. But He was more than that: He was the divine Son of God. He openly said, "My kingdom is not of this world." He was a king, of a divine kingdom.

In the third century, Eusebius spoke of the power of Jesus's anointing.

> That his anointing was divine is proved by the fact that he alone, of all who have ever lived, is known throughout the world as Christ and . . . is honored by his worshipers throughout the world as King, held in greater awe than a prophet, and glorified as the true and only High Priest of God.[6]

Evangelist Billy Graham saw Jesus as the culmination of all the history of Israel. Without Jesus's role as the divinely anointed Messiah, the Old Testament doesn't make sense.

> The prophecies about the Messiah were not a bunch of scattered predictions randomly placed throughout the Old Testament, but they form a unified promise-plan of God, where each promise is interrelated and connected into a grand series comprising one continuous plan of God. Thus, a unity builds as the story of God's call on Israel, and then on the house of David, progresses in each part of the Old Testament.[7]

GETTING TO KNOW THE REAL JESUS

We can read of many different reactions to Jesus. The common people obviously reacted to the benefits of His miracles. Along with their adulation, we have the venomous statements of leaders who were threatened by Jesus, and even the rather offhand remarks of the Roman rulers who wondered why they were so threatened. We have spontaneous testimonies from those who experienced miracles, and the heartfelt testimonies of the Apostles. For me, one of the most convincing things about the New Testament is the number

---

6. Eusebius. *Eusebius: The Church History,* trans. Paul L. Maier (Grand Rapids, MI: Kregel Publications, 2007), 30.
7. Walter C. Kaiser Jr., "The Promise of the Messiah," *Billy Graham Evangelistic Association,* November 22, 2006, https://billygraham.org/decision-magazine/november-2006/the -promise-of-the-messiah.

of negative remarks about Jesus that are recorded there right along with the positive. There is no spin, no attempt at making Him anything other than what He is. It's breathtaking.

Along with a study of His cultural context, His sayings, and His actions, we have another means of knowing Christ that is unique. We can ask His Father about Him. Christ is different from any other being who lived, because He was both divine and human. This means, simply, that we can communicate with God through the medium of the Holy Spirit and ask about Him. He instructs us to ask His Father to help us know Him.

> When Jesus came to the region of Caesarea Philippi, he asked his disciples, "Who do people say the Son of Man is?"
>
> They replied, "Some say John the Baptist; others say Elijah; and still others, Jeremiah or one of the prophets."
>
> "But what about you?" he asked. "Who do you say I am?"
>
> Simon Peter answered, "You are the Messiah, the Son of the living God."
>
> Jesus replied, "Blessed are you Simon son of Jonah, for this was not revealed to you by flesh and blood, but by my Father in heaven." (Matthew 16:13–17 NIV)

We have a special conduit of knowledge to which we may turn; Heavenly Father will teach us about Jesus, through the Holy Spirit. He promises us that, when we ask ourselves, "What would Jesus do?" God, through His Spirit, will reveal Christ to us. Joseph Smith relied upon this gift as he carved out a

In Christ, we see a maturity of love that flowers in self-sacrifice and forgiveness; a maturity of power that never swerves from the ideal of service; a maturity of goodness that overcomes every temptation, and, of course, we see the ultimate victory of life over death itself.
—Vincent Nichols

new theology and taught startling new insights about the role of Jesus Christ:

I have an old edition of the New Testament in the Latin, Hebrew, German and Greek languages. . . . I thank God that I have got this old book; but I thank him more for the gift of the Holy Ghost. I have got the oldest book in the world; but I have got the oldest book in my heart, even the gift of the Holy Ghost. [The Holy Ghost] is within me, and comprehends more than all the world; and I will associate myself with him.[8]

With the Holy Spirit as our guide, let's take a fresh look at the New Testament and try to edge a little closer to knowing the real Jesus. As we do, let's see if we can also find ourselves in these stories, and perhaps gain more understanding about what He would have us do to be worthy followers of Him.

HOW TO USE THIS BOOK

This book is meant as a springboard to help you think about Jesus. We will look at the way the New Testament text was made, because it is brilliant. We will look at the cultural context, because it is important, and we will try to make some connections between our modern, daily dilemmas and the teachings of Jesus. We won't cover every verse or even every book, but hopefully we will touch on some things that will inspire you and enrich your study of the Savior.

You may have already noticed I like to reference various translations of the Bible. Although we in the Latter-day Saint community recognize the King James Version of the Bible as the most correct translation available, I find that some passages are so familiar that my mind tends to wander as I read. Using different translations keeps the language fresh and my mind awake to the message behind the words. When I have quoted directly from the Bible, you will notice in the source that follows a "KJV" for the King James Version or an "NIV" for the New International Version.

---

8. Joseph Smith, "The King Follett Sermon." *Ensign*, April 1971.

Chapter Two

THE NATIVITY: WHERE THE ATONEMENT BEGINS

The Gospels are not biographies, nor are they histories by our modern definition; they are testaments. The purpose of each of the Gospels is (paraphrasing Luke) to take those things that had been written and spoken by the actual witnesses of Jesus's ministry and pass them along to *those who love God's word* (one meaning of the word *Theophilus*[9]) that we "[might] know the certainty of those things, wherein [we have] been instructed" (Luke 1:1–4 KJV).

As a result, we can expect that the stories of Jesus will be presented to us in a deliberate fashion. Each of the Gospels is carefully structured, reflecting the unique perspective of the author. We must shake off the expectation that the accounts will be

Christmas is built upon a beautiful and intentional paradox; that the birth of the homeless should be celebrated in every home.

—G. K. Chesterton

just alike, but instead expect them to be as different as the authors

---

9. Luke Timothy Johnson, *The Writings of the New Testament* (Minneapolis, MN: Fortress Press, 2010), 188.

themselves and appreciate the added depth and breadth they give to our understanding of Christ's mission. This is a good foundation with which to begin an examination of the birth narratives.

MATTHEW: THE NEW MOSES AND THE NEW LAW

Matthew's birth narrative emphasizes the similarities between Christ and Moses, which is a fitting preface to a Gospel that focuses on Christ as the new Moses, the giver of the higher law. Defending Christ's messianic role in a Pharisaic community, Matthew opens with a genealogy that links Jesus to the Davidic line of kings. In addition, the genealogy gives him an opportunity to address the issue of Jesus's lowly birth and even suspicions about His paternity that would have been part of His upbringing.

Though today we revere Mary as a paragon of womanly virtue, this would not have been her experience in daily life. It was not uncommon for betrothed young women to be raped by Roman soldiers, since it was known that their families would protect their reputations by going ahead with the marriage. (Thus sparing the soldier any embarrassing consequences.) Mary became pregnant before she was married, and her claim of a divine father for her son would have been met by more than skepticism. In the eyes of her neighbors, this otherwise virtuous young girl would either have had relations with Joseph, or she might have been a victim of rape. Though Joseph stepped forward and married her, protecting her reputation, people would still have talked, and the taint of scandal would have followed her all through her life.

> One second-century tradition cast Mary as a hairdresser who had an affair with a Roman soldier by the name of Panthe; another imagined her as a prostitute; while a medieval legend suggested that she had been raped. What all these traditions have in common is their stress on Jesus's illegitimacy.[10]

---

10. Helen K. Bond "Who Was the Real Virgin Mary?" *The Guardian*, US Edition, December 19, 2002, https://www.theguardian.com/world/2002/dec/19/gender.uk1.

14

Matthew responds to these scurrilous accusations by stressing the virtue of Mary and the trust Joseph had in her. In addition, in the genealogy of Jesus, Matthew introduces four women: Tamar (1:3), Rahab (1:5), Ruth (1:5), and Bathsheba (simply called "Uriah's wife," 1:6 NIV). Why include these four women among the list of Jesus's ancestors? Scholar Luke Timothy Johnson explains:

> The genealogy helps Matthew deal with Jesus' suspect parentage. All were outsiders to Israel; all were sexually suspect; and through all of them God had worked surprisingly for the salvation of the people. They prepare for the birth of a messiah by the virgin Mary.[11]

The first two chapters of Matthew leave us with a sense of the royal lineage of Jesus whose destiny, like that of Moses, is hidden at first. Born in obscurity, each rises to be God's mouthpiece on earth.

LUKE: THE MARGINALIZED AND THE HOLY SPIRIT

Luke, the Greek chronicler, emphasizes the miraculous virgin birth, so similar in many ways to the Greek legend of Isis and Horus. Rather than seeking to differentiate the two stories, Luke uses that resonance to strengthen the case for Jesus's divinity. Later, as Christianity spread to the Gentiles, temples and shrines once dedicated to Isis (represented in sculpture with her son Horus on her lap) were converted to shrines dedicated to Mary and Jesus.[12]

In addition (perhaps because he was a physician), Luke pays attention to the process of birth, to the afflictions of the people Jesus healed, and to the suffering of the marginalized in society. In Luke's narrative, the itinerant shepherds, not the wealthy Magi, are featured. Above all, Luke notices and records the thoughts and feelings of women, so often neglected in scripture. Throughout his Gospel these preoccupations give us a beautifully balanced reflection of Jesus's impact on everyone around Him.

---

11. Johnson, *The Writings of the New Testament*, 171.
12. Meg Baker, "Isis and the Virgin Mary: A Pagan Conversion," Columbia University, http://www.columbia.edu/~sf2220/Thing/web–content/Pages/meg2.html.

WHAT IS IMPORTANT ABOUT JESUS'S BIRTH?

We know what is important about the death of Christ; it is a vital part of the Atonement. But what about the birth of Christ? We are interested in the births and upbringing of the great figures in history, and Jesus is no exception. About His upbringing we know very little; after considerable detail about His birth, we are told almost nothing about nearly thirty years of Jesus's life. Why then, is so much attention given to the circumstances of His birth?

> *The Almighty appeared on earth as a helpless human baby, needing to be fed and changed and taught to talk like any other child. The more you think about it, the more staggering it gets. Nothing in fiction is so fantastic as this truth of the Incarnation.*
>
> —*J. I. Packer*

As Latter-day Saints we have a third birth narrative in the Book of Mormon. It is in the form of a vision that Nephi is given of Christ's nativity. To understand the role of Christ's birth in the Atonement, we may turn to this third narrative. The context of this vision is presented in such a way that we can readily relate to it: its components symbolize each person's search for faith. Nephi has been taught about the tree of life by his father and decides to seek his own understanding of his father's vision. In fact, he boldly asks "that I might see, and hear, and know of these things, by the power of the Holy Ghost" (1 Nephi 10:17). In response, God gives him far more than he bargained for. The Spirit of the Lord tells Nephi that he is about to be shown a "sign" that will be a sure witness of the divinity of Christ.

> And behold this thing shall be given unto thee for a sign, that after thou has beheld the tree which bore the fruit which thy father tasted, thou shalt also behold a man descending out of heaven, and him shall ye witness; and after ye have witnessed him ye shall bear record that it is the Son of God. (1 Nephi 11:7)

At this point the Spirit simply says, "Look," and Nephi is shown the tree of life from his father's vision.

> I looked and beheld a tree; and it was like unto the tree which my father had seen; and the beauty thereof was far beyond, yea, exceeding of all beauty; and the whiteness thereof did exceed the whiteness of the driven snow. (1 Nephi 11:8)

When he asks to know the interpretation of the tree, Nephi is commanded to once again, "Look!" and beholds the city of Nazareth. Notice that the same describing words are used for both the virgin and the tree: "In the city of Nazareth I beheld a virgin, and she was exceedingly fair and white . . . A virgin, most beautiful and fair above all other virgins" (1 Nephi 11:13, 15).

Now comes the great question, the question the Spirit asks of every person who comes seeking an understanding of the Atonement, and the key to why the birth narratives are crucial parts of the Gospels. "And he said unto me: Knowest thou the condescension of God?" (1 Nephi 11:16). This is not a rhetorical question; God expects an answer. And, to be honest, Nephi admits that he doesn't quite get it. He replies, "I know that [God] loveth his children; nevertheless I do not know the meaning of all things" (1 Nephi 11:17).

What an understatement! When you think of what Nephi has been through, and what he is yet about to go through, it is fair to say that his life was more confusing than most of ours. Yet his great faith is evident when he says, in effect, "I know that God loves his children, yet I don't know the meaning of everything." How many of us would have the faith, after leaving home, getting stranded in the wilderness, enduring persecution from older siblings, and being separated from everything that was familiar, to testify that God is loving and to humbly admit our ignorance? I love Nephi in this moment.

And so it is with us. We know God loves His children, but we cannot understand all the strange things that happen in this world. We try not to think about the suffering of children, about the way evil often triumphs, about the seemingly pointless pain and sorrow endured by millions on this earth. If we think about it too hard, we may lose faith. And why, if the gospel is indeed true, do even people in our own families believe differently? Why does God sometimes seem absent when we need Him most?

The questions that took Nephi up on that mountain are common to all of us. Yes, we know God loves His children, but it is hard to believe He truly loves me, after all the ways I have failed and disappointed Him. I'm not important, I'm just one of billions. Does He really know who I am and care about the little things that occupy my unceasingly worried mind? What is the meaning of the things that my parents taught me, and does it apply to me?

THE MEANING OF THE TREE OF LIFE

And now for the thunderbolt. Rather than engage in any more gospel discussion, the Spirit simply tells Nephi who this mother and baby are, and Nephi gets it all, the whole picture, in one breathtaking, life-altering moment:

> Behold, the virgin whom thou seest is the mother of the Son of God, after the manner of the flesh. . . . Look!
>
> And I looked and beheld the virgin again, bearing a child in her arms. And the angel said unto me: Behold the Lamb of God, yea, even the Son of the Eternal Father!
>
> Knowest thou the meaning of the tree which thy father saw? And I answered him, saying: Yea, it is the love of God, which sheddeth itself abroad in the hearts of the children of men; wherefore, it is the most desirable above all things. And he spake unto me saying: Yea, and the most joyous to the soul. (1 Nephi 11:18–23)

Nephi was a great man before he received this vision; he was brave, righteous, and obedient. But after this vision, he was born again. In that moment, he became a disciple of Christ and never looked back. As a young man, he concentrated on perfect obedience. As a reborn child of Christ, he understood what the obedience was for; it was to lead him to Jesus. His transformation sets the tone for the entire Book of Mormon. Decades later he beautifully expresses how this focus on Jesus has become the one driving force of his life:

> We talk of Christ, we rejoice in Christ, we preach of Christ, we prophesy of Christ, and we write according to our prophecies, that our children may know to what source they may look for a remission of their sins. . . . Wherefore ye must bow down before him, and worship him with all your might, mind, and strength, and your whole soul; and if ye do this ye shall in no wise be cast out. (2 Nephi 25:26, 29)

The commandments are the iron rod, but the iron rod only leads to the tree of life. Jesus is the tree of life. It is Jesus that brings peace, hope, vitality, beauty, energy, and the *life* to eternal life. Only by tapping into Christ's loving grace can we experience the true joy of the gospel. Otherwise, we are just cherry pickers in the orchard; we may measure, pack, and even preserve the fruit, but we never actually taste it!

THE BIRTH OF JESUS AND THE ATONEMENT

In addition to the gospels we are blessed to have this beautiful birth narrative from the vision of Nephi, a prophet who lived centuries before it occurred. This passage of scripture changed my life at the age of nineteen, and in the decades since I have never been able to read it without feeling the same flow of emotion it evoked at that time. I have loved to ponder its message: that there is no person on this earth who need ever

It is impossible to conceive how different things would have turned out if that birth had not happened whenever, wherever, however it did . . . for millions of people who have lived since, the birth of Jesus made possible not just a new way of understanding life but a new way of living it. It is a truth that, for twenty centuries, there have been untold numbers of men and women who, in untold numbers of ways, have been so grasped by the child who was born, so caught up in the message he taught and the life he lived, that they have found themselves profoundly changed by their relationship with him.
—Frederick Buechner

feel alone, for Jesus has been there before us. Christ was willing to condescend, or literally to *go down with,* each of us into whatever terrifying, painful, and humiliating circumstances life might bring upon us. And to show us how low He would go, He was born in a stable and slept in a trough, amid the dung and debris of animals and the sights and smells of the lowest level of human existence. Elder Jeffrey R. Holland imagines the events of that fateful night:

> Now, alone and unnoticed, [Joseph and Mary] had to descend from human company to a stable, a grotto full of animals, there to bring forth the Son of God. I wonder what emotions Joseph might have had as he cleared away the dung and debris. I wonder if he felt the sting of tears as he hurriedly tried to find the cleanest straw and hold the animals back. I wonder if he wondered: "Could there be a more unhealthy, a more disease-ridden, a more despicable circumstance in which a child could be born? Is this a place fit for a king? Should the mother of the Son of God be asked to enter the valley of the shadow of death in such a foul and unfamiliar place as this? Is it wrong to wish her some comfort? Is it right He should be born here?" But I am certain Joseph did not mutter and Mary did not wail. They knew a great deal and did the best they could. Perhaps these parents knew even then that in the beginning of his mortal life, as well as in the end, this baby son born to them would have to descend beneath every human pain and disappointment. He would do so to help those who also felt they had been born without advantage.[13]

As happens so often if we are not careful, the symbols can cover that which is symbolized. In some of our lives the manger has already been torn down to allow for a discount store running three-for-a-dollar specials on gold, frankincense, and myrrh.
—*Jeffery R. Holland*

Later in the Book of Mormon, Alma elaborates on the importance of each of Christ's earthly experiences, beginning with the lowly manner of His birth and including all of the episodes we read about in the gospel narratives:

---

13. Jeffrey R. Holland, "Maybe Christmas Doesn't Come from a Store," *Ensign,* December 1977.

And he shall go forth, suffering pains and afflictions and temptations of every kind; and this that the word might be fulfilled which saith he will take upon him the pains and the sicknesses of his people. . . . And he will take upon him their infirmities, that his bowels may be filled with mercy, according to the flesh, that he may know according to the flesh how to succor his people according to their infirmities. Now the Spirit knoweth all things; nevertheless the Son of God suffereth according to the flesh that he might take upon him the sins of his people, that he might blot out their transgressions according to the power of his deliverance; and now behold, this is the testimony which is in me. (Alma 7:11–13)

Christ's Atonement began long before His birth, in fact, "before the foundation of the world," and the events of His birth were an important part of the Atonement process (Ephesians 1:4 KJV). As we approach the birth of Christ, it is wonderful to let the wonder in, to stand all amazed that He was willing to descend below all things in order to lift us up.

Chapter Three

WHAT WOULD MARY DO?

Mary, the mother of Jesus, is mentioned in just a few places in the Gospels. We see her at the time of His birth, and during His visit to the temple (probably for His bar mitzvah), and at the time of His death and Resurrection. Mary is also there to initiate the first miracle, at the wedding in Cana. Otherwise we know very little about her in canonized scripture. But by the second century, she had become a person of interest as the Latin, or Western, church split from the Greek, or Eastern, faction, with celibacy as one of the major issues. (To this day, Eastern Orthodox Catholics have married clergy.) For the Latin church, with its emphasis on celibacy, the image of Mary as perennial virgin became important. Legends grew up around her that have altered her image for all of us.

Non-Catholics may be surprised to learn that the "immaculate conception" does not refer to the birth of Jesus; it refers to the birth of Mary. By the time Constantine was establishing Christianity as the state religion in the fourth century, the church fathers had begun to believe that Mary could not have been conceived and born the way that all of us are. They decided that if Jesus was truly pure, He could not have been infected by what was called the "vitiated seed" of Adam. When Adam fell, he became corrupt, and that corruption infected every person in the world, and this would have included Mary if she had been born in traditional fashion. So they created a legend that made Mary the product of a virgin birth, just as Jesus was. It seems that for the early Catholic church, it became necessary to have Mary be less human and more divine in nature.

Mary's immaculate conception was first proposed as early as the fourth century and proceeded to be a subject of debate in councils for another fourteen hundred years. In 1854, the Pope declared as doctrine the immaculate conception of Mary, which is to say that Mary was born to Anna and Joachim without any sexual involvement. She was conceived, as was Jesus, by a divine miracle.[14] This helps us understand why Mary is worshipped along with Jesus in the Catholic church.

Eve brought forth children through having sexual relations and was, as a result, cursed with travail and sorrow; all of that is part of the Fall of Adam. Conversely the Catholic doctrine developed to say that not only did Mary have this child without sexual congress, but that she herself was born immaculately. Then they took it further to say that she did not even suffer the pains of childbirth, but that the child just miraculously appeared. (One account states that as Jesus was born Mary did not cry out, so the midwife, surprised, checked her and confirmed that she was still in a virginal state.) As celibacy became increasingly valued, Mary's virginal status became the ideal for women, and Jesus's virginal status, (as well as John the Apostle's) became the ideal for men. The Roman Catechism of the Council of Trent explains it thus:

> To Eve it was said: "In pain you shall bring forth children" (Genesis 3:16). Mary was exempt from this law, for preserving her virginal

14. Diana Severance, "Immaculate Conception Became Catholic Doctrine," Christianity.com, edited by Dan Graves, last updated July 2017, https://www.christianity.com/church/church-history/timeline/1801-1900/immaculate-conception-became-catholic-doctrine-11630497.html.

integrity inviolate, she brought forth Jesus the Son of God, without experiencing, as we have already said, any sense of pain.[15]

HOW THIS DOCTRINE AFFECTS US STILL

As a Western society, we have some leftovers from the Catholic view of both Eve and Mary. There prevails a sort of residual idea that there's something wrong with sex and with the sexual relations that occur in marriage that has lasted all the way to our day. One of the most revolutionary and wonderful things that Joseph Smith received through modern revelation was the concept that the Fall did not result in a corrupt race, with all of us being born in original sin. It was, instead, a choice between a good, and a greater good. The Church website states:

> *Jesus Christ raised women above the condition of mere slaves, mere ministers to the passion of man, raised them by his Sympathy, to be ministers of God. He gave them moral activity. But the Age, the World, Humanity, must give them the means to exercise this moral activity, must give them intellectual cultivation, spheres of action.*
>
> *—Florence Nightengale*

Because of the Fall of Adam and Eve, all people live in a fallen condition, separated from God and subject to physical death. However, we are not condemned by what many call the "original sin." In other words, we are not accountable for Adam's transgression in the Garden of Eden. The Prophet Joseph Smith said, "We believe that men will be punished for their own sins, and not for Adam's transgression" (Articles of Faith 1:2).[16]

So Mary did not need to reverse the curse of original sin, nor was she divinely conceived; she was a normal woman who was chosen to fill a remarkable role: the mother of the Son of God.

---

15. Mark Miravalle, "Mary's Virginity during the Birth of Jesus: The Catholic Church's Perennial Tradition," *General Mariology*, October 15, 2012, http://www.motherofallpeoples .com/2012/10/marys-miraculous-birth-of-jesus-the-catholic-churchs-perennial-tradition.
16. "Original Sin," Gospel Topics, topics.lds.org.

WHAT DO WE KNOW ABOUT MARY?

What was Mary like? We can tell from her encounter with Gabriel that she was a person of great strength. Her response to Gabriel, though filled with humility, also contains some astute questions. We also know that she was a literate scriptorian. Her response to Elizabeth's blessing, framed in poetic language, is known as the Magnificat (called that because Magnificat is the first word of the Latin translation). Mary's poem is modeled on the song of Hannah, and shows a tremendous awareness of scripture, of the political situation of the Jews, and of the eternal role of the Messiah.

Mary was also an outsider; she was technically an unwed mother. She was probably between the ages of twelve and fourteen when she was betrothed, and to the outside world there would have been only two explanations for her pregnancy: either she and Joseph had engaged in sexual relations, or she had been raped. (It was not uncommon for young Jewish women to be raped by Roman soldiers, as I mentioned previously.) Mary knew what the truth was, but who was going to believe her? She undoubtedly suffered the judgement of her neighbors. Without Joseph's protection, she might have suffered much more; she could have been stoned as a fornicator. Even if she had been allowed to live, she would have been subject to physical and mental abuse, with curses charged at her by her neighbors, with a bleak future ahead.[17]

> *To women there belongs a right which lies deeper than suffrage, higher than education, and sweeter than enforced virtue. It is the right of choice, the right to choose what she shall be.*
>
> —*Young Women's Journal*

---

17. Richard N. Holzapfel and Jeni Broberg Holzapfel, *Sisters at the Well: Women and the Life and Teachings of Jesus* (Salt Lake City: Bookcraft, 1993).

A MODEL FOR UNWED MOTHERS AND MOTHERS OF BLENDED FAMILIES

Gabriel understands what Mary will be facing, and he advises her to seek out her kinswoman Elizabeth, also miraculously pregnant in her old age. As she comes to meet Elizabeth we have that wonderful moment when Elizabeth turns, sees her, and the baby leaps in her womb (Luke 1:41–44). It's beautiful to me that Gabriel's mission includes placing Mary with a woman friend; God knows that the most important thing for Mary right that minute would be the support of someone who would understand her situation as no one else in the world could. And so a sister had been prepared to sustain Mary. She is no longer alone in her strange and frightening situation. This gives Mary the strength she needs, and she stays with Elizabeth quite a while. Following Elizabeth's example, we as a community of saints can strengthen someone who is misunderstood or an outcast.

> *There is a reason Mary is everywhere. I've seen her image all over the world, in cafés in Istanbul, on students' backpacks in Scotland, in a market stall in Jakarta . . . Images of Mary remind us of God's favor. Mary is what it looks like to believe that we already are who God says we are.*
> —Nadia Bolz-Weber

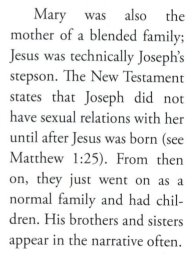

Mary was also the mother of a blended family; Jesus was technically Joseph's stepson. The New Testament states that Joseph did not have sexual relations with her until after Jesus was born (see Matthew 1:25). From then on, they just went on as a normal family and had children. His brothers and sisters appear in the narrative often.

A DISCIPLE OF CHRIST

Mary's own discipleship began when the angel of the Lord first appeared to her, and as Jesus grew, she learned the cost of discipleship in following her son. It became more challenging as the young child escaped a death threat from the king. More particularly, she understood the cost as the adult Jesus became hated, persecuted, and finally was brutally executed. Yet she was there for Him at all the crucial moments. Her discipleship grew as she came to know, love, and follow her son as Master and Redeemer.

> Mary's discipleship continued after her son's mission began. She was recorded as being present on several occasions through Jesus's three-year mission, and she faithfully reappears at the cross as both mother and follower.[18]

Mary was also a facilitator and an inspiration to her son. When Jesus was thirty, and His mission was ready to start, it was His mother that provided the impetus.

> On the third day a wedding took place in Cana of Galilee. Jesus' mother was there, and Jesus and his disciples had also been invited to the wedding. [Jesus apparently had disciples at this point.] When the wine was gone, Jesus' mother said to him, "They have no more wine."
>
> "Woman, why do you involve me?" Jesus replied.[19] "My hour has not yet come." (John 2:1–4 NIV)

She ignores that comment as far as I can tell and turns to the servants, and says, "Do whatever He tells you." This has put Jesus in a position, now, where all the servants are looking at Him with the empty wine jars and (whether His hour has come or not) His mother has decided she wants Him to do something about it! Before Him there are six stone water jars for the Jewish rites of purification, each jar holding twenty or thirty gallons. Jesus says to the servants, "Fill the jars with water." They fill them up to the brim. He says, "Now draw some out and take it to the master of the banquet." It turns out to be the best wine anybody's ever had. "What Jesus did here in Cana of Galilee was the first of the signs through which he revealed his glory; and his disciples believed in him."

---

18. Ibid., 62.
19. The word "woman" used here is the same word in Hebrew used for Mother Eve, meaning "womankind."

Then, notice what happens next. "He went down to Capernaum with his mother and brothers and his disciples. There they stayed for a few days" (John 2:1–12 NIV).

I find this passage very moving. Jesus's family surrounds Him as He begins His mission. It's as if they are saying, "Come on, Son. We'll go with you. We'll get you started because we know that this is going to be hard. We're taking the first steps with you." I think mothers and fathers can do a great deal as facilitators and initiators to help our daughters and sons experience the power of the Spirit and the power of the priesthood. We can help them take those first steps onto their missions in life.

Mary is relatable to almost every kind of woman. She was an unwed mother. She was an outsider. She was a woman of incredible righteousness and spirituality, who, in the most difficult of circumstances, had to hang on to her knowledge of self. She was thrown into life's problems when very young, and experienced the sorrow of having to bury a child. In Mary, we have a woman who needs the strength of her sisters. We have a woman who's a mother of a blended family. Like Jesus's life, Mary's was a microcosm of women's lives all over the world. Best of all, in Mary we have a role model: a woman who is a facilitator and an inspiration to her children and who helps them find their mission. She is a courageous follower of Christ.

THE COST OF DISCIPLESHIP

We could say that Mary was also the first Christian. Holding Jesus in her arms, she watched the shepherds arrive within hours of His birth and fall on their knees, saying an angel had appeared to them. She knew she had a special son, but this must have been an impressive moment. Then, a couple of years later, a group of men came from the East with gold, frankincense, and myrrh, all symbolic gifts that would be given to a king. "Mary kept all these things," it says, "and pondered them in her heart." One translation of that phrase is "preserved," so she may actually have written down the things that she pondered. What a journal that would be!

We see Mary at the foot of the cross, courageously sharing her son's last hours on this earth. I don't know if I would have had the courage to stand at the cross and watch what Mary watched, but she was there, even

> *The upside of painful knowledge is so much greater than the downside of bliss-ful ignorance.*
> —Sheryl Sandberg

though it could have cost her life. Most of the disciples ran away, but she was there. She was a witness at the tomb and one of the first witnesses of the Resurrection. Finally, we see Mary as one of the first members of the new Christian faith, meeting with the Apostles in the upper room in Jerusalem. At all of the most important moments of Jesus's life, Mary was there.

MARY IS A SYMBOL

Mary, because of her unique role, has a special place in our theology. She knew as early as her visit to Elizabeth that she was a symbol of Israel (see Luke 1:46–56). Her acceptance of God's will was a symbol of Israel's coming acceptance of Christ. In addition, she symbolizes Christ Himself. Nephi's vision of the tree of life portrays her as a tree that is the parent of the tree of life (see 1 Nephi 11). Finally, Mary is a symbol to all women; no matter what our challenges may be, we can look to Mary for an example of strength, courage, and resiliency.

Each figure in the scriptures has something to teach us. It is said, "I cannot be what I cannot see," and in Mary I can see a woman whom I can emulate. I want my daughters and granddaughters to

> *Mary is the chiefest figure, the regal queen, mother of mothers—holding center stage in this grandest of all dramatic moments.*
> —Jeffrey R. Holland

know her. There are great female role models in the scriptures, but our daughters are not going to see them unless we take the time to know them better, and then help those we love see them, too. There's not a woman in the world that can feel alone when she looks to the life of Mary and the trials she went through as a part of the Savior's mission.

Chapter Four

MATTHEW: SCALING THE SERMON ON THE MOUNT

I have a lot of questions about the Sermon on the Mount. My first question is this: Is Jesus really talking to me here? Because so much of what I find in this collection of sayings seems so far from the kind of life I actually live, I hardly know how to take it in. I mean seriously, if I really did what Jesus is teaching here, Craig and I would sell the house, pile our belongings in a shopping cart, and just wander through the world loving and teaching others, trusting God to provide for us. Does He mean for us to do that? I've actually heard people say that that part of the sermon was just meant for the Apostles and missionaries, and I kind of hope that is true.

Okay, even if that part is just meant for missionaries or Church leaders, what about all of the other teachings? If I followed the Sermon on the Mount, I wouldn't swear, judge wrongly, or do things to impress other people. I would pray in faith, all the time, in my heart or hiding in my closet, because I would never pray just to be heard by other people. I would give to everyone in need, and when people hurt me, I would stay all soft and vulnerable, and "turn the other cheek" (Matthew 5:39 KJV).

Worst of all, I would have to love *everyone*, even creepy people like serial killers and school shooters, who barely deserve to live, let alone be loved. And (even harder) I would have to forgive and even love people who might have personally abused or injured me or the people I love. I don't see that happening any time soon.

(Just to further discourage me) Jesus also says that the gate to heaven is so narrow that only a few people find it, but the way to hell is so wide and easy to travel that there is practically a traffic jam headed that direction. And He tops it off by saying this: "Be ye therefore perfect, even as your Father which is in heaven is perfect" (Matthew 5:48 KJV). Okay, now I know I'm in big trouble.

> "Above all else, God wants our hearts. Imperfect performance can be corrected, sins can be remitted, mistakes can be erased—but God can do nothing with an unwilling and rebellious heart until it repents. However, all those who really want and work for the kingdom of God with all their strength, however great or little their strength may be, will inherit that kingdom.
> —Stephen Robinson

I first read the Sermon on the Mount at the age of ten. I'm in my sixties now, and I'm not really too much better than when I first began to think about these things. I'm going to be honest with you: if I stub my toe, the first words that come out of my mouth are not "yea yea and nay nay" (Matthew 5:37 KJV). I'm a pretty nice person, as long as you don't come after one of my family members or close friends or keep me waiting too long in a restaurant. (In fact, when someone offends one of us, my husband and kids smile and say, "Well, shall we just sic Mom on them?") There isn't any reason to bore you with the rest of my failings, how I laugh at the wrong jokes and can hardly sit through three hours of church, but you get the idea. I really believe in the Sermon on the Mount, but my life doesn't look like it.

Then, on top of that, the things that you need to do to be like God and go to heaven are just *really hard*. When I read the whole Sermon I feel like I need to go lie down; it's exhausting just thinking about all the ways I don't measure up! Becoming "perfect" seems as hard as going from a standing position to leaping up onto my kitchen table. I know it is physically possible for a person to do, but it does not seem possible for *me*.

I'm clearly not making much progress. Should I just give up and go with the flow of people that are (as my dad used to say) headed to hell in a hand basket?

At least I am not alone in my discouragement. C. S. Lewis had his own response:

> As to "caring for" the Sermon on the Mount, if "caring for" here means "liking" or enjoying, I suppose no one "cares for" it. Who can like being knocked flat on his face by a sledge-hammer?[20]

MAYBE I'M LOOKING AT IT THE WRONG WAY

Is there another way to look at the Sermon on the Mount? Thinking of the gospel as a "sin management program"[21] can be very discouraging. In other words, the gospel consists of a list of things you should do and a list of things you shouldn't do. To be righteous, you have to eliminate all your bad behaviors and replace them with righteous acts. It's like a zero-sum game; you can't be good until you get rid of all the bad. That is not very inspiring, is it? Well, before I give up on the whole idea of trying to be perfect, I'm going to try looking at this a different way.

What if I look at the Sermon on the Mount as a list of symptoms? When someone comes in to the emergency room, doctors ask this question, "How does the patient present?" In other words, what can we observe about the patient that is indicative of problems within the body? What can we see that will give us information about hidden maladies that need fixing?

For example, if a patient is doubled over with pain in the right lower quadrant of the abdomen, and this pain seems even worse

20. C. S. Lewis, "Rejoinder to Dr. Pittenger," in *God in the Dock*, ed. Walter Hooper (Grand Rapids, MI: Eerdmans, 1970), 182.
21. A phrase coined by Nadia Bolz Weber in *Accidental Saints: Finding God in All the Wrong People* (New York: Random House, 2017).

when pressure on the spot is released, no good doctor would simply treat the pain and send the patient home. Nor would the doctor scold the patient for having severe pain. ("Come on, just walk it off, soldier!") And it would seem silly for the patient to believe that just by trying to be tough or pretending that the pain wasn't there he or she could overcome it. No, the pain is a symptom of something that may threaten the life of the patient if not treated. The doctor would do further tests and probably prep for an appendectomy.

Looking at the Sermon on the Mount in this way is helpful, because what Jesus is talking about is not a list of behaviors that need to be eliminated for us to become smiling, loving, cookie-cutter versions of righteousness. He is describing the symptoms of a spiritually sick person, and also characteristics of a spiritually healthy person. Since God is the source of all life, drawing closer to Him makes us more alive, healthier in an eternal sense, and drawing away from Him makes us ill. And this spiritual illness always presents itself in certain symptomatic behavior.

> "You will notice that, in all those cases, the Law is fulfilled by being made harder rather than easier; it is being radicalized rather than liberalized.
> —Marcus J. Borg & John Dominic Crossan"

So let's go back and look at just a few of the statements in this light.

> You have heard that it was said, "You shall not commit adultery." But I tell you that anyone who looks at a woman lustfully has already committed adultery with her in his heart. If your right eye causes you to stumble, gouge it out and throw it away. It is better for you to lose one part of your body than for your whole body to be thrown into hell. And if your right hand causes you to stumble, cut it off and throw it away. It is better for you to lose one part of your body than for your whole body to go into hell. (Matthew 5:27–30 NIV)

If you entertain lustful thoughts or feelings, it is a symptom that you are not leading a Christ-centered life. If you are focused on Christ, when a lustful thought pops in your mind, you do not let it stay. You recognize that it is unfaithful to your spouse, or even to yourself, if you are hoping to achieve a lasting, happy marriage. Those who center their lives on Christ recognize that breaking the law of chastity jeopardizes the most important possession we can have in life—our family. And if you never let a lustful thought stay, you will never find yourself in danger. Jesus is giving us clues to identify spiritual illness in ourselves. Here is another one:

> You have heard that it was said to the people long ago, "You shall not murder, and anyone who murders will be subject to judgment." But I tell you that anyone who is angry with a brother or sister will be subject to judgment. Again, anyone who says to a brother or sister, "Raca," is answerable to the court. And anyone who says, "You fool!" will be in danger of the fire of hell.
>
> Therefore, if you are offering your gift at the altar and there remember that your brother or sister has something against you, leave your gift there in front of the altar. First go and be reconciled to them; then come and offer your gift.
>
> Settle matters quickly with your adversary who is taking you to court. Do it while you are still together on the way, or your adversary may hand you over to the judge, and the judge may hand you over to the officer, and you may be thrown into prison. Truly I tell you, you will not get out until you have paid the last penny. (Matthew 5:21–26 NIV)

If you are angry, it could lead to violence, and even fatality. If you long for revenge against someone who has cheated you, and you want to sue that person in court, it will probably bankrupt you financially. But even worse, it will bankrupt you spiritually. No matter how much you win, you won't ever be satisfied. You'll be treating the symptom, but you will still have the disease in your heart.

You notice that Jesus isn't talking about the legal justice system, where people need to pay for their crimes. That is a given; people need to be accountable to the society in which they live. He is talking about the personal vendettas and hatred that arises between people over wrongs, both imagined and real. That is what destroys the soul.

You have heard that it was said, "Love your neighbor and hate your enemy." But I tell you, love your enemies and pray for those who persecute you, that you may be children of your Father in heaven. He causes his sun to rise on the evil and the good, and sends rain on the righteous and the unrighteous. (Matthew 5:43–45 NIV)

When you consider the amount of time we spend wondering why life isn't "fair," this statement of Jesus is all the more startling. Apparently, God does not worry about fairness in the same way we do; he just lets the world roll as it rolls, with storms and sun shed on everyone. So Jesus says, love and forgive your enemies, not because they deserve it, but because in that way you will be more like God, who sends rain and sunshine to everyone. In other words, you ought to forgive people because that is life. People do right and they do wrong, and sometimes we receive wonderful gifts of grace from people and sometimes we receive terrible harm. But just as we accept both rain and sunshine from God, we should accept good and bad from people and just keep going forward the best we can.

CONSIDER THE LILIES

Taken from this perspective, the statements about accumulating possessions and wealth make more sense. Rather than taking the statements as a prescription that we need to sell our houses and cars and become itinerant rabbis, considering them as indicators of our spiritual health is illuminating:

Therefore I tell you, do not worry about your life, what you will eat or drink; or about your body, what you will wear. Is not life more than food, and the body more than clothes? Look at the birds of the air; they do not sow or reap or store away in barns, and yet your heavenly Father feeds them. Are you not much more valuable than they? Can any one of you by worrying add a single hour to your life?

And why do you worry about clothes? See how the flowers of the field grow. They do not labor or spin. Yet I tell you that not even Solomon in all his splendor was dressed like one of these. If that is how God clothes the grass of the field, which is here today and tomorrow is thrown into the fire, will he not much more clothe you—you of little faith? So do not worry, saying, "What shall we eat?" or "What shall we drink?" or "What shall we wear?" For the pagans run after all these things, and your heavenly Father knows that you need them. But seek first his kingdom and his righteousness, and all these things will be given to you as well. Therefore do not worry about tomorrow, for tomorrow will worry about itself. Each day has enough trouble of its own. (Matthew 6:25–34 NIV)

Notice how many times Jesus uses the word *worry*. Worry is a symptom of spiritual illness. It is possible to be constantly worrying about money, no matter how much you have. And if you have enough to meet your needs but are constantly worrying about having more, your spirit is ailing. This makes the following statement about the foundation of the house even more meaningful.

Therefore everyone who hears these words of mine and puts them into practice is like a wise man who built his house on the rock. The rain came down, the streams rose, and the winds blew and beat against that house; yet it did not fall, because it had its foundation on the rock. But everyone who hears these words of mine and does not put them into practice is like a foolish man who built his house on sand. The rain came down, the streams rose, and the winds blew and beat against that house, and it fell with a great crash. (Matthew 7:24–27 NIV)

What is the house? I would say my house is me. It is who I am. And who are you? Are you the sum of your accomplishments, the wealth you have accumulated, or your career? If any of these things are your foundation, your house is built on sand.

Jesus is clear on what the foundation of our house

*Disturb us, Lord, when
We are too well pleased with ourselves,
When our dreams have come true
Because we have dreamed too little,
Having fallen in love with life,
We have ceased to dream of eternity
And in our efforts to build a new earth,
We have allowed our vision
Of the new Heaven to dim.*
—*Sir Francis Drake*

should be; it must be built on a rock, and He is the rock. He is the foundation upon which, if we build, we will never fall. He is saying, *You are my child. That is all that matters about you. That is what is eternal about you. As long as you keep that central in your mind, you will be able to see clearly and the things that are wrong with you will melt away.*

SPIRITUAL PROPRIOCEPTION

Scientists have a term for the sense that each of us has, the awareness of our body in space. It's called proprioception. This sense is something that is easy to ignore until it is lost. Oliver Sacks, a neurologist and essayist, wrote about a woman he treated who, as a result of a brain injury, lost her proprioception. She couldn't sense where the parts of her body were in space. For example, she couldn't raise her arm to feed herself unless she could see her arm. Her mind could not sense the parameters of her body, and it was a serious handicap.[22]

I think we sometimes lose our spiritual proprioception, our sense of where our spirit is in the daily workings of God's plan. The Sermon on the Mount is the best medicine in the world for this. Jesus gives us the clues, or symptoms, of a soul that is losing track of itself. Anger, lust, bitterness, or a crying need to be the center of attention are symptoms that we need to address if we are to become who God would have us become. Only when we regain our spiritual proprioception can we begin to know what Jesus would do in any situation. Our sinful behaviors are not evidence of incurable corruption, but instead are symptoms that point to illnesses that can be healed, leaving behind only that which is healthy and beautiful.

Here is another thing about spiritual maladies: some of them can be cured, but others may remain with us as long as we live. Those behaviors that are symptoms of illness will abate as we take our medicine by shunning sin, but we may find that no matter how hard we try, we will still have certain weaknesses that are part of

---

22. Oliver Sacks, *The Man Who Mistook His Wife for His Hat* (New York: Touchstone, 1998).

just being human. These will keep us humble and turning toward Christ until the day we die. So, though we may never take another drink, we may crave alcohol as long as we live. Though we may hold our temper, we may still have it, simmering inside! The behavioral guidelines in the Sermon on the Mount shows us how to keep our weaknesses from taking over our lives. Bruce R. Hafen says this:

> The Savior desires to save us from our inadequacies as well as from our sins. Inadequacy is not the same as sinfulness—we have far more control over the choice to sin than we may have over our innate capacity. The Lord will not save us in our sins, but from them. However, he can save us in our inadequacies as well as from them. A sense of falling short or falling down is not only natural, but essential to the mortal experience. But, after all we can do, the Atonement can fill that which is empty, straighten our bent parts, and make strong that which is weak.[23]

WHY IS IT SO HARD TO GET INTO HEAVEN?

I'm starting to feel better about the Sermon on the Mount, but there is still that one statement that haunts me, about how hard it is for a regular person like me to get into the kingdom of Heaven.

> Enter through the narrow gate. For wide is the gate and broad is the road that leads to destruction, and many enter through it. But small is the gate and narrow the road that leads to life, and only a few find it. (Matthew 7:13–14 NIV)

Why is the gate to heaven so hard to get to? Well, maybe the way to heaven is not so much like an obstacle course, where we have to climb over sin after sin. It might be more like a maze; it gets confusing when we leave the straight road of the commandments and wander into unknown territory. It is easy to get drawn off that path when we follow the loud, persistent messages that demand our attention. Jesus talks about being quiet, controlling

---

23. Bruce C. Hafen. "Beauty for Ashes: The Atonement of Jesus Christ," *Ensign*, April 1980.

your worst emotions, and listening to your better judgment. The way to heaven is fairly straightforward if we look toward Him and let Him guide us.

> Ask and it will be given to you; seek and you will find; knock and the door will be opened to you. For everyone who asks receives; the one who seeks finds; and to the one who knocks, the door will be opened. (Matthew 7:7–8 NIV)

> *There are two sets of virtues, the resume virtues and the eulogy virtues. The resume virtues are the skills you bring to the marketplace. The eulogy virtues are the ones that are talked about at your funeral.*
> —*David Brooks*

Maybe being righteous isn't so much about never doing anything wrong. Maybe it is more about continually asking for help and leaving the judging, anger, and concern about fairness to God. Maybe life is not a zero-sum game, where we replace sins with good deeds. It's more like peeling a banana, stripping off the rough, bitter outer covering that hides a sweet, beautiful inner soul that was always there, just waiting to be revealed.

No matter how I look at the Sermon on the Mount, it stands, for me, as the most challenging document in Christianity. I know that I will never truly understand it until I am "all in," committed to living according to its lofty ideals. Dietrich Bonhoeffer sums it up nicely:

> Humanly speaking, it is possible to understand the Sermon on the Mount in a thousand different ways. But Jesus knows only one possibility: simple surrender and obedience—not interpreting or applying it, but doing and obeying it. That is the only way to hear his words. He does not mean for us to discuss it as an ideal. He really means for us to get on with it.[24]

---

24. Diedrich Bonhoeffer, *The Cost of Discipleship* (New York: Touchstone, 1995), 196–97.

Chapter Five

MARK: A LESSON IN CELESTIAL BRANDING

Recently I attended something called a "branding seminar" that was taught by my daughter Alison, who is an expert in this area. People come from all over to have her teach them how to establish themselves as a "brand." To begin with, she took us through an exercise to narrow our personal priorities down to just a few vital ones, and then, based on those, we each established a mission statement. We even wrote down words that we tend to use often to describe our goods and services. Then she taught us how all of our "public facing" content, such as websites, advertisements, and even business cards should contain these elements, and even these key words, so that our brand is easily recognizable. It was surprisingly difficult to do, yet quite revealing for all of us.

I had this in mind when I sat down to study the Gospels and found to my surprise the

> *We are most blessed when we see ourselves as we are seen by [the Savior] and know ourselves as we are known by Him. In this world, we do not really grasp who we are until we know whose we are. He will never forget us nor our real identity. We should never forget whose we are. We are His.*
> —*Truman G. Madsen*

four Gospels are quite recognizable as "brands." In other words, each Gospel has a certain objective (mission statement) and a few strong priorities, and the way the story of Jesus is presented in that gospel supports and reflects that perspective. There are even key words that recur, such as the word "signs" in the Gospel of John, and the word "immediately" in Mark. That is an interesting reminder that we each have a "brand," whether we mean to or not. Through our words and actions we convey an overriding message to others. And we can think about that as we dive into the gospel of Mark.

WHO WAS MARK?

Mark was not one of the original Apostles; he never personally met Jesus. He was converted with his mother, whose name was Mary (everybody's mother seems to be named Mary), and lived in Jerusalem, where he met Peter and Paul at some point. We do not have the story of his conversion, but he may have received the gospel from Barnabus, with whom he appears to have had a close relationship. (They might even have been cousins.) Mark is writing just before the fall of Rome, at a time when the Early Christians were facing much persecution. The historian Tacitus noted:

> Nero punished with the utmost refinements of cruelty a class of men despised for their vices, whom the crowd called Christians. . . . The confessed members of the sect were arrested and mocking accompanied their end. They were covered with the skins of wild animals and torn to death by dogs; or they were hung on crosses and when sunlight failed they were burned to serve as lamps at night.[25]

In a time of terrible persecution, when it must have seemed that the entire fabric of the Christian movement was unraveling, Mark set forth the life of the Savior in a way that showed a steady, purposeful mission of salvation, rather than a confusing collection of random episodes.

---

25. *The Annals of Tacitus*, book XV:44, in the Loeb Classical Library edition of Tacitus, vol. V (1937), http://penelope.uchicago.edu/Thayer/e/roman/texts/tacitus/annals/15b*.html.

Mark first appears in the book of Acts, chapter 12, where he is mentioned as being one of the disciples of Jesus, but of course this is after the Savior's death. Though he wrote his gospel in Greek, Mark did not speak Greek or Hebrew as his first language—he spoke Aramaic, just as Jesus had. (Scholars tell us that his Greek is a very conversational, active Greek, rather than the Greek of a scholar.[26]) Mark is by far the shortest Gospel, about 11,000 words. All the others have about 18,000–20,000 words; Mark is only about two-thirds as long as the other Gospels, but 19 percent of it is about the events connected with Christ's atoning sacrifice.

Mark is writing from a very strong oral history, and this poses some challenges for the reader. Have you ever noticed when you go back and read your old journals you find references to people, places, and things that you thought you would always remember? And now, you can't remember who "Bob" was? Oh, for a last name! (In my case, many times when I'm looking at our old family pictures, I can't even tell which baby I'm holding! It's embarrassing.) We realize too late that we should have always written names and dates on the backs of photos, but we never imagined we would forget so many important events.

This is certainly the case with Mark. He will refer in passing to an event in the life of Jesus that would have been a part of the oral tradition at the time, but has since been lost, and occasionally he leaves us needing more detail. Both Matthew and Luke appear to have relied heavily on Mark's Gospel as they composed theirs, and many details were filled in by those two later writers.

Mark spent a lot of time with Peter, which is evident by his choice of subject matter, and by comments from historians over the next few centuries. Eusebius said of him:

> The Gospel according to Mark had this occasion. As Peter had preached the Word publicly at Rome, and declared the Gospel by the Spirit, many who were present requested that Mark, who had

---

26. Luke Timothy Johnson, *The Writings of the New Testament* (Minneapolis, MN: Fortress Press, 2010), 146.

followed him for a long time and remembered his sayings, should write them out. And having composed the Gospel he gave it to those who had requested it. When Peter learned of this, he neither directly forbade nor encouraged it.[27]

As a result, some scholars go so far as to call the Gospel of Mark the "Memoirs of Peter."

Peter, with his powerful, impetuous nature, is the one person (besides Christ Himself) who comes through most strongly in Mark's Gospel. His encounters with the Savior show a growing relationship that is by turns heartwarming and heartrending and reveals the personality of Jesus in a unique way.

MARK CREATES A NEW GENRE

Mark's Gospel is definitely the story of Jesus's life, but is it a biography? Certainly, the story is told in a somewhat linear fashion, but it does not begin with Jesus's birth; it begins with His baptism. The Gospel of Mark represents a new genre. It is different from our modern biographies; it has, as it were, a brand of its own. Ancient biographers did not worry about getting each event organized in order, and Mark follows this tradition. Instead, experiences from the life of Christ are deliberately placed in small groupings to make a point. Mark uses a technique called "intercalation," more commonly known as a "Markan sandwich." Luke Timothy Johnson explains how groupings of three create framing and filling for a thematic presentation of events.

> For Mark, the triad becomes an architectonic principle. This can be seen first in his frequent use of literary intercalation. In its smallest form, two fragments of one story frame a third passage in something of a sandwich arrangement. Mark's reader is forced to see the frame and the middle together, in tension. The central story is illuminated—or

---

27. J. Warner Wallace, "Is Mark's Gospel an Early Memoir of the Apostle Peter?" Cold-Case Christiantiy, July 25, 2018, http://coldcasechristianity.com/2018/is-marks-gospel -an-early-memoir-of-the-apostle-peter.

darkened—by its placement within the frame, whereas the outer story is given density by being filled in this fashion.[28]

This sandwiching of events occurs in almost every chapter. I call it an example of "celestial branding," because through this use of a repetitive structure, Mark is able to reveal what was most important (at least in his view) about the events in Jesus's mission. The term 'sandwich' naturally draws our attention to the middle of the passage, which will contain the meat. So each chapter is structured as a chiasmus. The beginning of the pericope will relate to the end, and both will frame, and in some way illuminate, the 'meat' of the sandwich.

Then one of the synagogue leaders, named Jairus, came, and when he saw Jesus, he fell at his feet. He pleaded earnestly with him, "My little daughter is dying. Please come and put your hands on her so that she will be healed and live." So Jesus went with him. A large crowd followed and pressed around him. (Mark 5:22–24 NIV)

(Part one—first slice of bread. Jairus is a ruler and has power, a name, and status.)

And a woman was there who had been subject to bleeding for twelve years. She had suffered a great deal under the care of many doctors and had spent all she had, yet instead of getting better she grew worse. When she heard about Jesus, she came up behind him in the crowd and touched his cloak, because she thought, "If I just touch his clothes, I will be healed." Immediately her bleeding stopped and she felt in her body that she was freed from her suffering.

At once Jesus realized that power had gone out from him. He turned around in the crowd and asked, "Who touched my clothes?"

"You see the people crowding against you," his disciples answered, "and yet you can ask, 'Who touched me?'"

But Jesus kept looking around to see who had done it. Then the woman, knowing what had happened to her, came and fell at his feet and, trembling with fear, told him the whole truth. He said to her,

---

28. Johnson, *The Writings of the New Testament*, 147.

"Daughter, your faith has healed you. Go in peace and be freed from your suffering." (Mark 5: 25–34 NIV)

(Part two—the story within the story, the filling. This woman is no one, with no name, an outcast. She is alone while Jairus is surrounded by attendants. She touches Jesus. Jairus does not.)

While Jesus was still speaking, some people came from the house of Jairus, the synagogue leader. "Your daughter is dead," they said. "Why bother the teacher anymore?" Overhearing what they said, Jesus told him, "Don't be afraid; just believe." He did not let anyone follow him except Peter, James and John the brother of James. When they came to the home of the synagogue leader, Jesus saw a commotion, with people crying and wailing loudly. He went in and said to them, "Why all this commotion and wailing? The child is not dead but asleep." But they laughed at him.

After he put them all out, he took the child's father and mother and the disciples who were with him, and went in where the child was. He took her by the hand and said to her, "Talitha koum!" (which means "Little girl, I say to you, get up!"). Immediately the girl stood up and began to walk around (she was twelve years old). At this they were completely astonished. He gave strict orders not to let anyone know about this, and told them to give her something to eat. (Mark 5:35–43 NIV)

(Part three—the other piece of bread. The climax to the stories. The little girl is also nameless, the noisy mourners are like the noisy crowd.)

Mark uses this chiasmic structure to ensure that we read the stories together and understand their interrelation. In the beginning of this this chapter, Jesus has just exorcised a demon, and it took place on Gentile soil. A large crowd is present; it is a noisy, public event. This sets the scene for these interconnected stories; the silent, suffering woman is sandwiched between the noisy crowd and the noisy professional mourners at the bedside of the silent girl. The exorcism for the Gentile is immediately followed by the petition from the leader of the synagogue, surely the most Orthodox of Jews. Jesus's responses to both petitions are identical; He simply goes into action to help. But along the way we come to the meat of the sandwich, as one lone, nameless woman with an issue of blood (leaving her ritually unclean for twelve years) reaches out and takes hold of His robe and is healed. The action stops. Jesus takes a moment to state the theme of all of these stories: "He said to her, 'Daughter, your faith has healed you. Go in peace and be freed from your suffering'" (Mark 5:34 NIV).

And then things begin to move again. Jesus is told that the daughter of Jairus is dead. He moves into action, going to the home and, in a most private way, raising the girl from the dead. Three kinds of uncleanness, three varieties of healing, three settings, three different echelons of society. One Jesus. Details balance the chiasmus. The daughter of Jairus is twelve years old. The woman has suffered twelve years.

> *We who lived in concentration camps can remember the men who walked through the huts comforting others, giving away their last piece of bread. They may have been few in number, but they offer sufficient proof that everything can be taken from a man but one thing: the last of the human freedoms—to choose one's attitude in any given set of circumstances; to choose one's own way.*
> —*Victor Frankl*

Both are nameless. The Devils are named "Legion," which is what a Roman cohort is called. The ruler of the synagogue falls on his knees before Jesus. Both men, the centurion and the leader of the synagogue, symbolize the two great powers in Jesus's life. But neither brings Jesus to His knees. Only the humble faith of the hapless woman stops Him short. Jairus speaks openly but Jesus asks him to keep the raising of his daughter a secret. The woman tries to be healed secretly but Jesus brings it into the open, cleansing her not only of her illness but of the shame imposed on her by an overzealous application of the law.

Mark's genius is to take episodes in Jesus's life and combine them in a way that enriches our understanding of each. Whether the recipient is a Gentile; a poor, marginalized woman; or the rich ruler of a synagogue, the healing is the same and the source of power is the same. The two vital elements are the power of Christ and the faith of the believer. Race, ethnic affiliation, or even the degree of righteousness, have nothing to do with this healing grace. Certainly, worldly wealth or power hold no sway; they are just part of the noise.

Scholar Micah Kiehl notes,

> In chapter 5, Jesus does not discriminate between Jew and Gentile; both are healed and transformed. The rules and structures of either society are irrelevant to him. He demolishes the demoniac's isolation. He honors the ritually unclean—the bleeding and the dead—with no heed for the consequences. Neither Jew nor Gentile has an inherent advantage. In the words of St. Paul, 'God shows no partiality' (Galatians 2:6 New Revised Standard Version).[29]

FINDING OURSELVES IN MARK'S GOSPEL

I have faith that if we caught hold of God's living candle on that truth and went out in the world being true to the vision, we would not need to defend the cause of Jesus Christ. People would come and ask; "Where have you found the radiance that I sense in your eyes and in your face? How come you don't get carried away with the world?" And we would answer that the work of salvation is the glorious work of Jesus Christ. But it is also the glorious work of the uncovering and recovering of your own latent divinity.
—*Truman G. Madsen*

Certain dramatic motifs work well because the same patterns are reflected in our lives. It is a common saying that "things come in threes." Have you ever had events come to you in a grouping, where there seems to be a beginning, a middle and an end? I experienced this during my third year of college. I was enjoying my schoolwork and stayed through the summer instead of going back to California. A friend was majoring in

29. Micah Kiel, "Commentary on Mark 5:21–43," Working Preacher, January 29, 2012, https://www.workingpreacher.org/preaching.aspx?commentary_id=1188.

linguistics and decided to take Japanese. He knew I was interested in Japan, and invited me to take it with him. It sounded fun for some reason, and I spent that summer learning the rudimentary basics of the language. Japan was so fascinating I took a class on the history during the next block. I thought that perhaps God might be preparing me for service in that part of the world.

I had always wanted to serve a mission, but in the next year I got into a serious relationship. It began to look as if my life was taking a different course, so I set that first goal to the side and went forward in a different direction. Then, quite suddenly, I felt a change in my heart, and that relationship ended. I remember feeling very confused at the time, because the young man I was involved with was a wonderful person. Why couldn't I feel good about going forward with that relationship? And why had I let go of my mission goal for that period of time? In both instances, I felt I was guided. Was I just imagining all of it?

Nonetheless, as soon as I was "free" again, I was constantly thinking about missionary work. My twenty-first birthday came right around this time, and another friend reminded me that I was now old enough to serve if I wanted to. I remember a feeling of pure joy when he said this, and I took that as an answer and turned in my papers. I was pretty sure that if I felt that strongly about Japan, I wouldn't be going there, so I arranged to open my mission call all by myself. (I didn't feel up to reacting to a call to Wisconsin in front of lots of people.) Before I opened my call, I spent some time in prayer, until I felt

Imagine yourself as a living house. God comes in to rebuild that house. But presently He starts knocking the house about in a way that hurts abominably and does not seem to make any sense. What on earth is He up to? The explanation is that He is building quite a different house from the one you thought of - throwing out a new wing here, putting on an extra floor there, running up towers, making courtyards. You thought you were being made into a decent little cottage: but He is building a palace. He intends to come and live in it Himself.

—*C. S. Lewis*

really thrilled for the opportunity to go to Cleveland, or Mexico, or anywhere I might be sent. With shaking hands, I opened the letter. I was called to Sendai, Japan.

My mission to Japan was a special time in my life. It was very difficult, as every mission is, but I felt sustained in the experience by the memory of the preparation the Lord had put me through two years before I left. And the preparation wasn't just the study, it was also the relationship I had been in. I learned so much from that association, and also learned to know my own heart. That relationship was the center of a Markan sandwich in my life. The fact that it was bracketed on the one side by the year of study about the language and the people of Japan, and then on the other side by the actual experience with them in my mission, combined to leave me with a life-long faith in the process by which God can lead our lives if we let Him.

Mark's testimony of Jesus is also a testimony to us about how our lives can unfold. God will send promptings to prepare us for upcoming challenges. If we follow them, we will be started on the road, as Jesus moved toward the home of Jairus. Then, something will occur that stops us, that asks us to pivot, as it were, and do something different than we expected, like the woman who reached out and stopped Jesus with her touch. It may seem at that point that we have been derailed from our original course, as the disciples must have thought the death of Jairus's daughter derailed Jesus. But that is where the miracle will occur. Something will ensue that will make that earlier preparation make sense. And we will have an unshakeable witness that God is present in our lives. The raising of Jairus's daughter meant more somehow, because of the stop along the way.

MARK CHALLENGES US TO DISPLAY OUR CELESTIAL BRANDING

What then, is your brand? What is the overriding message of your life? Mark shows us that if we invite the Lord into the process, we will find our unique voice. You don't have to be a great public speaker. You don't have to be particularly talented. You don't have to write a book. All you need is the testimony of Jesus and He will help organize your life so that the message of Christ's gospel is evident in every aspect of it. And we can watch in the life of Jesus the process by which God builds that witness in us. It is often by leading us on rather circuitous routes through life! So, rather than taking the unexpected turns of our lives as disappointments, we might view them as God's branding exercise. He is helping us narrow down our priorities. He is ensuring that our language, our actions, and even our countenances reflect Him, because we know He is the one that has been in charge of the route.

As God guides our steps, we will have a witness to bear that will bring comfort to others at a moment when there is no other comfort. We will speak the truth in love. We will give hope to those who have lost faith. With Jesus as our guide, we will have the courage and the sensitivity to know what to say and what to do to let His power shine through us, having "received His image in [our] countenances" (Alma 5:14). That's celestial branding at its best.

Chapter Six

A SABBATH-KEEPING SELF-HELP SESSION

Here's a confession: Keeping the Sabbath day holy is not my strong suit. In fact, the recent emphasis by the Church on the Sabbath makes me downright uncomfortable. I'm not sure why I feel so guilty, because when I examine my Sabbath behavior, it's not shocking. I go to church; I'm not hanging out poolside, at movies, or in shopping malls. It's just that by the time I get home from church, I want to get my comfy clothes on, hunker down, and relax. So I feel sort of rebellious and grumpy when they talk about proper Sunday behavior, because somehow I feel that I am not quite measuring up. I'm going to have a little self-therapy session about this with myself, and you are invited to participate if you have a few issues in this area.

Issue #1:

Let's start with the expression: "Keeping the Sabbath Day Holy." I have to say that the word "holy" doesn't really describe me! I know that it's good to be holy, but it doesn't sound all that fun. In fact, when I think about the word "holy," I get an image of the "church lady" as portrayed by Dana Carvey and am tempted to smirk and say, "Well isn't that special!" Yet "holy" is how God commands me to keep the Sabbath day. So let's start right there. It's obvious that I need to reexamine the definition of holiness.

Merriam-Webster gives this definition:

holier; holiest
> 1: exalted or worthy of complete devotion as one perfect in goodness and righteousness
> 2: Divine
>> - for the Lord our God is *holy*—Psalms 99:9 (King James Version)
> 3: devoted entirely to the deity or the work of the deity: a *holy* temple, *holy* prophets
> 4a: having a divine quality: holy love
>> b: venerated as or as if sacred: *holy* scripture, a *holy* relic[30]

I notice that these definitions build on one another. God is holy, and as people show devotion to Him they may also be described as holy or, in other words, partaking of His divine nature. The emotions we feel toward God (like reverence and veneration) and even the objects that remind us of Him (like the temple or our scriptures) may also be described as holy.

A Venn diagram might be helpful here, showing my nature, which is "wholly human," and God's nature, which is "wholly holy," as it were. Holiness could be viewed as that little section where my lifestyle overlaps with God's lifestyle.

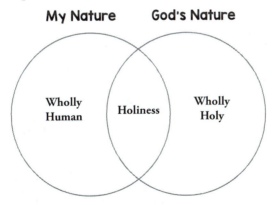

My Nature   **God's Nature**

Wholly Human   Holiness   Wholly Holy

---

30. *Merriam-Webster Online*, s.v. "Holy," https://www.merriam-webster.com/dictionary/holy.

To keep the Sabbath day holy might be seen as an opportunity to spend time in a sacred space with God. This can be done by moving as many sacred activities as possible into the Sabbath day. Hopefully there are portions of every day that are devoted to divine pursuits, but on Sunday, we have the chance to really move several hours into that shared, sacred space and spend some quality time with the Lord.

Thinking about it that way helps me overcome my rebellious attitude a little. God isn't asking me to not have any fun on Sunday; He is asking me to share as much of the day with Him as I can. I'm definitely on board for that.

Sabbath Action Item #1:

I'm going to redefine "holiness" as spending time in a sacred space with God and try to fill my Sabbath with activities that Jesus would want to share in.

Issue #2:

Why do we make a lot of restrictions for Sunday behavior?

Jesus was very critical with the Jewish leaders for overregulating the Sabbath. What's wrong with going to 7-Eleven or indulging in a nice Netflix binge?

> Inherent gospel holiness, or what
> Terms else they please to give it; for 'tis that,
> And that alone, by which all graces come
> Into the heart; for else there is no room
> For ought but pride, presumption, or despair,
> No love or other graces can be there.
> —John Bunyan

Jesus was raised in a time of great imbalance when it came to the Sabbath. In response to the warnings of prophets like Ezekiel—who listed Sabbath breaking as one of the reasons the Israelites had been overthrown and drawn into captivity by the Babylonians and the Assyrians—Sabbath keeping had become a top priority for the Jews. Over time, the rabbinical commentary on the simple commandment to keep the Sabbath day holy grew to include thirty-nine principal classes of prohibited actions, including sowing, plowing, reaping, cleansing, grinding, sifting, baking, and so on. Each class of actions was protected by additional rules, so that by the time of Jesus there were several hundred prohibited actions for the Orthodox Jew to avoid on the Sabbath day.[31]

Common sense had long ago taken flight in this theological maelstrom. For example, spitting on the ground was defined as plowing, because the dirt might be moved by the spittle. Printing two letters in a row was writing, which was interpreted as work. Any knot that required two hands to untie also constituted working. Wearing shoes with nails in them was bearing a burden. Walking through grass was threshing. And looking in a mirror was forbidden to women because they might be tempted to pull out a gray hair!

A key word in the theological discussion about the Sabbath was "lawful," and this also becomes a key word in the interactions between Jesus and the leaders of the synagogue. The Pharisees were obsessed with "lawfulness." What was lawful to do on the Sabbath and what was not? For example, one day when the disciples were hungry, they picked grain as they walked through the fields, causing the Pharisees to object that to do so was not "lawful."

> One Sabbath Jesus was going through the grainfields, and his disciples began to pick some heads of grain, rub them in their hands and eat the kernels. (Luke 6:1 NIV)

When the Pharisees used the term "lawful," they were not referring to the commandments regarding Sabbath observance found in the Torah but to the rabbinical commentary that had grown up around Sabbath observance. As Jesus often did, He used the same word in a challenge to the Pharisees. If anyone knew the law, our Savior did. And He knew the difference between "lawful" and those restrictions that constituted a "hedge around the law."

---

31. "Jesus Christ and the Sabbath: How Did Jesus Christ View the Sabbath Day?" United Church of God, accessed September 10, 2018, https://www.ucg.org/bible-study-tools/booklets/sunset-to-sunset-gods-sabbath-rest/jesus-christ-and-the-sabbath.

One of the restrictions that most irritated the Savior was the injunction against helping anyone in need unless his or her life was in danger. Since most of the healings performed by Jesus were for people whose lives were not in imminent danger, the Pharisees accused Him of breaking the Sabbath.

On one occasion, He healed a woman who had suffered for years from a disease that did not threaten her life (just made it miserable), and He was immediately rebuked by the leader of the synagogue:

> Indignant because Jesus had healed on the Sabbath, the synagogue leader said to the people, "There are six days for work. So come and be healed on those days, not on the Sabbath." (Luke 13:14 NIV)

The leader of the synagogue is referring to a rabbinic injunction that states: "Any danger to life overrides the prohibitions of the Sabbath" (Mishnah Yoma 8:6). This tradition was a good one, but here the ruler is extending the "hedge" to say that healing of any kind, unless it actually saves a life, is a type of work that should be left to the other six days. Jesus will have none of it.

Jesus responded sharply,

> "You hypocrites! Doesn't each of you on the Sabbath untie your ox or donkey from the stall and lead it out to give it water? Then should not this woman, a daughter of Abraham, whom Satan has kept bound for eighteen long years, be set free on the Sabbath day from what bound her?" (Luke 13:15–17 NIV)

WHAT'S WRONG WITH A HEDGE?

There is no question that one of the purposes of organized religion is to suggest rules and guidelines that help us keep the commandments. In other words, to make a hedge around the law! Is this inherently wrong? Some would argue that it is. Making rules to help people keep the rules can lead to a worship of rules, rather than a worship of God. Karl Barth warned that "a religion adequate to revelation and congruent to the righteousness of God . . . is unattainable by human beings."[32] The human tendency to make rules around rules around rules is what can make religion go terribly wrong.

ARE WE HEDGE BUILDERS?

We are not exempt from this tendency. In fact, as members of The Church of Jesus Christ of Latter-day Saints, we excel at hedge building! For example, we believe in sexual purity before and fidelity after marriage. For this reason, we encourage our youth to dress modestly, we outline proper behavior between the sexes, and we encourage young people not to date before the age of sixteen. These useful guidelines for behavior are not in themselves commandments, but over time they can grow to be an end in themselves. I've known parents who adamantly refused to let their son or daughter attend the school prom because it fell a week before that sixteenth birthday. Their dedication in keeping this injunction so exactly comes from a great desire to be obedient, but it can also lead to a judgmental attitude toward those with a more relaxed attitude.

We must be careful that our desire to maintain the "hedge" doesn't interfere with the greater goal, which is to help every person come unto Christ. For example, when I've seen leaders turn kids away from an activity for the lack of a skirt or a tie, I've

In the spiritual life, discipline means to create that space in which something can happen that you hadn't planned or counted on.
—*Henry Nouwen*

wondered what Jesus would do in that situation. They are there, in front of us, asking to come in, even though they may not have the right clothing, or a dance card, or even the right attitude! At that moment, what is "lawful," in the way that Jesus defined it? Is there

---

32. Fleming Rutledge, "Fleming Rutledge: Why Being 'Spiritual' Is Never Enough," *Christianity Today*, May 2018, https://www.christianitytoday.com/women/2018/may/fleming-rutledge-why-being-spiritual-is-never-enough.html.

a way that we can show that the person is more important than the policy, while still respecting the rules?

One might ask oneself in any church situation, "Right now, is my behavior more like the Pharisees or more like the Savior?" If we are making hedges around the law, and then mistaking the hedge for the law itself, Jesus's many rebukes to the Pharisees on this issue might be instructive. How many times have we judged our neighbors in the Church for not adhering to guidelines that are actually not commandments? On the other hand, how many times have we excused our own behavior (even though it was not really appropriate) because it technically fell within the established guidelines?

Sabbath Action Item #2:

I'm going to adopt Jesus's definition of "lawful," to mean "doing good."

I realize that this will relax some restrictions, and in other cases it will raise the bar on my Sabbath behavior. In any case I am going to resist the temptation to judge others, who may define "lawful" differently than I do.

Issue #3:

I like my new definitions of "holiness" and "lawfulness." Now, how do I put them into practice? How do I decide what to do, and what not to do, on the Sabbath day?

Sabbath keeping, like any commandment, starts with asking the question, "What would Jesus do?" Jesus was, in fact, very strict about the Sabbath. He obeyed the fourth commandment as he obeyed all of the commandments, perfectly and for the right reasons. What He reacted against were endless guidelines that actually detracted from the spirit of

> When I had to make a decision whether or not an activity was appropriate for the Sabbath, I simply asked myself, "What sign do I want to give to God?" That question made my choices about the Sabbath day crystal clear.
>
> —Russell M. Nelson

the Sabbath, and the way that those who kept them judged others who did not.

When I excuse my lazy behavior by noting what seems to be a relaxed attitude toward Sabbath observance on the Savior's part, I am missing the point. The idea of reorganizing our behavior in order to avoid transgressing God's laws is a good one, but can lead to an overemphasis on what shows, rather than what it truly good. Jesus approaches each commandment differently. He starts with what doesn't show; He approaches the commandments by looking at our hearts. Each Sabbath activity should be viewed through His loving lens.

When Jesus tells the rulers of the synagogue that it is "lawful" to do good on the Sabbath, He sets a standard for all of us. Doing good on the Sabbath is positive, active, and very easy to identify. It is different than just not doing anything bad. It is different than doing nothing. (So much for Netflix.) It is actively looking for ways to show love, give service and advance the kingdom of God.

This positive, active approach to the Sabbath doesn't seem discouraging to me. I like the idea of loading up some good things to do on Sunday, rather than just refraining from fun. Sunday can be its own kind of fun. The scripture says that the Sabbath should be a "delight." I like the sound of that.

Sabbath Action Item #3:

I'm going to concentrate on making the Sabbath a "delightful" day.

There are so many ways I can be of use to my Savior! I'm going to actively plan my Sundays so that they include time with family,

ministering to others, reading, studying, listening to great music, enjoying nature, and taking care of my church responsibilities. As I concentrate on making the Sabbath a "delight," I know He will bless me.

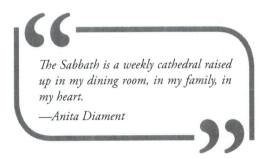

The Sabbath is a weekly cathedral raised up in my dining room, in my family, in my heart.

—Anita Diament

I'M SORRY, YOUR THERAPY SESSION HAS TIMED OUT

Well, it's time to end our session, but I'm feeling better, aren't you? It turns out that if I define holiness in the way that God defines it—as sharing in His preferred activities—I'm already holy! (Well, at least a little bit anyway.) And rather than waiting until I turn into a different kind of person, I can choose holiness by spending more time worshiping, serving, and learning about the Savior on His special day. Rather than focusing on what I shouldn't do, or judging others for their Sabbath choices, I can redefine "lawful" as Jesus did—simply doing good. And I can find creative ways to love and interact with those God has placed in my sphere of influence, making the Sabbath a "delight" for others as well as for myself.

D. Todd Christofferson says this:

> If we yearn to dwell in Christ and have Him dwell in us, then holiness is what we seek, in both body and spirit. We seek it in the temple, whereon is inscribed "Holiness to the Lord." We seek it in our marriages, families, and homes. We seek it each week as we delight in the Lord's holy day. . . .
>
> Sister Carol F. McConkie has observed: "We recognize the multitude of tests, temptations, and tribulations that could pull us away from all that is virtuous and praiseworthy before God. But our mortal experiences offer us the opportunity to choose holiness. Most often it is the sacrifices we make to keep our covenants that sanctify us and make us holy."[33]

Holiness, like forgiveness or humility, is a virtue that cannot be cultivated without divine grace. But with God's help, we can learn to choose holiness a little at a time, and Sunday is a great place to start.

---

33. D. Todd Christoferson, "The Living Bread Which Came Down from Heaven," *Ensign*, November 2017.

Chapter Seven

LUKE: JESUS AND THE HERO'S JOURNEY

The first thing to know about the book of Luke is that it is only the first half of a book; the other half is the Acts of the Apostles. These two were originally composed as one scroll. In our Bible the Gospel of John comes between them, so it's hard to get the continuity, but for the past century scholars have agreed that they make up two parts of a single literary composition by a man named Luke, who may have been a companion of Paul.[34]

The second thing that is very interesting about this Gospel is the way that Luke frames his narrative as a journey. The use of geography to reflect the spiritual life of a people is beautifully illustrated in the Old Testament,

> *Every day we step into the unknown on our journey. From moment to moment we do not know where it will take us. This is the refining nature of the Wilderness we travel in and the Light and Power by which we are led. Understanding the nature of the journey makes all the difference in our experience in the wilderness world. We learn to cry to the Lord and to cultivate the power to hear the Voice.*
> —*M. Catherine Thomas*

---

34. Luke Timothy Johnson, *The Writings of the New Testament* (Minneapolis, MN: Fortress Press, 2010), 189.

with the wandering in the wilderness of the Israelites. Luke references that journey as a starting point to Jesus's ministry, as Jesus enters the wilderness for forty days. During that time, He fasts, is ministered to by angels, prepares Himself for His mission, and has interactions with the adversary. Luke wants us to make a connection between the life of Christ and the House of Israel.

Luke's Gospel follows a chiasmic structure. The first part of his narrative shows us Jesus, heading toward Jerusalem at the age of twelve. In the ensuing years the Savior is always traveling, but the narrative concludes in Jerusalem. Why do the most important events in the life of the Savior take place in and around Jerusalem, especially in and around the temple? Johnson explains:

> Why is Jerusalem so central? The city and its temple were obviously of historical importance for Judaism and . . . for the Christian movement—after all, it is where Jesus was killed and the church was born. . . . But more than historical recollection is at work for Luke. The city and the temple, for him virtually identical, symbolize the people of Israel.[35]

After Jesus's death and Resurrection, geography is again important in the Acts of the Apostles. The narrative opens in Jerusalem as the new Church is established, then moves outward into the regions just beyond Jerusalem, then into the diaspora (Jewish settlements in Gentile territories) and finally ends in Rome, the end of the known world. For the early Christians that would constitute the fulfillment of Jesus's injunction to take the gospel "to the ends of the earth" (Acts 1:8 NIV).

Once we understand the importance of geography in Luke's testament, we can see why on occasion he places Jesus in some different settings than the other Gospels do. Scholars believe that the Gospel writers depended both on oral histories and on written sources, but Scholar F. F. Bruce warns us not to assume too much about just what sources they used:

---

35. Ibid., 194; italics added.

The Gospel as preached in those early days emphasized what Jesus did more than what He said. The message that proved effectual in the conversion of Jews and Gentiles was the Good News that by His death and rising again He had procured remission of sins for all believers. But once they were converted, they learned much more, and in particular they were taught the wonderful Sayings of Jesus. Now it is striking that the greater part of the material common to Matthew and Luke, but not found in Mark, consists of Sayings of Jesus. This has led to the conjecture of another early document on which Matthew and Luke drew for their common non-Markan material, the document usually referred to as "Q." But it is safer to regard "Q" not as the name of a hypothetical document, but as a convenient symbol for the non-Markan material common to Matthew and Luke.[36]

Whatever its format, we can assume that Matthew, Luke, and John had access to a collection of the teachings or sayings of Jesus. As Mark used the narrative structure to frame the message of Jesus, Luke used geographical settings, to symbolize His physical journey. Perhaps the most notable examples of this are the ten chapters in which Jesus travels through Perea (Luke 10–19), the traditional route taken by Jews to avoid going through Samaria. It is in these chapters that Luke records some of the most important teachings of Jesus about inclusiveness, such as the parables of the good Samaritan and the prodigal son. He uses the fact of Jesus being on an actual detour (one created to avoid a hated group of people) to show how racial, ethnic, and religious prejudice can take us off the straight path toward God.

Geography as a literary motif both predates and postdates Luke's gospel. From Homer's *Odyssey* (approx. 650 BCE) to Tolkein's *The Hobbit* (AD 1937), the journey to spiritual awakening is often mirrored by a physical journey through a wilderness. Mythologists call this the Hero's Journey. Joseph Campbell describes it thus:

---

36. F. F. Bruce, "The Sources of the Gospels," *Journal of the Transactions of the Victoria Institute* 75 (1943): 7.

> A hero ventures forth from the world of common day into a region of supernatural wonder: fabulous forces are there encountered and a decisive victory is won: The hero comes back from this mysterious adventure with the power to bestow boons on his fellow man.[37]

Jesus's forty days in the wilderness prepare Him for His three-year journey toward His atoning sacrifice in Jerusalem. Both journeys alert us, as readers and followers, to consider our own mortal journeys. Luke has Jesus begin His spiritual journey in the temple in Jerusalem, and we are sadly aware that this is also where it will end, but the journey itself is the main focus. Though the narrative does state a series of destinations (for example, "He steadfastly set his face to go to Jerusalem" [Luke 9:51 KJV]), we never think of this as the most important element of the story. We are reading to see what Jesus does along the way.

YOUR HERO'S JOURNEY

The first line of Dicken's masterwork, *David Copperfield*, famously begins: "Whether I shall turn out to be the hero of my own life, or whether that station will be held by anybody else, these pages must show."[38]

Each of us may be said to be the "hero" of our own life journey. What can we learn from Jesus's journey about our own? There are three elements in the mythical hero's journey that I think are helpful for each of us as we understand our own journey on this earth.

1. Choose the right guide and traveling companions
2. Understand the agenda
3. Have a worthy destination

---

37. Joseph Campbell, *The Hero with a Thousand Faces* (New York: MJF Communications, 1949), 30.
38. Charles Dickens, *David Copperfield* (London: Penguin Books, 1996), 1.

GUIDES AND COMPANIONS: CHOOSING THE TEAM

Among the traveling companions of the hero are the mentor, or travel guide, and the followers, or traveling companions.[39] In the book of Luke, Jesus's travel guide is the Holy Spirit. In the first chapter, Mary receives a visit from Gabriel with the startling news of Jesus's impending birth. When Mary asks, "How will this be, since I am a virgin," the angel responds to her, "The Holy Spirit will come on you, and the power of the Most High will overshadow you. So the holy one to be born will be called the Son of God" (Luke 1:34–35 NIV).

Luke again describes the Holy Spirit descending on Jesus at His baptism (see Luke 3:21–22). It is interesting that Jesus did not consider Himself unique in the possession of this divine helper: In fact, He was adamant that His followers could experience the same step-by-step guidance:

But when he, the Spirit of truth, comes, he will guide you into all the truth. He will not speak on his own; he will speak only what he hears, and he will tell you what is yet to come. (John 16:13 NIV)

> I think a spiritual journey is not so much a journey of discovery. It's a journey of recovery. It's a journey of uncovering your own inner nature. It's already there.
> —Billy Corgan

But when they arrest you, do not worry about what to say or how to say it. At that time you will be given what to say, for it will not be you speaking, but the Spirit of your Father speaking through you. (Matthew 10:19–20 NIV)

---

39. These three characteristics of the hero's journey were distilled from part one of Joseph Campbell's *The Hero with a Thousand Faces*.

HOW TO GET THE HOLY SPIRIT AS YOUR GUIDE

Guidance from a divine source is an essential component of the hero's journey. Joseph Campbell explains:

> Protective power is always and ever present within the sanctuary of the heart and even immanent within, or just behind, the unfamiliar features of the world. One has only to know and trust, and the age-less guardians will appear. Having responded to his own call, and continuing to follow outrageously as the consequences unfold, the hero finds all the forces of the unconscious at his side.[40]

During the period of wandering in Perea, Jesus's disciples observed the Lord seeking guidance in prayer and asked Him to teach them how to receive that same guidance.

> When he finished, one of his disciples said to him, "Lord, teach us to pray, just as John taught his disciples."
> He said to them, "When you pray, say: 'Father, hallowed be your name, your kingdom come. Give us each day our daily bread. (Luke 11:1–3 NIV)

When Jesus speaks of "daily bread," He is speaking of more than three square meals a day. He is again referencing the children of Israel and their sojourn in the wilderness. For forty years, they received "daily bread," or manna, from God. Jesus goes on to encourage His disciples to keep praying, using the homely comparison of God to a sleeping neighbor, tucked into bed with his children and unwilling to be disturbed. And yet, He says, if you keep knocking,

> I tell you, even though he will not get up and give you the bread because of friendship, yet because of your shameless audacity he will surely get up and give you as much as you need.
> So I say to you: Ask and it will be given to you; seek and you will find; knock and the door will be opened to you. For everyone who asks receives; the one who seeks finds; and to the one who knocks, the door will be opened. (Luke 11:8–10 NIV)

---

40. Campbell, *The Hero with a Thousand Faces*, 72

I have to admit that at times, when I've read that passage, I've thought, "You know, I don't think that's really true, because I've asked for certain things, sometimes for years, and I didn't receive them." But finally I connected these three components of the hero's journey. We ask for daily bread, for guidance, for protection. Then the vicissitudes of life test us to the limit, and we learn what asking really means. We keep knocking and knocking when there appears to be no answer forthcoming. Finally, we receive not what we have asked for but what we need. For in our ignorance we may not recognize the dangers in what we seek. Our guide must show us what we really need.

> Which of you fathers, if your son asks for a fish, will give him a snake instead? Or if he asks for an egg, will give him a scorpion? If you then, though you are evil, know how to give good gifts to your children, *how much more will your Father in heaven give the Holy Spirit to those who ask him!* (Luke 11:11–15 NIV; italics added)

Jesus is not promising to give us everything we want, or even what we think we desperately need, but He is promising the most essential thing: the Holy Spirit. This, by the way, is the only promise in the sacrament prayer. If we "always remember Him and keep His commandments," we will "always have His Spirit to be with [us]" (D&C 20:77). You know you have the right traveling companion in life when you feel the Spirit is with you. It's not necessarily when life goes right or everything you undertake is successful: it's when you have the Spirit with you.

That plays out beautifully in Acts, or the second half of Luke's gospel. If we skip John, and go right from the book of Luke to Acts, we see how Jesus moves from commanding the Apostles to go out into the world and preach the gospel to the Day of Pentecost where they are blessed with the gift and power of the Holy Ghost that enables them to do so. Jesus was guided by the Spirit, and up to that point He personally guided the Apostles. Now, on the Day of Pentecost, He replaces His physical presence with the Spirit to guide them.

LET JESUS CHOOSE YOUR TRAVELING COMPANIONS

Jesus chose an unusual group as His traveling companions. They included a few fishermen, a tax collector, and a thief. These were obscure people, who probably didn't have very good table manners, and who certainly weren't well educated. For a brilliant man like Jesus, they might not have been the most interesting people with whom to spend time day after day. They tended to quarrel with each other and found it difficult to grasp what Jesus's mission really meant. They could be disappointing, but these were the people Jesus chose for His friends, and I think one of the reasons He chose them was that He saw the greatness in them. He knew what they could become.

I had a wonderful mentor, Arthur Henry King, who served as a kind of adopted father to many young people at BYU over the decades. Dr. King didn't have children of his own—just the students who became a part of his family. (When I became one of those children, I think there were about forty of them.) He often said, "Jesus used to say, 'You have not chosen me, but I have chosen you.' I am exactly the opposite of Jesus; I don't know how to choose my friends, so I let Jesus choose them for me." He didn't fool us though. Dr. King would invite into his circle those students who seemed to need him the most, and in this way, he was very much like Jesus. For those of us who were lucky enough to stumble into his fatherly embrace, his influence and love changed all of our lives. He had a vision; he saw what we could become, and he helped us see it. He showed me an example of a person who asks Jesus to choose his traveling companions, and then imitates the way Jesus treated those who followed Him. As Joseph Campbell remarked, "the way to become human is to learn to recognize the lineaments of God in all the wonderful modulations in the face of man."[41]

The Church is one place where Jesus chooses our traveling companions. In the Church, we are placed in a group of people that

---

41. Ibid., 390.

we wouldn't otherwise know, and through our various callings we are thrown together with people whom we would not necessarily choose as friends. Yet many times these strangers turn out to be some of the most wonderful people we will ever meet. Craig and I have made such wonderful friends over the years of people that we were called to visit or home teach. Jesus brought those friends to us, and we truly would have missed something great without them.

I have a young friend who chose some very poor traveling companions in high school, who got him involved in stealing and selling items. One night they found that they were being pursued by the police, so they ran away in one of their parents' cars. When they ran out of money and ended up robbing a store, they were caught. This fine young man, up to that point an A student, was suddenly arrested and tried as a criminal. You can imagine how devastated he was, and how desperately his parents prayed for him to be shown mercy. Instead, the judge sentenced him to the maximum sentence of three years in prison. It seemed that the damage to his life was irreparable.

In prison, he was assigned a home teacher who lived in the area. The first time this man came to see the boy he said, "Okay, you're going be here for a while, so let's set some goals." The first goal they set was to finish high school. Then the home teacher said, "I hear you played an instrument in the school band and you're really good at it. Let's get a teacher to come in and keep your skills up." That was a second goal. And a third goal was to work and save some money while he was there.

> Nobody grows old by merely living a number of years. People grow old by deserting their ideals. You are as young as your faith, and as old as your doubt; As young as your self-confidence, as old as your fear; As young as your hope, as old as your despair.
> —Douglas MacArthur

By the end of the three years, this boy had graduated from high school, taken some online college courses, kept up his music, and saved some money from a job with the airlines. Throughout his difficult sojourn in the prison (his own wilderness) this home teacher was a faithful friend and guide. Instead of being lost, this young man found himself there. He came out, went to college, and went on to have a wonderful, successful life with a tremendous family and is one of the finest people I know. On the day he was sealed to his sweetheart in the temple, that home teacher was invited to attend. Those of us who loved that boy looked on the home teacher as an angel, and the joy he experienced that day was truly heavenly. Jesus chose a traveling companion for our young friend in the wilderness, and his life was changed forever.

As Jesus chooses traveling companions for us in the Church, we might try to avoid the short-sighted response: "Hey, wait a minute. I had my friends all picked out. I had a calling that I wanted to do, and I was going to ask my two friends to work with me in it, and it was going to be just great. But now you've reorganized my ward, and none of the people I like are there, and I'm with all these other people that I don't really relate to. I bought a house in this area just to be in the ward I wanted, and I'm really angry about this whole thing. I had my journey mapped out, and I had my friends all chosen, and you, Heavenly Father, have messed up my life by changing my journey!"

It may sound silly when I say it out loud, but I admit that I have prayed prayers that sound like that. Stephen Covey said, "Our frustrations are determined by our expectations." When we get the expectation going that our journey is going to go a certain way and it goes a different way, we can get very angry.

HAVE A WORTHY DESTINATION

Our destination should determine our agenda. Jesus's destination was the Atonement, which included suffering for our sins in Gethsemane, His death on the cross, and His Resurrection. As a result, worldly accomplishments meant little to Him; interactions with the people for whom He would give His life meant everything.

70

Though it may look like Jesus is just an itinerant preacher, wandering from place to place, He is following a specific agenda: to meet and interact in a meaningful way with a cross-section of God's children, and through these interactions to demonstrate to all of us that He is working out the Atonement for each of us. What then, as Christians, is our agenda?

I must admit that I love a good agenda. I print them up for every gathering, every vacation, even for family dinners! It sometimes causes problems, so I have tried to loosen up. Last Thanksgiving when the family was all coming I said to my daughter, "My goal for this family gathering is not to try to orchestrate everything." She just started laughing and replied, "You've sent out two agendas via email already, Mom, and we didn't even get here yet!" I thought, "Well, that's only two. I mean, I've sent out more in the past." I do have a hard time trying not to, well, run everything. All moms understand this, right? We try to organize the lives of our children, of our family. We want everything to go a certain way. But life doesn't always work like that.

Whenever I go to our temple in San Diego and go into the celestial room, I look at the spot (right by the stairs) where our family stood together after the dedication service many years ago. We were lucky to be able to sit in the celestial room to hear the dedicatory prayer given by Gordon B. Hinckley. It was magnificent. When it was over, we gathered those four children who were with us in a little circle at the bottom of those stairs, and we put our arms around each other and promised that we would all come back there, that our children would be married there, and we would all be together.

That was my agenda, and it was a good one, but I understand now that in this life that may not happen in my family. Unfortunately, when it began to seem like maybe that wasn't going to all come together quite the way I had orchestrated it, my response was to continually push, and push, and push in every way I could to get those people who seemed to be edging out of the circle back into the circle, so that we could get that agenda going that I had set as an ideal.

Painful experience taught me that I needed to let go of that specific agenda (as nice as it sounded) and just open my heart to the Lord's agenda for my family, which is, of course, that each member be allowed to choose his or her own path. Agency is much more important to God than it is to parents! But I have learned that this sacred right to choose one's own path is our most precious possession. I am assured that eventually we will all be in the arms of Jesus, but there may be a more scenic path to that end for our family than I had envisioned. It is a path that has very little to do with my ability to control it. In fact, it is very different from what I had thought would be best, using my limited vision. Yet even now I can see how many great things have come to our family as we have learned to respect and love each other—not in spite of, but because of, our differences.

UNSCHEDULED STOPS

We can learn a lot about this by watching Jesus in His day-to-day life. As far as I can tell, His agenda was mostly made up of "unscheduled stops." He usually was headed somewhere, but what He did along the way is what we remember. Though these stops appeared unscheduled, they were the most important moments of His day. As we find our lives screeching to these unexpected halts, Jesus can teach us how to handle them. Many of His teachings and parables deal with unexpected stops as well.

Two of the most important unexpected stops He talks about happened during His detour into Perea. In the tenth chapter of Luke, Jesus tells the story of the good Samaritan, who stops on a journey to save a stranger. Now, I have good Samaritan moments all the time; I just don't take advantage of them. I often see people who are suffering in some way or stopped on the side of the road with car trouble. I'm sorry for them, but I hope there's a Samaritan right behind me, because I'm busy, I have an agenda! Once in a great while I have actually stopped and had a good Samaritan experience, but I'm sorry to say they've been relatively few in my life.

The story of the good Samaritan opens with a man who wants to justify himself. (That's me, by the way: I'm that guy.) "Who is my neighbor?" he says. Jesus responds:

> A man was going down from Jerusalem to Jericho, when he was attacked by robbers. They stripped him of his clothes, beat him and went away, leaving him half dead. A priest happened to be going down the same road, and when he saw the man, he passed by on the other side. So too, a Levite, when he came to the place and saw him, passed by on the other side. But a Samaritan, as he traveled, came where the man was; and when he saw him, he took pity on him. He went to him and bandaged his wounds, pouring on oil and wine. Then he put the man on his own donkey, brought him to an inn and took care of him. The next day he took out two denarii[42] and gave them to the innkeeper. 'Look after him,' he said, 'and when I return, I will reimburse you for any extra expense you may have.' Which of these three do you think was a neighbor to the man who fell into the hands of robbers? . . . Go and do likewise. (Luke 10:25–37 NIV)

What a simple story. But it is life changing if we let it be. It invites us to become the person who stops, rather than the person who passes by. Jesus is the master of the unscheduled stop. He will be walking with His disciples and somebody comes along and says, "Would you go and heal this person?" He starts that way, and then somebody else needs something, so He stops and does that, then He goes back, and just keeps moving until he gets around to everyone. You could call Jesus's whole three-year ministry a series of divine, unscheduled stops.

As Christians, it might behoove us to think, "The more unscheduled stops of mercy that are in my days, the more I am on Jesus's path." Rather than at night having a wonderful feeling that you got your whole checklist done (which is a good thing, too) you might ask yourself: "Did I have an unscheduled stop today, where I showed

---

42. One denarius would be equivalent to about one day's wage.

mercy to a stranger, or did something that Jesus needed me to do?" We might even write that down on the list: schedule an unscheduled stop! You might think, "Okay, I'm going to do one thing today that's not scheduled, I'm going to pray to have a moment where the Spirit is guiding me to do something that I hadn't thought to do."

I once heard President Thomas Monson say that he kept two checklists. One was his actual calendar, with all that he had scheduled. And another he called "the Lord's to-do list." There he would jot down any thoughts that came into his mind of service that needed doing. He went on to say that he always tried to do the Lord's list first. This a great call to repentance for me. Jesus seemed to take joy in His everyday life, and I want my life to be happier. I want to enjoy today more, and the days when I feel really fulfilled are days that I have felt I have been, as Thomas Monson said, "on the Lord's errand."

WHAT BRINGS YOU JOY IN THE JOURNEY?

The great reward of viewing your life as a celestial journey is that it can bring a sense of meaning. Joseph Campbell says, "We're so engaged in doing things to achieve purposes of outer value that we forget that the inner value, the rapture that is associated with being alive, is what it's all about. . . . We're not on our journey to save the world, but to save ourselves. . . . But in doing that you save the world. The influence of a vital person vitalizes."[43]

Elder Uchtdorf says:

> To what end were we created? We were created with the express purpose and potential of experiencing a fullness of joy. Our birthright—and the purpose of our great voyage on this earth—is to seek and experience eternal happiness. One of the ways we find this is by creating things. . . . In the end, the number of prayers we say may contribute to our happiness, but the number of prayers we answer may be of even greater importance. Let us open our eyes and see the

---

43. Joseph Campbell and Bill Moyers, *The Power of Myth* (New York: Anchor Books, 1991), 5, 183.

heavy hearts, notice the loneliness and despair; let us feel the silent prayers of others around us and let us be an instrument in the hands of the Lord to answer those prayers.[44]

Along with the spiritual things that make us happy, there are many other things that enrich us. By adding those things into our lives and into our journey, we become better traveling companions for others. My friend, Jo Clark, who's approaching ninety years old and is a great example to me, advises, "Always have something you're looking forward to; have a trip, or a project, or something in your mind that's engaging you creatively."

For me, joy comes from learning something new. I have carried a quote around for forty years that has been a mantra for my life. It is the advice that Merlin gives to the young King Arthur in the book *The Once and Future King*, by T. H. White, (which became Disney's *The Sword and the Stone*).

> The best thing for being sad . . . is to learn something. That is the only thing that never fails. You may grow old and trembling in your anatomies, you may lie awake at night listening to the disorder of your veins, you may miss your only love, you may see the world around you devastated by evil lunatics, or know your honor trampled in the sewers of baser minds. There is only one thing for it then—to learn. Learn why the world wags and what wags it. That is the only thing which the mind can never exhaust, never alienate, never be tortured by, never fear or distrust, and never dream of regretting. Learning is the only thing for you. Look at what a lot of things there are to learn.[45]

I find whenever I'm really sad or discouraged, I will feel better if I learn something, so I set my mind to learning something that has a beginning, a middle, and an end, something that stretches my thinking. It gets my mind off myself, and I always feel a little rush of joy when something comes together in my mind that I feel might be interesting to share. The traditional methods of reaching out to

---

44. Dieter F. Uchtdorf, "Happiness, Your Heritage" *Ensign*, November 2008.
45. T. H. White, *The Once and Future King* (New York: Ace Books, 2011).

God (prayer, fasting, scripture study) always help, but I find that just opening our eyes to the world around us and rediscovering the things that we like to do can be another form of spiritual effort. We are getting in touch with who we really are.

Finding those things along the way is a key to joy in the journey. I see Jesus doing this in the narrative. He is interested in things, He is interested in food, in what people do for a living, in their families. When He tells His parables, you can tell that He understands housekeeping, child rearing, business, politics, and even tax collecting! He is deeply intellectual but is also a fisherman. He appreciates good food and wine, and He even cooks! He understands the world around Him, and that is part of taking joy in the journey.

So as heroes on the journey of life, let's take a lesson from Jesus. How much are we seeking that traveling companion of the Spirit? If we had the Spirit with us even 10 percent more often, how might that change our lives? Do we invite Jesus to choose traveling companions for us on this dangerous road, remembering that the friends that Jesus chooses for us are the ones that will really change our lives? Whenever we get upset that the path isn't going the way we want, do we try to remember that it's because God is setting the agenda? Do we remember that He is setting us on a path toward eternal life, and the unscheduled stops along that path are the ones that will save us in the end? Paul sums it up:

> There is a great work for the saints to do. Progress and improve upon and make beautiful everything around you. Cultivate the Earth. Adorn your habitations. Build cities. Make gardens, orchards, and vineyards, and render the Earth so pleasant that when you look upon your labors you may do so with pleasure, that angels may delight to come and visit your beautiful locations. In the meantime, continually seek to adorn your minds with all the graces of the Spirit of Christ.
>
> —Brigham Young

Therefore, since we are surrounded by such a great cloud of witnesses, let us throw off everything that hinders and the sin that so easily entangles. And let us run with perseverance the race marked out for us, fixing our eyes on Jesus, the pioneer and perfecter of faith. For the joy set before him he endured the cross, scorning its shame, and sat down at the right hand of the throne of God. Consider him who endured such opposition from sinners, so that you will not grow weary and lose heart. (Hebrews 12:1–4 NIV)

Jesus knew that the tomb lay ahead of Him. Yet His was a joyful journey, for He looked forward to His ultimate destination, coming out of the tomb, and the joy of His Resurrection. Though sorrows lie ahead for all of us, a joyful resurrection is what is what we can look forward to, and why these wonderful days of our lives give us the opportunity to feel joy even in the midst of difficulty. As we walk in Jesus's footsteps, we'll feel joy in every step of the journey.

> *Our commitment to the gospel is supposed to be a test, it's supposed to be hard, it's supposed to be impractical in the terms of this world.*
> —*Hugh B. Nibley*

Chapter Eight

KNOCKING ON HEAVEN'S DOOR: THE PURPOSE, PROCESS, AND POWER OF PRAYER

Recently, we visited with a friend who, after years of excellent health, had developed a debilitating heart condition. Like my husband, he had been shocked when a serious health complication came, and we commiserated on life's strange turns. Later, as we drove away, our son Blake had some thoughtful questions. "In the case of something that is 'incurable,' what is appropriate to pray for? Are we trying to exert our faith for a miraculous cure? And what if the person we pray for doesn't get well? Was our faith not strong enough?" These questions are a good place to start in any discussion of prayer.

Frankly, one reason I am writing about this subject is that I need to think more about it. I don't think I'm very good at prayer. I find it hard to pray for even a few minutes, and yet we are commanded to pray without ceasing. What does this really mean? (Since we do it so much, it's much easier to just pray without thinking!) Be honest, how many times at a Church social have you asked God to miraculously make sugar cookies, donuts, and red punch "nourishing and strengthening to our bodies?" Are we seriously asking for a molecular change to take place in these foods, or are we just saying words? I feel like the disciples, who regularly watched Jesus disappear into the wilderness to commune with His Father for hours, even days at a time. Finally, in exasperation, they asked Him, "Lord, teach us to pray" (Luke 11:1 NIV).

WHY DO WE PRAY?

Before we get to Christ's prayer tutorial, let's reexamine the reasons why we pray. There are so many that I just randomly wrote down a few:

Purposes of Prayer

1. Understanding
2. Making something happen
3. Healing/Finding relief from suffering
4. Repenting
5. Connecting with God

I can't help but notice that the purposes of prayer I wrote down start with me at the center and eventually move outward. The first three are all about me, and how I am feeling. Finally, by the fourth one I am starting to worry a little about getting my behavior in line, and finally on the last one I am really reaching up, rather than drawing in, as I pray.

The LDS Bible Dictionary has the best definition of prayer I've ever read:

> Prayer is the act by which the will of the Father, and the will of the child are brought into correspondence with each other. *The object of prayer is not to change the will of God* but *to secure for ourselves and for others blessings that God is already willing to grant but that are made conditional on our asking for them.* Blessings require some work or effort on our part before we can obtain them. Prayer is a form of work and is an appointed means for obtaining the highest of all blessings.[46]

Blake's question about whether we pray to make something happen is pertinent here. Do our prayers really impact the world around us? The answer is, unequivocally, yes, and no. (Sorry.) Yes,

---

46. Bible Dictionary, "Prayer;" italics added.

in that our prayers can be a catalyst for a change in the environment and sometimes even the events about which we are praying. The scripture says, "The effectual fervent prayer of a righteous man availeth much" (James 5:16 KJV). But no, in that what our prayer "availeth" may not be exactly the thing we were asking for!

My husband, Craig, spent his teenage years watching his mother suffer with breast cancer that metastasized into her bones and caused her untold suffering. She received many blessings during the five years of her illness, but she only got worse and eventually died when he was seventeen. I asked him once if that long ordeal, during those very formative years, affected his faith in a negative way. "Actually," he responded, "it was just the opposite, because my mom received something positive from every blessing. She felt strengthened, supported, was sometimes miraculously able to do something she wanted to do (like participate in her daughter's wedding). Above all, she felt that the Lord was with her. She had the promise she would live as long as God needed her to be here, and she was at peace."

> Sometimes during solitude, I hear truth spoken with clarity and freshness; uncolored and untranslated it speaks from within myself in a language original but inarticulate, heard only with the soul, and I realize I brought it with me, was never taught it nor can I efficiently teach it to another.
>
> —Hugh B. Brown

Now that Craig is two years into a battle with multiple myeloma, his mother's example is his guide. He is very pragmatic about his illness; when it gets him down, he pays attention to it, otherwise he goes on without worrying too much.

But I am not so sanguine. I want him to get well! And my question is this: What is appropriate for me to ask? Can I beg for healing? Can I campaign for a miracle? With this in mind, let's look at the Lord's tutorial on prayer. He instructs us to pray "after this manner." As an exercise I would invite you to join me in creating a sample prayer using this template.

After this manner therefore pray ye:
> Our Father which art in heaven, Hallowed be thy name.
> Thy kingdom come, Thy will be done in earth, as it is in heaven.
> Give us this day our daily bread.
> And forgive us our debts, as we forgive our debtors.
> And lead us not into temptation, but deliver us from evil:
> For thine is the kingdom, and the power, and the glory, for ever.

Amen. (Matthew 6:9–13 KJV)

Let's unpack this little batch of sentences and see what we find.

"Our Father which art in heaven, Hallowed be thy name."

Do you praise the Lord in your prayers? Formal prayers, like the dedicatory prayers in the temple and the Psalms, praise God. Other faiths are better at praising God than Mormons are; I don't know why this is. I sometimes think it is our rather grim pioneer heritage. We are like that old married couple where the wife complains, "You never tell me you love me!" and the husband growls back, "Dear, I told you I loved you when I married you fifty years ago, and if I change my mind, I'll let you know!"

But praising God is important. To hallow God's name is to acknowledge its sacredness. So in this test prayer we are creating, let's add a few expressions of praise for God. I can't think of the holiness of God without thinking of all the ways I have felt His love, grace, and care. This is the gratitude part of the prayer. Praise and gratitude are interchangeable, almost. We are good at

There is locked in all of us more faith than we presently know. We are heard, but the response of God may not be what we would hear and now wish. Yet, haven't we lived long enough to say to the Lord, "Disregard previous memo." How many times have you prayed, and prayed, and prayed for something, and a few years later thought, "That would not have been the best thing." Look what we would have missed if we hadn't gone through that thing that I was trying to avoid. To thank Him that He answered, "No," and to ask that He erase some of the requests that we now realize were foolish.

—*Truman Madsen*

thanking God; we need to get a little better at praising Him too. Psychologists tell us that parental criticism has a greater impact than praise because we tend to praise generally and criticize specifically. (Example, "You're such a good girl!" vs. "You never make your bed!") We respond to the specific; we remember it, and we value it as more accurate feedback than general statements.

So when we pray let's think of some specific things to thank God for and specific things for which to praise Him. I'm going to do three. (And if you will excuse me, I will use the familiar pronouns, because that is how I pray when it is just God and me.) I will be thanking and praising Him for Craig's remission, for the peace we feel, and for the closeness our family is experiencing in this tough time. From my prayer you can see what is uppermost in my mind these days. Yours will look different, but it should be personal and specific to what is happening in your life right now.

"Thy kingdom come. Thy will be done in earth, as it is in heaven."

This is a big, big sentence, and it comes right at the first. It's as if we are saying, "Look, I don't know what is right to ask; I can't know the mind and will of God, but I'm saying right up front that the rest of this prayer only applies if it meets this first criteria. Let Your will be done, and let events roll forward so that Your kingdom will fill this world. My requests come second to that."

And with that caveat, I think Jesus is letting us know that we can go on to ask about our daily concerns, anything from help finding a next meal to help losing weight!

"Give us this day our daily bread."

Everything we need, every day, is a fit subject for prayer. "Sustain us, keep us alive, heal us, and help us find our keys, pass this test, and make it through another session of dialysis. Just as You kept the Israelites alive every day with manna, keep us alive with Your living bread. And just as that bread only lasted a day at a time, we know that we will need to come back tomorrow and ask again."

82

"And forgive us our debts, as we forgive our debtors."

I know that some translations of this scripture use "trespasses," and some use "sins," but the word "debts" speaks to me. I owe so much to God, to my parents, to family members who forgive me, to people who serve me when I don't deserve it, etc. When I spend a moment thinking about all that I owe, I can hardly even focus on anything that is owed to me; it is so little. The tendency to stew over small insults and hurts just melts away. Jesus shows exactly how that process works: focus first on what has been forgiven you, and you will find it easy to forgive others. And He makes it conditional; you only get to ask for forgiveness when you are willing to forgive. Isn't that just brilliant?

"And lead us not into temptation, but deliver us from evil"

Rather than the endless talking and worrying about our behavior, where it comes from, what causes us to do what we do, why we can't do better, Jesus simply invites us to ask for help. "Please God, don't lead me into temptation. Deliver me from evil." Does this imply that God leads us into bad situations? I really don't know. It's a very strange statement, and I don't presume to understand what God means by it. But I will say that most people who stop believing in God stop praying and stop keeping the faith because they feel that God has betrayed them in some way. God knows this about us. He knows that we cannot see what He is really up to. When we ask for bread, He gives us the bread of life, but we often become upset that He doesn't give us what we really asked for, which was some fake thing that just looked like bread. We get hurt and angry and turn away from Him, often when we need Him most.

Since He can't make us understand more than we are ready to, He tells us to pray that He won't test us too much, or push us harder than we can bear, but that He will deliver us from the evil that is all around us. And that is what we should pray for. I need another few decades to understand this line in the Lord's Prayer, but in the meantime, I know what to pray for.

"For thine is the kingdom, and the power, and the glory forever. Amen."

This is the only thing that gets repeated twice. Jesus bookends His prayer with statements about God's power and kingdom and glory. We are back to praising, adoring, and giving credit where credit is due: to God. We are ending where we began, asserting that He is in charge, it is His kingdom, His glory, and we are just trying to fit into that great pattern.

This is a template that helps us establish a prayer process for ourselves. I first heard the phrase "prayer process" in a talk by Neill Marriott, then serving as a counselor in the general Young Women's presidency, at a women's conference I attended with my daughters. She said, in an offhand way, "Now I'm sure you all have a prayer process. Here is mine." The three of us looked at each other and said, "What? A prayer process? I want one of those!" Sister Marriott went on to describe her process: the room where she liked to go, how she began by bearing her testimony to her Father, how she asked, how she listened, and so on. I was impressed that she had thought so much about prayer.

I remember being challenged by a religion professor in college to pray out loud fifteen minutes every day for a month. That sounded like an excellent prayer process but turned out to be pretty grueling work! I'd kneel down, Enos-like, ready to pour out my soul for hours. Three or four minutes later, I had blown through my usual concerns and caught myself wondering where we might go for lunch, or if so-and-so might call, etc. It seemed virtually impossible to simply talk to an empty room for fifteen minutes. (At least it seemed empty.) But, after several days of trying, I found myself having more to say and a greater ability to listen quietly for a few minutes. I'm embarrassed to say that this did not become a daily, or even a weekly process for me. But the exercise taught me that there is a great well of power from which I might draw when I need to, and I have been to that well a few times since.

In the delightful book *Flunking Sainthood*, Jana Reiss describes her attempt to pray while going about her daily chores, a recommendation from a Catholic mystic for finding God. Finding conventional prayer too difficult, Jana tests the Monk's assertion that if our hands are busy with a menial, repetitive task, our minds will be free to focus on God:

> In practice I learn that this kind of spiritual multitasking feels artificial . . . I do my chores in silence, but instead of enjoying the quiet as an accompaniment to my growing spiritual bliss, my mind zips around like the bamboo plants we keep trying to kill off in the backyard, which preserve themselves by sending off industrious hardy shoots all the way to the other end of the lawn. My mind cannot stay present in the moment."[47]

I haven't got a specific prayer process to recommend, but I am sensitive to the fact that we need certain, designated ways to bring ourselves into the spirit of prayer. The last couple of years I have been studying meditation, and I have developed a couple of meditations that help me focus and open myself to God's Spirit. In addition, I have one or two spots that are prayer-friendly for me. As the mother of many children, one of these places has always been the shower! For many years, it was virtually the only time I was alone during the day. I began regularly praying during that time, and over the years, I've had some strong impressions come to me somewhere between rinse and repeat. One day my sister Diane called me and said, "Marilyn, have you taken a shower yet today? I need an answer to a prayer!" We laughed, but it did make me realize that patterns can strengthen our prayer prowess.

Having a prayer process doesn't mean we get hung up on a set of rules. The scriptures are full of warnings about how letting the form get in the way can destroy the function of prayer. I was taught this

---

47. Jana Reiss, Flunking Sainthood: A Year of Breaking the Sabbath, Forgetting to Pray, and Still Loving My Neighbor (Brewster, MA: Paraclete Press, 2011), 33.

in a powerful way as a missionary in Japan. We almost never had an opportunity to teach a family, so we were thrilled when a father actually invited us back to the home to give a family night. As my companion and I sat on the tatami mat together, we explained to the father that we would like him to open our meeting with prayer. He said he had never prayed before, so we simply invited him to speak to God and say what he felt. He looked up into heaven and said, "Lord, these women have come to us like angels from God with a message for our family. Help us to understand what they have come to teach us." I still rank this as one of the greatest prayers I have ever heard.

I wish our story went on to say how that family joined the Church, but our experience was different than I expected that night. They agreed to take the lessons, and soon we taught a lesson on how to pray: how to address God properly, follow the steps, and close in the name of Jesus Christ. Now, there is nothing wrong with this pattern, it's great. But after the lesson on prayer, we never again heard our investigator speak from his heart to God. Instead, he humbly said the things we suggested, in order. And somehow, we never got back to the Spirit we felt that first night. After a while, they dropped the discussions.

Now, this is not the fault of any program. It is the fault of those of us who valued the program above the passion of the Spirit in the heart of the investigator. If we really thought about who we were addressing when we pray, our prayers would change significantly.

THE POWER OF PRAYER

The power of prayer brings us back to Blake's original question. What is the use of prayer? Does it really change things, or just our hearts? I believe that prayer can change things, including but not limited to hearts. Jesus believed in it, and taught us to ask, ask, ask. In the temple, we see Adam and Eve praying for messengers from God, and those messengers are sent. Our temple worship culminates in a sacred prayer that calls upon the power of our covenants.

The Book of Mormon tells us that through prayer angels are dispatched from God to help mortals have faith in Christ. Christ spends His last few minutes with His disciples praying on their behalf, and then kneels down and prays for the Nephites in such a way that their hearts are filled with joy beyond expression (3 Nephi 19). And in my own life, prayers have been answered in startling, unexpected ways. I couldn't make it up; it simply came from God.

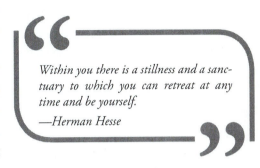

Within you there is a stillness and a sanctuary to which you can retreat at any time and be yourself.
—Herman Hesse

It is worth learning how to pray, practicing the skill, and developing a process. It is worth studying the impact that covenants have on prayer, and the impact that fasting might have. It is worth writing down our prayers and sending them to our children. It is worth having them hear us pray for them, plead to the Lord on their behalf, and thank Him for their beautiful spirits. It is worth having a spouse hear us do the same for him or her, every night, on our knees. We may find that gradually, over the decades, what we ask for shifts, and how we ask it shifts, as we grow closer to aligning our mind and will with God's. Or not. It doesn't really matter, as long as we keep trying.

PRAYER AS A PART OF THE BIGGER PICTURE

I think that there are many factors involved when we pray for something. It is said that when Joseph Smith went into the grove to pray, he not only asked the question of one fourteen-year-old boy but also carried with him the question of millions of people who had prayed, "Where is the truth?" Sometimes when we pray for things there's more involved than we realize, so if it seems like something doesn't happen as quickly as we think it should happen, or it doesn't happen at all, don't give up.

John Groberg says:

Just stop and think for a moment of the whole world, the whole universe literally filled with pleas for help. . . . We must spend effort to hear the cry of others—those unborn, those untaught, those unhappy, those unbaptized, those unwell, and those unsealed. We must even strain to comprehend what is being requested, what is needed, and how we can best fill that need. We must, in fact, move into the unknown, become a full partner with God, and attune our souls to the hearing and answering of those pleas.[48]

> *Grant me the ability to be alone, May it be my custom to go outdoors each day among the trees and grasses, among all growing things and there may I be alone, and enter into prayer to talk with the one that I belong to.*
> —*Rabbi Nachman of Bratzlav*

When Jesus talks about becoming a Savior on Mount Zion, He is referring to our part in helping Him answer the prayers of others. At the most difficult times of my life, when the heavens seem closed, I have learned that I can always get an answer to one prayer, and that is this: "Give me something to do." That's my default, fallback prayer. Asking "Why is this happening?" and "What does it all mean?" just doesn't work that well; my understanding is always just catching up with events too slowly. Yet I can pray, "Give me something to do," and I can get an answer almost immediately. Something will come into my mind that somebody needs, and it gets my mind off my doubts, or my fears, and gets my mind back where it should be, which is helping God bring to pass the happiness, immortality, and eternal life of other people. Whenever we jump on that train there's joy there.

Another reason that we pray is for repentance, and I thought Brigham Young had a great perspective on this:

---

48. John Groberg, "Investing for Eternity," *Ensign*, April 1986.

I do not recollect that I have seen five minutes since I was baptized that I have not been ready to preach a sermon, lay hands on the sick, or pray in private, or public. I will tell you the secret of this. If you commit an overt act, repent of that immediately and call upon God to give you the light of His Spirit.[49]

If Brigham did something that he felt was a mistake, he didn't do like I do, which is to obsess about it afterward and say, "I can't believe I said that. I just can't believe I said that." He went right to prayer. *Heavenly Father, forgive me. That was unkind. I didn't need to say that. I shouldn't have done that. Forgive me, just forgive me, please,* and then he was ready to move forward. What if we spent less time castigating ourselves and just relied on a fervent prayer for forgiveness? I like that proactive sense of prayer.

> *Your problem and mine is not to get God to speak to us; few of us have reached the point where he has been compelled to turn away from us. Our problem is to hear.*
> —Henry B. Eyring

The last purpose for prayer on my short list is to connect with God. The great David O. McKay, who was doing meditation long before it was hip and who was everyone's embodiment of what a prophet should look like, said this, "Prayer is the pulsation of a yearning, loving heart in tune with the Infinite. It is a message of the soul sent directly to a loving Father. The language is not mere words."[50] President McKay had a process of prayer that included six things: virtue, faith, reverence, sincerity, loyalty, and humility. I'm beginning to notice that deeply spiritual people have a process of prayer.

PRAY, PRAY, PRAY

The more we know about prayer, the more we will be inclined to turn to prayer rather than to our own wisdom. Hugh B. Brown was

---

49. Brigham Young, in *Journal of Discourses*, 12:103.
50. *Teachings of the Presidents of the Church: David O. McKay* (2011).

a great Apostle and an incredible orator. But I was touched recently when reading one of his devotional addresses at BYU. Instead of ending with a stirring conclusion, he simply started to pray for the students he was addressing. This is how he concluded his talk:

> Heavenly Father, wilt thou bless this wonderful audience of young people. Let Thy Spirit be with each of them that they may know of Thy presence and be lifted up thereby, that they may keep themselves clean and pure in Thy sight, so that when the Savior shall come again, they may be numbered among those who are worthy to meet Him at His coming. I pray for this blessing upon you and leave you this testimony and my own special blessing humbly, in the name of Jesus Christ, Amen.[51]

Jeffrey R. Holland emphasizes the power of praying for and with our children, rather than just lecturing them about the importance of it:

> Have our children ever unexpectedly opened a closed door and found us on our knees in prayer? Have they heard us not only pray with them but also pray for them out of nothing more than sheer parental love?[52]

I have a sweet memory of an afternoon when I was about fourteen years old. My mother had just been called as the Relief Society president. She was a very shy lady, and being the president of anything was not something that she would welcome. I remember walking by her bedroom one day and seeing her on her knees in prayer at her bedside. I'll never forget it. I just stood there for a moment and looked at her. It was a greater lesson than she could have ever taught me. Elder Holland says, "Let's live the gospel conspicuously. Leave that door open now and then."

It is useful not only to rethink the great blessing of prayer in our lives, but to rethink the importance of sharing that blessing with our children and our grandchildren. How easy it is to take a moment

---

51. Hugh B. Brown, "Father, Are You There?" (Brigham Young University devotional, October 8, 1967), speeches.byu.edu.
52. Jeffrey R. Holland, "A Prayer for the Children," *Ensign*, May 2003.

and pray together, rather than just be together. How easy it is to mention to a child that you've been praying for him and what you've been praying, or to send her a text and let her know just what you said. This, like everything else, was shown to us by Jesus. In Luke 11, it says, "It came to pass that as [Jesus] was praying in a certain place, when he ceased, one of His disciples said unto Him, Lord, teach us to pray" (Luke 11:1 KJV). That is the introduction to the Lord's Prayer. They asked to learn to pray, because they saw the Lord in prayer, and so our children, our grandchildren, our spouses and the people we care about will know that we have faith in God, and that prayer means something to us when they see us pray often.

Imperviousness to the promptings of the still small voice of God will also mean that we have ears but cannot hear, not only the promptings of God, but also the pleas of men.
—*Neal A. Maxwell*

I'm still not sure about the best way to pray, but I'm so thankful that you don't have to be very good at it to do it. I'm thankful that it does not require a sophisticated skill set, or even four exact steps. (You can do the steps backwards if you want. Thank Him at the end and ask to get home safely at the beginning.) As long as you reach out and talk to your Heavenly Father, He will listen, He will answer, and things will happen. As you invite Him into the daily dilemmas of your life, the things that happen to you will make more sense and will seem part of a bigger reality. That is the purpose, the process, and the power of prayer.

PRAYER MEDITATION

One of the hardest things about praying is to pay attention! Here is a meditation to help you quiet your mind and connect your mind, body and spirit in preparation for prayer.

1. Sit comfortably with your hands relaxed in your lap. Take a few deep cleansing breaths and then slow your breathing a bit so that it gently flows in and out.

2. Take a look around you and then draw that attention in as you would pull the string on a laundry bag, gathering your attention to a spot about a foot in front of you. Your eyes are open, but you are not really focusing on anything. Your sight is beginning to go inward. Now, gently close your eyes.

3. Starting at the top of your head, quietly scan down through your body. Relax the muscles of your jaw, your neck, your gut. As your mind travels downward be aware of where your body is right now. What parts are touching the seat? The floor? What parts are sending you messages of pain, or pleasure, or anything in between? Observe your body as it rests on the earth. Explore the sensations it is feeling right now, the sounds it hears, and send a message of gratitude to God for the body that houses your spirit.

4. Now that you are truly still, go over in your mind other blessings God has given you. Just list a few specific, recent ones to place yourself in a spirit of gratitude. Bear your testimony to God about His importance in your life.

5. Now ask yourself one question: "What do I want?" What comes first to your mind? Let it rest there and expand the circle of attention just a little wider and ask this question: "What does God want for me?" Use that as a starting place for your prayer.

Chapter Nine

JOHN: JESUS, THE GOD OF MIRACLES

The Book of John stands alone amidst the Gospels; John's approach to the story of Jesus is unique. Rather than beginning with the birth of Jesus, John begins in the cosmos, placing Christ in the role of omnipotent creator before His humble incarnation into the realm of flesh. The book is traditionally divided into four parts, known as the Prologue, the Book of Signs (chapters 2–12) the Book of Glory (chapters 13–20) and the Epilogue (chapter 21).

THE WORD MADE FLESH

The Word of God means something very special to the Hebrews. During Jesus's day, there were no books—this was hundreds of years before the first printing press—and a little town like Nazareth would have possessed only a few precious scrolls, stored at the synagogue in a container called an ark. Each Sabbath, the Torah scroll would have been carried through the congregation by the Hazzan, while people danced and kissed their fingers before touching it. That God could be made manifest through the written word is a fairly sophisticated idea that set the Hebrew faith apart even then.

The Jews understood that there is power in the word. Genesis begins with God creating the world through the spoken word. His word was later etched on the stone tablets to cement His covenant with Israel. John's introductory statement, "In the beginning was the Word, and the Word was with God and the Word was God" (John 1:1, KJV), would have been perfectly understandable to the Jews. By bringing that creative force, the word, into the meridian of time, to be made flesh in the person of Jesus, John establishes the connection between the Old and New Testament views of God. John will pick up that theme again and again, tying the word of God and the power of God to the person of God in Christ.

SHOW ME A SIGN

In the next eleven chapters, John explores seven miracles of Jesus, which he calls "signs." "Miraculous signs" (NIV) or "miracles" (KJV) are translated from the plural of *sēmeion*, "a sign or distinguishing mark whereby something is known, sign, token, indication."[53] John's Gospel is bookended with the assurance that these "signs" were performed for a specific purpose, namely, to point the way to Christ as Messiah.

> *We believe that we have a right to revelations, visions, and dreams from God, our heavenly Father; and light and intelligence, through the gift of the Holy Ghost, in the name of Jesus Christ, on all subjects pertaining to our spiritual welfare; if it so be that we keep his commandments, so as to render ourselves worthy in his sight.*
> —Joseph Smith

What Jesus did here in Cana of Galilee was the first of the signs through which he revealed his glory; and his disciples believed in him. (John 2:11 NIV)

Jesus did many other things as well. If every one of them were written down, I suppose that even the whole world would not have room for the books that would be written. (John 21:25 NIV)

---

53. "Sēmeion," in *Bauer–Danker–Arndt–Gingrich Lexicon of the New Testament* 920, 2aα.

WHAT A MIRACLE IS AND IS NOT

"It is . . . inaccurate to define a miracle as something that breaks the laws of nature," says C. S. Lewis.[54] Joseph Smith taught the same doctrine in the School of the Prophets, and this is one of the things that makes us a little different from other faiths who believe in creation "ex nihilo." Nothing comes from nothing. In Latter-day Saint theology, God uses the laws of the universe, and the laws of nature, to mold spirit and matter into new creations. Thus, by extension, miracles are not something that occurs outside of natural law but are a manifestation of God's greater understanding of and command over those laws. Augustine is with Joseph Smith when he says, "Miracles are not contrary to nature, but only contrary to what we know about nature."[55]

So, a miracle is something that is removed from the natural course of events, as we perceive them, but is governed by higher laws than we understand. In that context, airplanes would have been a miracle to an Elizabethan. But a miracle has another component; by definition it implies divine intervention. God has stepped in and changed the course of events in our favor.

Jesus's miracles all brought abundance, healing, or nourishment. Many people followed Jesus because of these miracles, then left Him when those miracles stopped, or at least stopped benefitting them directly. As Jesus cryptically said to the people clamoring for more feedings like the great luncheon for five thousand: "Very truly I tell you, you are looking for me, not because you saw the

> *Being a child of God is a miracle. Receiving a body in His image and likeness is a miracle. The gift of a Savior is a miracle. The Atonement of Jesus Christ is a miracle. The potential for eternal life is a miracle.*
>
> *—Donald L. Hallstrom*

---

54. C. S. Lewis, *Miracles: A Preliminary Study* (New York: Simon & Schuster, 1996), 80.
55. St. Augustine of Hippo, *City of God* XXI, 8, as quoted in Percy Dearmer, *Body and Soul* (New York: E. P. Dutton, 1909), 119.

signs I performed but because you ate the loaves and had your fill" (John 6:26 NIV).

There may be something important for us to learn here. If we accept the miracles in our lives as signs that point us to Jesus, they are having the right effect. If we lose faith when God fails to come through with the exact kind of help we are looking for, we have lost the meaning behind the miracle. We are seeking the sign instead of God. John is a great place to go to get that perspective back.

WHAT HAPPENS WHEN THE MIRACLE DOESN'T ARRIVE?

Some friends of ours had a son who loved the outdoors. One day on a hike with friends, a storm arose, and he slipped and fell off a precipice, landing on a ledge some fifty feet below. His hiking companion, having no way to reach him, dived into the lake below and swam for help. By the time she reached help and the rescuers could make it to him, it was early the next morning. He died in the arms of his rescuers. His mother describes her feelings:

> I found out what a broken heart truly means and feels like. My heart was figuratively broken but truly, it felt physically broken as well . . . heavy, burning and hurting. I couldn't function for the first two days after the devastating, numbing news. All of my tears, prayers and wishes couldn't change the fact that Jeff was dead. How does a mother survive the heartbreak of losing a child to death—or any other type of devastating loss?[56]

> *Satan, our adversary, wants us to fail. He spreads lies as part of his plan to destroy our belief. He slyly suggests the doubter, the skeptic, the chic is sophisticated and intelligent, while those who have faith in God and His miracles are naive blind or brainwashed.*
>
> —Dieter F. Uchtdorf

Jeff's mother described how, along with the pain of losing him, the thought of

---

56. Personal recollection of Lise Brown.

her son's lonely suffering in the last hours of his life was almost unbearable to her. Where was the miracle for this young man and his parents? Why, when so many receive miraculous healing or are saved from mortal danger, did this young man experience this senseless, seemingly random fall that ended in a night of suffering, and then death?

Donald Hallstrom addresses this conundrum in a sermon titled "Has the Day of Miracles Ceased?"

> What about the innumerable faith-filled, priesthood-blessing-receiving, unendingly-prayed-for, covenant-keeping, full-of-hope Latter-day Saints whose miracle never comes? At least in the way they understand a miracle. At least in the way that others appear to receive miracles. What about those who suffer from profound afflictions—physically, mentally, emotionally—for years or for decades or for their entire mortal life? What about those who die so very young?[57]

Hallstrom goes on to say that it may be short sighted to define a miracle only as a providential escape from suffering or death:

> Often we describe a miracle as being healed without a full explanation by medical science or as avoiding catastrophic danger by heeding a clear prompting. However, defining a *miracle* as "a beneficial event brought about through divine power that mortals do not understand" gives an expanded perspective into matters more eternal in nature. This definition also allows us to contemplate the vital role of faith in the receipt of a miracle.[58]

What is the role of faith in the receipt of a miracle? Perhaps it is simply this: that we pray for the hand of God to be manifest in our lives, and then we look for the manifestations as they occur. We don't prescribe what those manifestations must be; we have faith that they will be there, and we look for them. Once when the Apostle David Bednar was about to give a blessing he said this:

---

57. Donald L. Hallstrom, "Has the Day of Miracles Ceased?" *Ensign*, November 2017.
58. Ibid.

If it is the will of our Heavenly Father that you are transferred by death in your youth to the spirit world to continue your ministry, do you have the faith to submit to His will and not be healed?[59]

WHAT ARE YOUR SEVEN SIGNS?

It is here that I want to return to the seven signs, or miracles, that John records. I believe it is useful to think about the miracles we have experienced in our lives as signs, in other words, as experiences given to us so that we will know that Jesus is the Messiah. Whether those miracles resulted in the things we were asking for is irrelevant. The point is that we understand the sign that was being given and where it is pointing us.

Ask yourself, do I have seven signs in my life that Jesus is the Christ? Or maybe five? Or even three? Can you look back and identify miracles that have occurred in your life that caused you to have a testimony of Jesus? And have you been faithful to the signs that have been given you? Have you kept them in your heart, recorded them, and borne witness of them to your loved ones?

Here is the first sign that I received. When I was six I had five brothers, and my mother was expecting her seventh child. The night she went to the hospital, we were all sitting at the dinner table eating pancakes. (That is how we knew something was wrong; when Mom didn't feel well, she made breakfast for dinner.) Mom turned at the door and took a hard look at me. "Put Marilyn to bed," she said to my older brothers. "She doesn't look well." She was right; I was coming down with what was called "two-week measles." In those days women stayed in the hospital for ten days with a baby, so I was destined to go through that illness without my mother to nurse me. It was a tough time for a little girl, and I was lonely and afraid.

That night, feverish and worried, I crawled out of bed in my yellow footed jammies and knelt to offer the first real prayer that I can remember. I pleaded with my Heavenly Father that my mom would be okay and that I would get a sister! Oh, how I longed for a

---

59. David A. Bednar, "Accepting the Lord's Will and Timing," *Ensign,* August 2016.

sister. (Even my cat was a boy!) As I was praying, I heard the phone ring. I heard my brother Steve answer the phone and then, in a few moments, heard his happy voice calling up the stairs, "Marilyn, that was Dad. It's a girl!" At that moment I had a perfect assurance that God heard my prayer, not just because He gave me my wish, but because of the timing of the call. He heard me. He knew me. He was there.

Now, I don't believe that Heavenly Father made the baby into a girl to answer my prayer. I do believe that He inspired me to get on my knees and pray so that I would know that He was there. It was a sign to point me toward Him, something that would build my faith. Many times since I have leaned on the sign I received as a little child, that God heard my prayer. There have been subsequent, sacred moments when I have miraculously received the assurance that my prayer was heard, and that I was not alone as I faced challenges.

GOD IS IN THE DETAILS

Sometimes we discount God's intervention in our everyday lives. Does he really speak to little girls or help teenagers face an exam? Would God really help you find your car keys? I think we underestimate the condescension of God when we limit Him that way. Jesus said that His eye is on the sparrow. He told stories of women finding coins in the house, and men finding lost treasure in a field. He understands what matters to us, and sometimes there is nothing more important in the world than finding your car keys!

This is a story from Sidney Reynolds:

I am grateful for a teacher who encouraged his students to keep a journal of the whisperings or promptings of the Spirit in their lives. He directed us to note what we felt and what resulted. Little things became evident. One day, I was frantically trying to complete some assignments and prepare for a trip. I had just been down to the laundry area of the dorm to move my clothes from the washer to the dryer. Unfortunately, all the dryers were in use, and they all had many minutes to go.

I went back upstairs discouraged, knowing by the time those dryers finished, I had to be on the road. I had barely returned to my room when I felt prompted to go back downstairs and check the laundry again. *Foolishness*, I thought—I had just been there, and I didn't have time. But because I was trying to listen, I went. Two of the dryers were empty—and I was able to meet all my commitments. Could the Lord possibly have been concerned about smoothing my way in such a small but, to me, important matter? I have learned since through many such experiences that the Lord will help us in every aspect of our lives when we are trying to serve Him and to do His will.

I believe that all of us can bear witness to these small miracles. We know children who pray for help to find a lost item and find it. We know of young people who gather the courage to stand as a witness of God and feel His sustaining hand. We know friends who pay their tithing with the last of their money and then, through a miracle, find themselves able to pay their tuition or their rent, or somehow obtain food for their family. We can share experiences of prayers answered and priesthood blessings that gave courage, brought comfort, or restored health. These daily miracles acquaint us with the hand of the Lord in our lives.[60]

As I look back over the most notable miracles in my life, not all of them involved me getting what I wanted. When my husband, Craig, was suddenly diagnosed with Multiple Myeloma a couple of years ago, we were devastated. This is a disease that can be treated, but as yet there is no cure. In our first days of—well, I find myself unable to think of a word to describe how we felt—coming to grips with this new and terrifying reality, our stake president called and offered to give Craig a blessing. We didn't know President Clark well; he was relatively new in the area and

> *I am led to believe that our Heavenly Father loves us so much that the things that are important to us become important to Him, just because He loves us.*
> —*J. Devn Cornish*

---

60. Sydney S. Reynolds, "A God of Miracles," *Ensign*, May 2001.

we hadn't had much interaction with him since his call. He came and visited with us for a while, and then he gave Craig the most powerful priesthood blessing I have ever heard. One line has stayed with us ever since. He said, "I bless you that you will live to the nanosecond that God intends you to be on this earth, and that miracles will occur to bring that to pass." When he said those words an almost tangible feeling of peace descended on us.

Since then, Craig has been filled with a steady, calm assurance that he is in the Lord's hands. (I'm not so steady or calm. He's the rock, and I'm the wreck.) As each challenge has occurred—including surgery for a disintegrating vertebrae, months in a wheelchair, a stem cell transplant, chemotherapy and radiation treatments, and at one point ten days in the hospital just to get the pain under control—he has maintained a sense of humor and optimism that amazes us all. He tells each doctor that treats him that he will do all he can to live, but that he is in the Lord's hands, and he is not afraid of the outcome. That is the greatest miracle either of us have ever experienced, and it does not involve us getting what we asked for. It is, in the true definition of the word, a sign. It points our hearts and minds toward Jesus. It comes directly from Him. As Alma said, "Is not this real?" (Alma 32:35) It is the most real thing in the world.

UNSEEN HELPERS

Finally, the discussion of signs and miracles is not complete without a nod toward all the heavenly helpers who carry out the work of getting us through this vale of tears. Wendy Watson Nelson shared this profound insight that changed her life:

> The Prophet Joseph Smith declared that if we "live up to [our] *privilege*," the angels will not be able to be restrained from being our associates. . . .
>
> . . . We could also say it this way: As we keep our covenants, we can ask for angels to help us, literally!
>
> It was during Elder Jeffrey R. Holland's April 2010 general conference address that I first learned this truth. . . .

He said, "Ask for angels to help you."

He said it with such clarity and yet he said it in a manner that implied this was something we all knew! But for me, it was an entirely new principle.

> *Very real help from heaven is always available to us as we keep our covenants. I'm talking about praying to our Heavenly Father in the name of Jesus Christ, for those on the other side to be "dispatched" to assist us. Perhaps a departed loved one could be sent to help you with whatever you need.*
> —Wendy Watson Nelson

I wanted to call out, "Wait! Wait! What? You mean I could have been asking for angels to help me all this time?"

Without intending to sound too dramatic, I can say with all candor that Elder Holland's six words changed my life: "Ask for angels to help you."

That counsel changed my prayers. It changed my understanding of the very real help from heaven that is always available to us *as we keep our covenants.* I started to ask for assistance from those on the other side of the veil from that moment on!

Now, I'm not talking about praying to fantasy angels with wings to magically fairy-dust our problems away. I'm not talking about praying *to* angels. I'm talking about praying to our Heavenly Father in the name of Jesus Christ, for those on the other side to be "dispatched" (Elder Holland's word) to assist us. Perhaps a departed loved one could be sent to help you with whatever you need.[61]

"Has the day of miracles ceased?" Moroni asked. To paraphrase his answer: *No, only if you want it to. It'll cease when you stop believing in Jesus.*

It is by faith that miracles are wrought; and it is by faith that angels appear and minister unto men; wherefore, if these things have ceased. . . it is because of unbelief, and all is vain. (Moroni 7:35–37)

---

61. Wendy Watson Nelson, "How Angels Can Help Us More in Our Lives," *LDSLiving Magazine,* accessed August 30, 2018, http://www.ldsliving.com/How-Angels-Can-Help-Us-More-in-Our-Lives/s/81465.

HELPERS FROM THE OTHER SIDE

Recently I was in my daughter's Gospel Doctrine class when she addressed this topic. Andrea asked class members to testify of times when angels had attended them. One woman shared an experience she had while defending her doctoral dissertation. It was a stressful, difficult session, and as she got to the second hour, she was so worn down and tired that she couldn't think straight anymore. She just felt like giving up.

She said, "I didn't know what to pray for, so I just prayed, "Heavenly Father, can you just help me get through this second hour?" She explained what happened next, "My father, who had died a few years earlier, came into the room and sat on the chair next to me for the rest of the session. He just sat there," she said. "He didn't say anything, but he was there, next to me. And I pushed through." When this sister counts up the sacred signs that point her to Christ, this miracle will be paramount among them.

At the beginning of this chapter, I touched upon the tragic hiking accident, and the agony Jeff's mother suffered as she imagined him alone and suffering through the night. A few days after we heard about Jeff's accident, I awoke in the night thinking about him. Jeff was a friend of our son, Evan, but I had actually never met him. Though we had known his parents for several years, we were not in close contact. But I had the strongest impression come into my mind, just seven words: "Jeff was not alone on that ledge." It hit me so hard that I couldn't stop thinking about it, and I couldn't go back to sleep. Finally, I picked up my phone (I think it was around 2:00 a.m.) and texted Jeff's mother and told her what I had felt. She was awake, of course, and texted back that she had felt the same thing. Later, our daughter attended the funeral service, and Jeff's parents told her that I had been one of several people that had felt the same impression and communicated it to them. This was a miracle. Jeff needed to leave this world, but angels attended him through the process, and then bore witness, through various people, that he had not been alone.

Pray for angels to attend you and your loved ones. They will attend, and if you are prayerful about it, you may be able to sense their presence. If you do, bear your witness about it. Don't be afraid to sound like you're superstitious. Bear witness to people that there are miracles in your life; acknowledge the angels that have come to your rescue. Because that is exactly why angels are sent to interact with mortals, and you may be one who is lucky enough to be part of a miracle.

> For behold, God knowing all things, being from everlasting to everlasting, behold, he sent angels to minister unto the children of men, to make manifest concerning the coming of Christ; and in Christ there should come every good thing. . . . Wherefore, by the ministering of angels, and by every word which proceeded forth out of the mouth of God, men began to exercise faith in Christ; and thus by faith, they did lay hold upon every good thing; and thus it was until the coming of Christ. (Moroni 7:22, 25)

THE POWER OF THE WORD

We end where we began, with the Word made flesh. There's a lovely Hasidic story of a rabbi who always told his people that if they studied the Torah, it would put scripture on their hearts. One of them asked, "Why *on* our hearts, and not *in* them?" The rabbi answered, "Only God can put Scripture inside. But reading sacred text can put it on your heart, and then when your heart breaks, the holy words will fall inside."[62]

The real miracle is not when God grants our every wish, but instead when He heals our broken hearts, when His word becomes our walk, and when His angels attend us. As we watch for, and take notice of, the miraculous signs He places in our lives, we will be guided safely home.

---

62. Anne Lamott, *Plan B: Further Thoughts on Faith* (New York: Riverhead Books, 2005), 73.

Chapter Ten

HOW TO BE BORN AGAIN AND AGAIN

Jesus was a master teacher, not only because He had a great understanding of all the doctrine, but because (like any good teacher) He knew how to tell a great story. He understood that connecting knowledge with emotion is what makes people sit up and pay attention. A great teacher once advised me, "Any time you get up to give a lesson, Marilyn, remember it doesn't matter what people know, it matters what they *feel* about what they know." Jesus understood this and used examples with topics that people could relate to, like money, food, and children. Joseph Klausner, for many years professor at the Hebrew University in Jerusalem, said of Jesus:

> In his ethical code there is a sublimity, distinctiveness, and originality in form unparalleled in any other Hebrew ethical code; neither is there any parallel to the remarkable art of his parables. The shrewdness and sharpness of his proverbs and his forceful epigrams serve in an exceptional degree, to make ethical ideas a popular possession.[63]

Everybody knows the panic of losing a wallet, or what it feels like to be hungry or thirsty. Most of us know the frustration of

---

63. Joseph Klausner, *Jesus of Nazareth; His Life, Times, and Teaching* (London: Macmillan, 1944), 414.

being awakened out of a deep sleep by a fussy child. Perhaps the most dramatic and emotional experience in life is that of giving birth or being present when a child comes into the world. Jesus chose that experience as the symbol for baptism.

WHY DO WE NEED SYMBOLS?

Symbolism is expressed in language through metaphor, or the use of a concrete object to represent a more abstract concept. Metaphor comes from the Greek word *meta*, which means a passing over or going from one place to another, and *pharein*, to move or to carry. Metaphors mentally carry us from one place to another; they enable us to cross mental boundaries that would otherwise be closed to us. Think about your own religious experiences and how symbols have affected them. Every religion is built on a group of symbols.

Spiritual truths that transcend time and space can only be born in metaphorical vessels whose meaning is found in their connotations. A connotation is something that is connected to a word, but not denoted by it. If we look at a picture of two pieces of wood placed in a certain way, it would be described, or denoted, as a cross. Yet if you used those two pieces of wood metaphorically as a symbol and said, "This illness is a cross I must bear," your mind has automatically crossed the mental boundary between two simple pieces of wood to the more abstract cross of crucifixion. The cross of Crucifixion has connotations; everything you have learned about Christ's life and mission is connected to that symbol of Christ's sacrifice for us.

> *Water symbolizes the whole of potentiality—the source of all possible existence.*
> —*Mercia Eliade*

When you speak or even think metaphorically, a tiny little explosion happens in your brain; a synapse fires. This happens when the side of your brain that does all the analytical thinking makes a connection with the side of your brain that handles the abstract concepts. This carves a little neural pathway, as each synaptic connection actually makes a physical impression, something like the groove in a record album. The more we deal with religious symbolism, the stronger this network of neural pathways becomes.

When our synapses fire, another interesting thing happens: very often our emotions become active. If both sides of your brain aren't firing, your emotions probably will stay dormant; you're in a passive state. You've got to wake up and your brain has to start working before your emotions start working. The effort involved in understanding a symbol wakes up more than the brain. Mercia Eliade wrote:

> A religious symbol conveys its message even if it is no longer consciously understood in every part. For a symbol speaks to the whole human being and not only to the intelligence.[64]

WHAT DID BAPTISM MEAN TO JESUS?

With that rather digressive preamble, we are ready to talk about the symbolic significance of baptism, why Jesus was baptized, and why it is important for all of us to follow Him in this. Let's talk for a moment about what baptism meant to Jesus. Ritual immersion was a part of Jewish life. Before entering the synagogue and at other times, faithful Jews immersed themselves in cleansing baths that can still be seen at the sites of ancient synagogues. When John was baptizing in Jordan, I would imagine that the Jews who accepted that ordinance viewed it as something like the ceremonial

> *But, someone, please give me—who is born again but still so much in need of being born anew—give me the details of how to live in the waiting cocoon before the forever begins?*
> —*Ann Voskamp*

---

64. Mircea Eliade, *The Sacred and the Profane: The Nature of Religion*, trans. Willard R. Trask (New York: Harcourt Inc., 1959), 129.

immersion, or *mikveh* (meaning a "collection of water") that was a part of their worship.

> Mikveh purification was required of all Jews before they could enter the Temple or participate in major festivals. Hundreds of thousands of pilgrims converged on Jerusalem for Passover and other major feasts. One hundred mikvehs, attesting to the need for water purification before entering into Temple rites, have been found by Hebrew University's Benjamin Mazar around the wall adjacent to Herod's Temple. Mikvehs, resembling large bathtubs or small garden ponds, have been found in Jericho and elsewhere in Israel.[65]

But for John and Jesus, baptism was a symbol of something greater.

John's converts were already Jews, as were the first disciples of Jesus. What then did baptism mean for John and those whom he baptized? The baptism of John was a variation from more traditional Jewish practices of washing or cleansing for purification; it also represented, he said, "the return of Israel to its covenants with God." Eschatology (the study of the last days or the last things) "is a key to understanding what baptism meant to these Jews. For many Jews, as for the Jewish Essenes at Qumran, the new age of the kingdom of God was about to begin."[66]

John baptized people to prepare them for this new kingdom of God, which, in fact, was coming in the person of Jesus. As Jesus entered the River Jordan and submitted to the ordinance of baptism, the act itself took on multiple layers of meaning. As the Spirit descended upon him, John (and those faithful who were sensitive enough to see it) received the answers to the great questions: Where is the kingdom of God? and When is the Messiah going to come? The answers were manifest in the presence of Jesus: *The Messiah has come and I am He, and the kingdom of God is already here: it is within you.* This was a hard doctrine for the literal-minded Jews to understand.

---

65. "Ancient Jews and Cleanliness," Early Church History, https://earlychurchhistory.org/medicine/ancient-jews-cleanliness.
66. Obert C. Tanner, Lewis M. Rogers, and Sterling M. McMurrin, *Toward an Understanding of the New Testament* (Salt Lake City: Signature Books, 1990).

It's a hard doctrine still. But everything about the mission of Christ is symbolized in baptism: the entrance to a new world, the birth of a new self, and death and resurrection to eternal life.

WHAT DOES BAPTISM MEAN?

John records that one of the Pharisees, Nicodemus, came to Jesus in the night and asked Him, in effect, "What does baptism mean?" By the way, when someone comes in the night in the scriptures, it's related to darkness and secrecy and the enemy. When they come in the day, as when Jesus meets the woman at the well at high noon, it symbolizes light. The irony is that it would be "normal" to meet a learned Pharisee in the day time and a promiscuous woman at night. But as usual, Jesus reverses that, and our Gospel writer notes it in order for us to understand the great irony: "the people living in darkness have seen a great light," but often they can't see the greater truth that comes with it (Matthew 4:16 NIV).

Jesus immediately takes Nicodemus into a symbolic realm by connecting baptism to the process of birth. He says, "I tell you, no one can see the kingdom of God unless they are born again." Nicodemus, literal minded, says, "How can someone be born when they are old? Surely they cannot enter a second time into their mother's womb to be born!" Jesus says, "No one can enter the kingdom of God unless they are born of water and the Spirit. Flesh gives birth to flesh, but the Spirit gives birth to spirit."

Jesus then says, "The wind blows wherever it

We consider that God has created man with a mind capable of instruction, and a faculty which may be enlarged in proportion to the heed and diligence given to the light communicated from heaven to the intellect; and that the nearer man approaches perfection, the clearer are his views, and the greater his enjoyments, till he has overcome the evils of his life and lost every desire for sin; and like the ancients, arrives at that point of faith where he is wrapped in the power and glory of his Maker and is caught up to dwell with Him.
—*Joseph Smith*

pleases. You hear its sound, but you cannot tell where it comes from or where it is going. So it is with everyone born of the Spirit" (John 3:3–6 NIV).[67]

Here Jesus combines a common physical experience, feeling the wind against your skin, with one of life's most transcendent mysteries, the first breath of a living child. In either case, he explains, you don't know where the wind, or breath comes from. You don't understand what makes the baby come alive, but you see that baby take that breath. We've all seen it, and we know there's not a miracle to compare to it. We don't know where it comes from, but we know it's the power of God.

When Nicodemus wonders, "How can these things be?" Jesus responds with a fairly sharp challenge, that all of us must feel. "Are you a teacher in Israel?" In other words, *You've been teaching all these years. You know the stories of Genesis, did you get their true meaning? You know how God breathed life into Adam. You have studied story after story of barren women who prayed for the miracle of birth, and God granted that miracle. All of that was to prepare you to understand how great God's power is. The breath of life that you have been teaching about is God's power, and it can cause a complete renewal in your life. That's what baptism is. It's a breath of life.*

ONE PICTURE IS WORTH A THOUSAND WORDS

If you had to tell somebody in one sentence what the gospel means, what would you say? When Nephi was trying to understand the vision that his father had of the tree of life, the angel did not give him a gospel lecture. The tree of life was a symbol, and the angel made a real-life connection to that symbol by showing him, in vision, Mary holding Jesus. And in that moment all the synapses started firing; Nephi understood the meaning of the tree, as Eliade said, because the symbol speaks to the whole human being.

---

67. The same word is used for "spirit" and "wind" in Greek. That word ("ruach") is also used for the "breath of life" that God breathes into Adam's nostrils.

And I looked and beheld the virgin again, bearing a child in her arms. And the angel said unto me: Behold the Lamb of God, yea, even the Son of the Eternal Father! Knowest thou the meaning of the tree which thy father saw? And I answered him, saying: Yea, it is the love of God, which sheddeth itself abroad in the hearts of the children of men; wherefore, it is the most desirable above all things. And he spake unto me, saying: Yea, and the most joyous to the soul. (1 Nephi 11:20–23)

The whole meaning of the gospel is the love of God, the condescension of God, how far God will descend to meet His children and how much He loves them, like a mother loves a child.

DEFINING OURSELVES BY WHAT WE HAVE BEEN GIVEN

It is easy to spend more time thinking about what we lack than what we have. We come into the world full of promise, and most of us are part of a sweet circle of love that includes our parents and other family members. But at some point, the negative aspects of the world have so much effect on us that we lose that shininess, that hope, and that belief in our eternal potential. When Jesus says to Nicodemus that being baptized is like being born all over again, He is holding out the possibility that we can get that shininess back again. The birth narratives in the Gospels and the glorious vision of Christ's birth in the Book of Mormon are there to reaffirm our belief in that

Through baptism we have become adopted members of the royal family of Jesus Christ, and that is the basic reason we now call each other "brother" and "sister." We have indeed become members of the Church or family of Jesus Christ. If we can keep that concept clearly in mind, that we are now children of Jesus Christ, it will change our lives. . . . We will do nothing to bring dishonor or shame to that holy name we carry as children of Jesus Christ. We will respect and honor our covenant Father, Jesus Christ, and be righteously jealous and protective of the holy name we bear.

—Theodor M. Burton

promise. The promise of the Atonement is the promise of a newness of life, where we are defined, not by our limitations but by our potential, which can find its fulfillment through the greatness of Christ and our participation in His saving grace.

As we concentrate on the saving grace of Christ, that feeling of newness can be renewed in us. Alma asks us, "[Have ye] felt to sing the song of redeeming love?" And perhaps more importantly, "Can ye feel so now?" (Alma 5:26). To keep that newness of spirit, all we have to do is focus on what baptism really means. Alma explains its meaning:

> Behold, here are the waters of Mormon (for thus were they called) and now, as ye are desirous to come into the fold of God, and to be called his people, and are willing to bear one another's burdens, that they may be light; Yea, and are willing to mourn with those that mourn; yea, and comfort those that stand in need of comfort, and to stand as witnesses of God at all times and in all things, and in all places that ye may be in, even until death, that ye may be redeemed of God, and be numbered with those of the first resurrection, that ye may have eternal life. . . .
>
> If this be the desire of your hearts, what have you against being baptized? (Mosiah 18:8–10)

Whenever we lose a little of the joy of the gospel, we might look at our daily lives and ask, "How many of my daily activities have something to do with my baptismal covenant?" A young mom taking care of children might say, "Well, I'm comforting those who stand in need of comfort a lot, so that is good. But am I standing as a witness of God in all things and at all times and in all places that I may be in? For example, am I really bearing my testimony to my children? Am I teaching them the gospel by the way that I live? Am I showing my faith? Am I using the principles of the covenant I have made?" An older man might say, "I'm retired now, so I have more time to spend serving others. How can my baptismal covenant guide me to prioritize the days I have left on this earth?"

USING THE BAPTISMAL COVENANT

My parents used the Church, and in particular the covenants we made there, as they raised us. One time I got drawn into some trouble with some older girls who took a few items from the local store. It wasn't the biggest deal in the world; many parents would have given the child a lecture and let it go at that. But my parents took it very seriously and told me that I should go and talk to the bishop about it. I was terrified! I realize now that the bishop may have been hiding a smile as Dad asked him to counsel with me. At the end of the session my father said to the bishop, "Do you feel that Marilyn is worthy to continue to take the sacrament?" I was shocked. The bishop looked very serious and said, "Well, Marilyn, have you repented?" By then, I was sobbing. I didn't want to be excluded from taking the sacrament. For the first time I appreciated the blessing of being in the covenant, and I vowed to live worthy of my promises.

My dad and the bishop were teaching me to be a covenant person. They were teaching me that my behavior had eternal consequences. If I wasn't as honest as I should be, it wasn't just a matter of getting around my parents. I had a covenant relationship with my Heavenly Father, and I had a responsibility as a covenant member of the Church that I needed to uphold. It had a huge impact on me; it was very smart of my parents. They were good members of the Church. We went to our meetings. We made church a priority, and doing so taught us that we were covenant people. My mother and father, all their lives, took their covenants very seriously, and they taught us to be serious about them too.

The covenant of baptism can help us with this process as we keep it humbly, as we think to ourselves, "So-and-so lost someone recently. What have I done to mourn with him?" or "So-and-so is struggling. Heavenly Father, can you help me know what to do to strengthen her?" or "I haven't borne my testimony lately. Is there someone who could be helped by hearing my witness of Christ's love?" Heavenly Father allows us occasionally to be useful at a time of need. He shows us what we can do if we are paying attention.

Opportunities to play a little part in other people's lives often come within the community of the Church, where we have the chance to practice Christian principles with each other. We may be clumsy at first, but then hopefully we get a little better at it and feel more confident to practice those principles out in the wider world. When Craig was diagnosed with cancer, there was such an outpouring of love and concern for us that we were overwhelmed. People found kind, creative ways to reach out to us. We have never, for one moment, felt alone in our struggle. That is one of the great blessings of the baptismal covenant.

I remember taking a meal one time to a lady that lived down the street. She had to have her jaw wired together for a time, so I just took her a little basket with some soups and some liquid things. There was nothing impressive about it; I didn't have time to make homemade soup. I didn't decorate it or make a clever card. I basically just took some cans of soup down there in a basket. But when she saw it, she burst into tears and said, "No one's ever done anything like that for me." I said, "You're in the wrong church. I don't know what church you go to, but if I were in your condition, my patio would be piled with containers of soup, and they'd be homemade too, way better than I did. People would be pureeing all sorts of things!" We laughed about it together, but I went home with a new appreciation for the way our church teaches us to serve each other and practice our baptismal covenant.

HAVE YOU BEEN BORN AGAIN?

In The Church of Jesus Christ of Latter-day Saints, we are sometimes reluctant to say we have been "born again." This comes, I believe, from misunderstanding the term. Rather than go into a doctrinal discussion of what it means to be born again, perhaps I could just pass on to you the greatest advice that was ever given to me. A bishop of mine in college challenged me to take the four gospels and read them carefully and prayerfully, and write my thoughts in a notebook as I read. At the beginning of that exercise, I believed in the Church, and the gospel, and all sorts of good things. At the end of that exercise, I believed in Jesus. He was my personal Savior. From that time to this I have considered myself a Christian first, before any other label that might be applied to me. I was born again. Like any baby, I stumble, fall, and have a lifetime of development ahead of me. But there is no question in my mind that I am in Jesus's hands. I have a hope in Christ. I know I am going home to Him even in all of my imperfection, because He is mighty to save, and He has promised me that "none of them that my Father hath given me shall be lost" (D&C 50:40). We need never be ashamed to say that we have been born again, just because we are not perfect. Christ is perfect. We just have to be on board.

If you feel that it's hard for you to say, "I've been born of God," perhaps it is because something is getting in the way of feeling that newness of hope. When we allow too much of the negative into our lives, it can make it hard

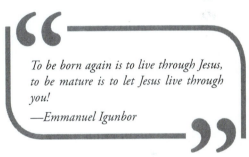

> To be born again is to live through Jesus, to be mature is to let Jesus live through you!
> —*Emmanuel Igunbor*

to feel the connection to the Savior that brings such joy. The image of being immersed in the waters of life is beautiful, and its opposite is equally powerful. We cannot spend hours and hours taking in negative images and narratives that cloud our eternal perspective. As the saying goes, "When a glove falls in the mud, it's not the mud that gets all 'glovey.'"

If we count the hours we spend bringing a lot of negative influences in, and how few minutes we may spend bringing wonderful things in, we can see how the joy of redemption can fade. Maybe we could just get into our scriptures a little bit more and get it back. Read about Christ's baptism and get your notebook out and write thoughtfully about what your baptism has meant to you in your life. Write about your memory of being baptized, and recreate that memory so that maybe your children could read it someday. When you take the sacrament on Sunday, what are you thinking about in terms of your covenant right now? What does your baptism mean to you right now? Each Sunday as we take the sacrament, we should feel that we are immersed in the waters of life all over again.

In a beautiful talk about Christ's birth, Elder Dale Renlund quotes this Swedish Christmas song:

> When Christmas morning gleams
> I want to go to the stable,
> Where God in the nighttime hours
> Already rests upon the straw.
>
> How good Thou wast to desire
> To come down to the earth!
> Now, I do not wish to waste
> My childhood days in sin anymore!
>
> Jesus, we need Thee,
> Thou dear children's friend.
> I no longer wish to grieve Thee
> With my sins again.

Then he goes on to say:

> When we figuratively transport ourselves to the Bethlehem stable, "where God in the night time hours already rests in the straw," we can recognize better the Savior as a gift from a kind, loving heavenly Father. Rather than feeling entitled to His blessings and grace, we develop an intense desire to stop causing God any further grief.[68]

As we read the New Testament, we can see ourselves as brand-new babies gasping our first breaths in the gospel. Then as we try to learn how to become spiritual adults, as we grow up in the family of Christ, His love will guide us. I'm often discouraged when I think of the blessings and knowledge that I have been given and how little I seem to do with it. Then I remember that

---

68. Dale G. Renlund, "That I Might Draw All Men unto Me," *Ensign*, May 2019.

that isn't the way that Christ looks at things. He says, in effect, *You may work as hard as you can, Marilyn, and your efforts may result in about 20 percent of what you need to do to be saved, or maybe only 2 percent of what you need to be saved. It doesn't matter, because I'm giving 100 percent, so your portion is just to get you into the game. You don't need to worry that you're not as good as you hoped you'd be, because I'm better than you ever dreamed. All you have to do is try as hard as you can. It may not look like much to anybody else, but I'm there with you, and it will be 100 percent.* He is mighty to save. As He assured the troubled Nicodemus, "For God so loved the world that he gave his one and only Son, that whoever believes in him shall not perish but have eternal life" (John 3:16 NIV).

> *A transformed life is the greatest of all miracles. Every time a person is "born again" by repentance of sin and faith in Jesus Christ, the miracle of regeneration is performed.*
> —Billy Graham

Chapter Eleven

THE LAST SUPPER AND FAMILY TRADITIONS

What would you do if you knew that tonight's dinner would be the last meal you would ever share with your family? Jesus was in the unique position of knowing that He had one last meal to share with His disciples. Let's pretend for a moment that we have been invited to the Last Supper. Try to imagine what the experience was really like. As we look at the elements of this incredible gathering, we might think about how we can incorporate some of the things Jesus did into our personal ministry, and even into our family gatherings. In addition, many components of the Last Supper are resonant of our worship in the temple. Connecting those two experiences can bring a deeper understanding of the time we spend there.

> For the past 33 years, I have looked in the mirror every morning and asked myself: "If today were the last day of my life, would I want to do what I am about to do today?" And whenever the answer has been "No" for too many days in a row, I know I need to change something.
>
> —Steve Jobs

A WASHING AND AN ANOINTING

It might be appropriate to begin a study of the Last Supper a few days before Passover, as Jesus and the disciples dined in Bethany at the home of Lazarus and his sisters.

> Six days before the Passover, Jesus came to Bethany, where Lazarus lived, whom Jesus had raised from the dead. Here a dinner was given in Jesus' honor. Martha served, while Lazarus was among those reclining at the table with him. Then Mary took about a pint of pure nard, an expensive perfume; she poured it on Jesus' feet and wiped his feet with her hair. And the house was filled with the fragrance of the perfume. But one of his disciples, Judas Iscariot, who was later to betray him, objected,
>
> "Why wasn't this perfume sold and the money given to the poor? It was worth a year's wages." He did not say this because he cared about the poor but because he was a thief; as keeper of the money bag, he used to help himself to what was put into it.
>
> "Leave her alone," Jesus replied. "It was intended that she should save this perfume for the day of my burial." (John 12:1–7 NIV)

Mary is inspired to offer this anointing to Jesus, because there will not be time after His Crucifixion to anoint His body properly before the Sabbath begins. And Jesus receives it from her with a humble and thankful heart. This is an anointing that has deep meaning for them both. Then, a few days later, the final supper begins with Jesus washing the feet of the disciples. So we have, in the last two recorded meals with the Savior before His death, a washing, and an anointing.

> Jesus knew that the Father had put all things under his power, and that he had come from God and was returning to God; so he got up from the meal, took off his outer clothing, and wrapped a towel around his waist. After that, he poured water into a basin and began to wash his disciples' feet, drying them with the towel that was wrapped around him. He came to Simon Peter, who said to him,

"Lord, are you going to wash my feet?" Jesus replied, "You do not realize now what I am doing, but later you will understand." (John 13:3–7 NIV)

Many times we interpret the scriptures, not the way they are written, but the way we see them in paintings. I've almost never seen a painting of Jesus washing the feet of the disciples when He is girded only in a towel, as a slave would be; in the paintings He's still fully clothed. But the image of Jesus taking off His robes and girding Himself in this simple way shows such vulnerability and humility; it is deeply moving. Also, there is a foreshadowing of His Crucifixion here. In this case, He is comfortable in the company of His most intimate friends, and voluntarily takes off His outer garments. But soon He will be forcibly stripped of His clothing in a humiliating fashion. This moment is another reminder that Jesus, of His own free will, chooses to humble Himself to save us.

> *Jesus gave us a model for the work of the church at the Last Supper. While his disciples kept proposing more organization—Hey, let's elect officers, establish hierarchy, set standards of professionalism—Jesus quietly picked up a towel and basin of water and began to wash their feet.*
>
> —*Philip Yancey*

Researcher Brené Brown reminds us, "Vulnerability is the birthplace of connection and the path to the feeling of worthiness. If it doesn't feel vulnerable, the sharing is probably not constructive."[69] There is something deeply vulnerable about a leader washing the dirty feet of his followers.

JESUS PREPARES US TO BE TAUGHT

Along with all the other important lessons of the Last Supper, there is a wealth of information here about how to minister to our families, and to others. Jesus, the Master Teacher, is showing us how to

---

69. Brené Brown, in Martha Rosenberg, "Author Brené Brown Discusses Embracing Our Ordinariness," *Huffpost*, February 21, 2011, https://www.huffingtonpost.com/martha-rosenberg/embracing-our-ordinariness_b_802808.html.

make a real impact on those we wish to teach, by involving all of their senses. Learning that involves all five senses stays in the mind longer than any other kind. St. Thomas Aquinas said:

> The senses are a kind of reason. Taste, touch and smell, hearing and seeing, are not merely a means to sensation, enjoyable or otherwise, but they are also a means to knowledge—and are, indeed, your only actual means to knowledge.[70]

Jesus had very little time with His disciples, so the importance He places on involving all of their senses is very impressive. Just imagine the touch of His hands on their feet (two areas so rich in nerve endings) and the smell of the fragrant oil. Hear the swish of the water, the breathing of the quiet observers. And imagine the sound of Jesus's voice in the hushed silence in that upper room. Then, during the meal, smell and taste the fresh bread and the wine. This homely, heavenly aroma mixes with the acrid smell of men's bodies, close together, leaning toward the Savior, reminding them (and us) of the condescension of God. Jesus, a heavenly being, is closing His ministry in a humble room with simple, unwashed men eating simple food. The Last Supper is the ultimate learning experience, one never to be forgotten.

CREATING LAST SUPPER MOMENTS

We can and ought to create special moments where we combine the physical with the spiritual to maximum effect, as Jesus did so beautifully. Here are a few examples that might encourage you to think more creatively about how to do this in your home or in your Church calling.

1. One year at girl's camp, we concentrated on the life of the Savior, with a special devotional each day given by the counselors, culminating in a final devotional on the Atonement. To keep camp from getting too somber, we planned a fun

---

70. St. Thomas Aquinas, as quoted by in *Modern Arts Criticism, Volume 1* (Detroit: Gale Research, 1991), 318.

"spa day," where we had the older girls do manicures, pedicures, and hair styling for the younger girls. What we didn't anticipate was the impact that this would have on all of them. Time after time, as older girls knelt down and washed the dirty feet of the younger girls, both shed tears. There was something so intimate and so selfless about that simple act that it became the one thing that girls, (both those who washed, and those who were washed) bore their testimony about. The carefully planned devotionals had far less impact than washing and drying the feet of those young girls. Who knew that there was such power in a simple act? When is the last time you gave a pedicure to your teenage daughter, or a foot massage to a tired son? It could help break down some barriers.

2. One young family I know has a special meal every year, one or two nights before Easter. First, they fix a simple Mediterranean meal and talk to their children about the Last Supper. Then the parents invite each child to sit in a special chair and they wash that child's feet, rub oils into them, and then talk about the Savior doing the same thing with His disciples. It is a simple, but incredibly moving experience each time. What a wonderful custom! I can't imagine that a child could be untouched by that.

3. One of the things I love about sacrament meeting is to watch the physical expressions of love that families show each other. I love to sit next to my husband and hold hands; we rarely have occasion to do that otherwise. One Sunday I sat next to Sister Joyce Zwick and witnessed a custom that they have in their family. She keeps a little bottle of lotion in her bag, and quietly massages the hands of whatever grandchild is lucky enough to be sitting next to her. She did this for a little granddaughter of ours, and it was so sweet. The sweet fragrance of the lotion, the healing touch of a loving hand; priceless.

4. One sister recalls: "My mother had a custom of gathering us children by the fire in winter and sharing oranges with us. She would sit and peel the orange, then break it into sections and hand it to each child. The act of preparing the orange, the lovely smell, even the random spurts of juice, are a precious memory for me. She did it for my children, too, who remember those moments fondly now that Grandma is gone. I keep oranges in my home now, and I do the same for my family when they come to visit." Such a lovely, simple act, involving all the senses.

Remember that when Mary anointed Jesus "the house was filled with the fragrance of the perfume" (John 12:3). There is fragrance connected with many homely duties, whether we are rubbing lotion into someone's skin, cooking something that has a spicy smell, or even decorating with flowers. The more senses we can involve, the better.

TAKING TIME TO BE HOLY IN THE TEMPLE

Part of what makes the Last Supper such a holy experience is the preparation provided by this ceremony of washing. Jesus stops time for a moment and allows His disciples to enter a sacred space with Him. Stepping into sacred space almost always involves a physical change; we change our clothes, we wash, we prepare food. These physical changes affect our spiritual state. The temple offers this to us, whenever we choose to take advantage of it.

Last year ,our daughter Alison was hit by a car, and for several months, she was in pain every day. I went up to help her for a few days, and one night she said, "Mom, I want to go over to the temple and be washed and anointed. Would you come with me?" She didn't talk of "doing initiatory work." She spoke of it as she felt about it; she wanted to be washed and anointed. She wanted to receive a blessing, and she knew that the blessing she needed was available in the temple. The temple involves our senses with its sweet, sacred ordinances.

No ordinance is effectual unless it changes our hearts, softens our spirits, and makes us more receptive to God's grace. If we use the ordinances of the sacrament and the temple the way they were intended, we can receive tremendous strength from them. Ordinances remind us that no spiritual teaching is complete without making a physical connection. Our bodies, minds, and spirits must all be a part of the experience.

JESUS SHOWS US WHAT TO TEACH OUR FAMILIES

After we have shown our vulnerability and humility to our families, after we have made sacrifices to feed and care for them, and after we have the Holy Spirit, we may, with confidence, teach them. And what should we teach them? Jesus shows us here.

John's Gospel is filled with sacramental symbolism. It begins with turning water into wine, contains both the great sermons on the living water and the bread that came down from heaven, and gives us the anointing of Jesus and the washing of feet. Then, just as we do in the temple, the disciples receive the most essential teachings that they will need in order to make their way safely through the world once the Savior is gone. These last teachings, the last words of the Lord, should be our guide.

> *The practice of having traditions to keep us close to the great heritage which is ours to enjoy should be something every family should try to keep alive. If we will build righteous traditions in our families, the light of the gospel can grow ever brighter in the lives of our children from generation to generation.*
>
> —L. Tom Perry

All this I have spoken while still with you. But the Advocate, the Holy Spirit, whom the Father will send in my name, will teach you all things and will remind you of everything I have said to you. Peace I leave with you; my peace I give you. I do not give to you as the world gives. Do not let your hearts be troubled and do not be afraid. (John 14:25–27 NIV)

Bishop Chris Waddell says:

The peace we all seek requires more than a desire. It requires us to act—by learning of Him, by listening to His words and by walking with Him. We may not have the ability to control all that happens around us, but we can control how we apply the pattern for peace that the Lord has provided—a pattern that makes it easy to think often about Jesus.[71]

FAMOUS LAST WORDS

We began by thinking about what we might say if we knew that tonight's dinner was the last we would share with our children. What did Jesus choose to say at the Last Supper? He had spent three years training His disciples, and in many ways I'm sure they were not really too much better than when He started. As the dinner progresses, Philip and Andrew are arguing about who gets to be first in the kingdom of heaven. Peter's all puffed up, telling Christ how he's never going deny Him. Judas meanwhile has been stealing money out of the bag and now he's about to go betray Jesus and cause His death.

But Jesus doesn't concentrate on these things. Instead He reminds His dear friends that He is the source of their strength. He says, in effect, *I am the tree of life you've been taught about. I'm the vine, you're just branches. You're not the tree, so you don't need to worry about being the whole tree. You've just got to be there and listen when I send a message to you. Do what I tell you, and you will bear fruit. Remember that without me you can do absolutely nothing* (John 13–15).

He concludes:

I have much more to say to you, more than you can now bear. But when he, the Spirit of truth, comes, he will guide you into all the truth. He will not speak on his own; he will speak only what he

71. W. Chris Waddell, "A Pattern for Peace," *Ensign*, May 2016.

hears, and he will tell you what is yet to come. I have told you these things, so that in me you may have peace. In this world you will have trouble. But take heart! I have overcome the world. (John 16:12, 13, 33 NIV)

WHAT JESUS PROMISES ALL OF US

President Henry B. Eyring was raised by a father who, though a dedicated scientist, was also very attuned to the influence of the Spirit. When his wife died after years of suffering, he took time to thank every nurse and doctor who cared for her. He saw them as angels who had given service to the Savior by caring for her. President Eyring says:

> The influence of the Holy Ghost continued with him as we arrived at the home of my parents. We talked for a few minutes in the living room. Dad excused himself to go into his nearby bedroom. After a few minutes, he walked back into the living room. He had a pleasant smile. He walked up to us and said quietly, "I was worried that Mildred would arrive in the spirit world alone. I thought she might feel lost in the crowd." Then he said brightly, "I prayed just now. I know Mildred is all right. My mother was there to meet her."
>
> Now, one of the reasons my father asked for and received that comfort was because he had always prayed in faith since his childhood. He was used to getting answers that came to his heart to give comfort and direction. In addition to having a habit of prayer, he knew the scriptures and the words of living prophets. So he recognized the familiar whisperings of the Spirit.[72]

In our family gatherings, in our conversations, are we teaching our children and grandchildren to know the voice of the Spirit? If we had a last meal together, we would surely promise them that the Spirit would be with them. Would they know how to recognize it because we had shown them that example in our own lives? Many times I have heard each of my parents say that their testimony of Christ was the most important possession they had. My father

---

72. Henry B. Eyring, "The Holy Ghost as Your Companion," *Ensign*, November 2015.

bore his testimony often in church. I remember being embarrassed because he was always very emotional. I treasure those memories now, and the way my mother would often speak of her testimony to me. I lean on their strength now, even though they are both gone. In essence they were teaching me to trust in the Spirit, as Jesus taught at the Last Supper, and elsewhere:

> And now, verily, verily, I say unto thee, put your trust in that Spirit which leadeth to do good—yea, to do justly, to walk humbly, to judge righteously; and this is my Spirit. I will impart unto you of my Spirit, which shall enlighten your mind, which shall fill your soul with joy. (D&C 11:12–13)

JESUS PRAYS FOR US

Finally, Jesus ends this heavenly session by offering what is known as the High Priestly Prayer, or the Intercessory Prayer. In simple words, it is a formal prayer of power. Jesus prays for His disciples, as He did often, but this time it is in their hearing. This type of prayer is also part of our own temple worship. I find it deeply moving that before we can go through the veil into God's presence, we must learn to pray for others through the strength and power of our covenants. Prayer on behalf of those we love is how we begin and end our days in our families, and Jesus shows us here just how to do that. There is a great power that comes as we pray for others, in their hearing. Here are a few excerpts from this final prayer that we can emulate in our prayers for our families:

> I pray for them. I am not praying for the world, but for those you have given me, for they are yours. Protect them by the power of your name...so that they may be one as we are one. Then the world will know that you sent me and have loved them even as you have loved me.
> Now this is eternal life: that they know you, the only true God, and Jesus Christ, whom you have sent. (John 17:9, 11, 23, 3 NIV)

DO OUR CHILDREN KNOW THAT WE KNOW?

By the end of the Last Supper, there was no doubt in anyone's mind who Jesus was, and what He expected His disciples to do. Are we creating moments that communicate the most important parts of our testimonies to our children? Elder Jeffrey R. Holland challenges us to "live the gospel as conspicuously as you can."

> We might we ask ourselves what our children know, from us, personally? Do our children know that we love the scriptures? Do they see us reading them and marking them and clinging to them in daily life? Have our children ever unexpectedly opened a closed door and found us on our knees in prayer? Have they heard us not only pray with them but also pray for them out of nothing more than sheer parental love? Do our children know we believe in fasting as something more than an obligatory first-Sunday-of-the-month hardship? Do they know that we have fasted for them and for their future on days about which they knew nothing? Do they know we love being in the temple, not least because it provides a bond to them that neither death nor the legions of hell can break? Do they know we love and sustain local and general leaders, imperfect as they are, for their willingness to accept callings they did not seek to preserve a standard of righteousness they did not create? Do those children know that we love God with all our hearts and that we long to see the face—and fall at the feet—of His Only Begotten Son? I pray that they know this."[73]

> *Live the gospel as conspicuously as you can. Keep the covenants your children know you have made. Give priesthood blessings. And bear your testimony! Don't just assume your children will somehow get the drift of your beliefs on their own.*
> *—Jeffrey R. Holland*

I love this quote: "If I could hear Christ praying for me in the next room, I would not fear a million enemies. Yet the distance makes no difference; he is praying for me."[74] Our children can feel

---

73. Jeffrey R. Holland, "A Prayer for the Children," *Ensign*, May 2003.
74. *The Works of Rev. Robert Murray McCheyne: Complete in One Volume* (New York: Robert Carter and Brothers, 1874), 138.

that we are praying for them, and that is the next best thing to having Jesus Himself do so.

THE SACRAMENT: OUR WEEKLY LAST SUPPER MOMENT

In culmination of all the beautiful components of this evening together, our Savior instituted the ordinance of the sacrament. Describing the bread and wine as His blood and body, He had each one of His disciples partake of it.

> While they were eating, Jesus took bread, and when he had given thanks, he broke it and gave it to his disciples, saying, "Take and eat; this is my body."
>
> Then he took a cup, and when he had given thanks, he gave it to them, saying, "Drink from it, all of you. This is my blood of the covenant, which is poured out for many for the forgiveness of sins." (Matthew 26:26–28 NIV)

The sacrament is the Last Supper in microcosm. It gives us a few quiet moments to recommit ourselves to the Lord. It involves all of our senses. It is a time of repentance and humility, when we ask ourselves, "Lord, is it I?" (Matthew 26:22, KJV). In other words, am I betraying you in some way? It is a time when we go over in our minds the promises we have made and "renew our vows" so to speak. It is a time to say thank you. Robert D. Hales said, "The sacrament gives us an opportunity to come to ourselves and experience 'a mighty change of heart'—to remember who we are and what we most desire."[75]

It can be difficult to truly pay attention during

> *When young men prepare, bless, and pass the sacrament in worthiness and reverence, they literally follow the example of the Savior at the Last Supper and become like Him.*
>
> *—Robert D. Hales*

---

75. Robert D. Hales, "Coming to Ourselves: The Sacrament, the Temple, and Sacrifice in Service," *Ensign*, May 2003.

the sacrament, to quiet the mind and enter into a state of meditation and prayer. At the end of this chapter, I will share a guided meditation that you might use to focus your thoughts during the sacrament. The most important point is this: if we don't take conscious time to connect with God, time will slip away and we will lose touch.

> Take time to be holy, the world rushes on;
> Spend much time in secret, with Jesus alone.
> By looking to Jesus, like Him thou shalt be;
> Thy friends in thy conduct His likeness shall see.[76]

LAST SUPPER MOMENTS, EVERY DAY

It is instructive as a parent to look at the amount of preparation that went into this evening of the Last Supper. I am sure the disciples, soon to be Apostles of the new Church of Christ, thought about it for the rest of their lives. We can create "Last Supper moments" for our children. We can touch them, humbly serve them, prepare food for them, pray for them, share ordinances with them, and testify to them of our love for the Savior. Let there be no doubt in the minds of anyone we love that we are committed, covenant Christians. That, for me, is the way we can share in the Lord's Supper.

GRATITUDE MEDITATION

The purpose of the meditation is to cultivate an open and gentle feeling of thankfulness for all that is good in your life—for the gift of life itself and for the blessings of God's grace. Cultivating gratitude can replace painful feelings with positive ones.

Go at your own pace and include anything else that comes to mind:

1. Settle yourself in a relaxed posture. Take a few deep, calming breaths to relax and center. Let your awareness move to

---

76. "Take Time to Be Holy (Dickman)," *Music for Choirs, Submitted Music (2007–2011)*.

your immediate environment: all the things you can smell, taste, touch, see, hear.

Thank God for the world right around you and for your body that can enjoy them.

2. Next, bring to mind those people in your life to whom you are close: your friends, family, partner, spouse, parents, etc.

   Thank God for the people who love you and whom you love.

3. Next, turn your attention onto yourself: You are a unique individual, blessed with imagination, the ability to communicate, to learn from the past and plan for the future, to overcome any pain you may be experiencing. You have the Savior and His teachings to guide you, and the opportunity to repent and change for the better.

   Thank God for the plan of happiness, the Atonement of Christ, and for His forgiveness.

4. Finally, rest into the realization that life is a precious gift. That you have been born into a period of immense prosperity, that you have the gift of health, culture, and access to spiritual teachings.

   Thank God for the many blessings that come to you every day and the many prayers that have been answered. Praise Him for His mercy and love.

Chapter Twelve

WHEN WE SURVEY THE WONDROUS CROSS

One thing that continually surprises me is the diversity of ways that we exit this life. It's messy getting into this world, but it's even messier getting out of it. For some it takes years and years of suffering for the body to finally lay itself down and be finished. In other cases, someone's gone before you even have a chance to say goodbye. And, even though death comes to every person on earth, most of us are surprised and devastated when our turn comes, or when we have to let go of someone we love. Part of living well involves dying well. As He does in every aspect of our lives, Christ has a great deal to teach us about that difficult transition.

A SORE SUBJECT

The events that make up what we call the Atonement of Christ—His suffering in Gethsemane, followed by His betrayal, arrest, trials and the Crucifixion—are difficult to talk about. A delicate balance exists between understanding something of the scope of Christ's suffering and what can become a morbid fascination with it. I'm reminded of the conversation I had with my mother soon after the birth of our first child. Mom had ten pregnancies and gave birth to seven children, yet I never heard her recount the "gory details" of her labor and birth experiences. I knew that her first child was born while my dad was in the service and unable to be with her. She gave birth in a base hospital, laboring more than twenty-four hours before the doctor, using forceps (which look like they belong in a museum of torture) extracted my brother in what must have been a truly terrifying and painful experience. But I only knew this because I specifically asked my mother to tell me about it, and she downplayed it in the telling.

My first experience with labor and delivery was not (mercifully) as long and tortuous as my mother's, but still, childbirth is no picnic. After Kirk was born I looked around at all the mothers I knew and felt a worshipful admiration for every one of them. (Especially considering

> "
> *Love was compressed for all history in that lonely figure on the cross, who said that he could call down angels at any moment on a rescue mission, but chose not to—because of us. At Calvary, God accepted his own unbreakable terms of justice.*
> —*Philip Yancey*
> "

the fact that, having suffered this unimaginable experience, most of them chose to repeat it!) Most of all, I marveled that my mother was not sharing in detail the harrowing stories of her suffering and sacrifice. Finally, I asked her why she said so little about these difficult experiences. "Well," she replied, "what would be the use of going on and on about it? It was painful and frightening, sure, but it was all worth it, and that is what matters."

And this is, perhaps, a useful guideline as we survey the wondrous cross. We need to know enough about Jesus's suffering to appreciate it. But then, like my mother with her birthing experiences, we should move on, inspired by the hope in Christ that was the whole purpose for His ordeal. I recognize the source of my mother's beautiful attitude toward childbirth in Christ's candid, yet measured, description of His suffering in Gethsemane:

For behold, I, God, have suffered these things for all, that they might not suffer if they would repent; Which suffering caused myself, even God, the greatest of all, to tremble because of pain, and to bleed at every pore, and to suffer both body and spirit—and would that I might not drink the bitter cup, and shrink— Nevertheless, glory be to the Father, and I partook and finished my preparations unto the children of men. (D&C 19:16, 18–19)

WHAT DID JESUS FEEL?

Even though we all prefer warm, fuzzy feelings and happy endings, the story of the Crucifixion is not a Hallmark Channel moment, and when we try to make it so, we miss something important. If we don't really try to understand what Christ went through in order to accomplish His atoning sacrifice, we will never comprehend how much He did for us, nor how His suffering is a vital component of His power to succor us.

Christ's "passion," or His atoning sacrifice, began in the Garden of Gethesemane, where He took upon Himself all of the sin of the world. Recently I asked the members of my scripture class to suggest what Jesus might have been feeling in the Garden of Gethsemane, during His trials and persecution, and at the Crucifixion. We got to twenty things very quickly. Here is what our chalkboard looked like after I took all the words and grouped them into four categories:

Emotions:	Afflictions:	Temptations:	Other:
Betrayed	Mental Illness	Lust	Amazed
Heaviness	Social Anxiety	Anger	Love
Pain	Behavioral Problems	Rage	Empathy
Loneliness	Physical Sickness	Envy	Compassion
Sorrow		Jealousy	Strengthened
Anguish		Addiction	by Angels
Fear		Obsession	Surrender to God
Remorse		Violence	

This list is not comprehensive, but it was interesting to see how uncomfortable we felt about ascribing many of these emotional states to our perfect Savior. For example, in Gethsemane did Jesus feel lust? Violent rage? Deep depression? If we are to believe the scriptures, He experienced the entire range of human emotions. Alma 7:11–13 emphasizes, by its repetition of the phrase, "according to the flesh," that there is a vast difference between knowing something in the Spirit and experiencing it in the flesh. And that it was necessary for the Savior to suffer all of these things "according to the flesh," in order to do more than simply save us from the punishment for our sins. He suffered so that He could "succor" us.

> And he shall go forth, suffering pains and afflictions and temptations of every kind; and this that the word might be fulfilled which saith he will take upon him the pains and the sicknesses of his people.
>
> And he will take upon him death, that he may loose the bands of death which bind his people; and he will take upon him their infirmities, that his bowels may be filled with mercy, according to the flesh, that he may know according to the flesh how to succor his people according to their infirmities.
>
> Now the Spirit knoweth all things; nevertheless the Son of God suffereth according to the flesh that he might take upon him the sins of his people, that he might blot out their transgressions according to the power of his deliverance; and now behold, this is the testimony which is in me.

This passage states that Jesus took upon Himself pains, afflictions, and temptations of every kind, sickness, infirmities, and death. Let's unpack a few of these terms just to get a sense of the "scope of work" Jesus faced in the Atonement:

- **Pains**: Everything that hurts, and has hurt, every person who has ever lived. That is a lot of pain, when you think about it.
- **Afflictions**: This is a category that holds all the miscellaneous things that we suffer. Afflictions might include deformities, handicaps, and emotional and mental illnesses. Afflictions might also include psychological scars from a traumatic upbringing, or damage from social, economic, or political hardships. It's a big category.

- **Temptations of every kind**: Human beings have a frightening capacity for evil. Even nice people may have dark corners in which lurk strange sexual fantasies, deep jealousies, and violent tendencies. In Gethsemane, Jesus opened Himself to the worst excesses of the decadent, depraved, and desperate. How could our perfect Savior allow such degradation to enter His sinless soul? He did it because somebody had to save us from ourselves.

- **Sickness:** Everything connected to the imperfect construction and the gradual corruption of the body. Every person suffers illnesses. Jesus took all of these illnesses upon Himself.

- **Infirmities:** Everything about us that isn't strong and healthy may be called an infirmity, or a weakness. In her outstanding book *Weakness Is Not a Sin*, Wendy Ulrich defines weakness:

> We might define weakness as the limitation on our wisdom, power, and holiness that comes with being human. As mortals we are born helpless and dependent, with various physical flaws and predispositions. We are raised and surrounded by other weak mortals, and their teachings, examples, and treatment of us are faulty and sometimes damaging. In our weak, mortal state we suffer physical and emotional illness, hunger, and fatigue. We experience human emotions like anger, grief, and fear. We lack wisdom, skill, stamina, and strength. And we are subject to temptations of many kinds.[77]

- **Death**: Death, in my mind, includes not just the cessation of physical life, but the fear of the process, the process itself, and the collateral damage that can occur as a result. Death can be a dirty bomb that blows families apart, destroys relationships, causes greedy inheritors to fight, leads to prison sentences for those who cause it (whether voluntarily or involuntarily) and so forth. Death is the great negator of life. Jesus takes death upon Himself.

---

77. Wendy Ulrich, "It Isn't a Sin to Be Weak," *Ensign*, April 2015.

JESUS TEACHES US ABOUT DYING WELL

The agony of the garden, the ignominy of the trials, and the suffering on the cross combined to make Jesus's death the most difficult one imaginable. This was on purpose, as was everything in His life and mission. For most people, death is not a painless slide into immortality; it can be a gritty, difficult battle that may last anywhere from days to years. It can be traumatic for those involved, and I imagine may even be traumatic for the spirit that is sometimes wrenched from the body.

When my mother-in-law died, it marked the end of many years of suffering from blood clots in her lungs. One night her condition suddenly deteriorated, and when we arrived at their home, she was sitting in a chair in terrible distress. She was leaning over, trying to breathe, and all she could say was "help me." I reached down to take hold of her shoulders and was shocked to see blood coming out of the pores in her back. Her organs were failing, and her body was under so much strain that she was experiencing *hematidrosis*, just as our beloved Savior did. I know that angels were there to strengthen her through those moments, as they were for Him. I was reminded that, when we suffer, He has literally been there before us.

> Having satisfied the demands of justice, Christ now steps into the place of justice; or we might say He is justice, just as He is love. Likewise, besides being a "perfect, just God," He is a perfect, merciful God. Thus, the Savior makes all things right. No injustice in mortality is permanent, even death, for He restores life again. No injury, disability, betrayal, or abuse goes uncompensated in the end because of His ultimate justice and mercy.
> —D. Todd Christofferson

Jesus had to suffer, and all of us have to suffer. But Jesus also got help from an angel in His darkest hours, and so will we. There is no need for any soul to suffer alone. Jesus is there to comfort us, and we can reach out and get that comfort from Him, just as He was strengthened in the garden. "An angel from heaven appeared to him and strengthened him" (Luke 22:43 NIV).

THE CROSS OF CALVARY

The Gospels don't go into great detail about crucifixion; it was such a familiar part of life that they probably assumed that nothing needed to be said beyond, "They crucified Him." Every person in that day had seen crucifixions; they happened all the time. Crucifixions were very public events; they were meant to last a few days, with the victims enduring the most gruesome suffering imaginable. Soldiers would often fasten a little seat to the cross, so that the person could sit and take the weight off his limbs. This gave temporary relief, but actually prolonged the suffering. Also, the soldiers were trained to put the spikes in so that they didn't hit a major artery; they didn't want the victim to quickly bleed to death, but to die slowly of asphyxiation and exposure. It was one of the worst forms of execution ever created. Jesus came into that world of sin and suffering and died a truly awful death. He descended below all the things that we might go through in our mortal experiences. No matter what we suffer, He can share and lift our burdens. Then He helps us try to be like Him and feel His joy by teaching us to lift the burdens of others.

> The cross is the center of the world's history; the incarnation of Christ and the Crucifixion of our Lord are the pivot round which all the events of the ages revolve. The testimony of Christ was the spirit of prophecy, and the growing power of Jesus is the spirit of history.
> —Alexander McLaren

Every one of the standard works testifies of the grim necessity of Jesus's death. Long before it occurred, and long after it was over, prophets have shared the sorrowful vision:

Doctrine and Covenants

Behold the wounds which pierced my side, and also the prints of the nails in my hands and feet; be faithful, keep my commandments, and ye shall inherit the kingdom of heaven. Amen. (D&C 6:37)

Book of Mormon

> And the world, because of their iniquity, shall judge him to be a thing of naught; wherefore they scourge him, and he suffereth it; and they smite him, and he suffereth it. Yea, they spit upon him, and he suffereth it, because of his loving kindness and his long-suffering towards the children of men. (1 Nephi 19:9)

Bible

> But he was pierced for our transgressions, he was crushed for our iniquities; the punishment that brought us peace was on him, and by his wounds we are healed. (Isaiah 53:5, NIV)

The beautiful hymn "When I Survey the Wondrous Cross" expresses the sorrow we feel for Christ's suffering, concluding with the resolution to be worthy of the hope His promise of redemption offers.

> See from His head, His hands, His feet,
> Sorrow and love flow mingled down!
> Did e'er such love and sorrow meet,
> Or thorns compose so rich a crown?
>
> Were the whole realm of nature mine,
> That were a present far too small;
> Love so amazing, so divine,
> Demands my soul, my life, my all.[78]

As the last component of this awful death, Jesus was shut away from His father's comforting spirit, which had sustained Him throughout His life. Jeffrey R. Holland speaks of those last lonely moments on the cross:

> I speak of the Savior's solitary task of shouldering alone the burden of our salvation. . . . I speak of those final moments for which Jesus must have been prepared intellectually and physically but which He may not have fully anticipated emotionally and spiritually—that concluding descent into the paralyzing despair of divine withdrawal

---

78. Isaac Watts, "When I Survey the Wondrous Cross," 1707.

when He cries in ultimate loneliness, "My God, my God, why hast thou forsaken me?"

Thus, of divine necessity, the supporting circle around Jesus gets smaller and smaller and smaller. . . . Essentially, His lonely journey back to His Father continued without comfort or companionship. . . . It was required, indeed, it was central to the significance of the Atonement that this perfect Son, who had never spoken ill nor done wrong nor touched an unclean thing had to know how the rest of humankind . . . would feel.

Finally and mercifully, it was "finished." Against all odds, and with none to help or uphold Him, Jesus of Nazareth, the living Son of the living God restored physical life where death had held sway and brought joyful, spiritual redemption out of sin, hellish darkness, and despair. . . . One of the great consolations of this Easter season is that because Jesus walked such a long, lonely path utterly alone, we do not have to do so.[79]

What can we say about the sacrifice of Christ? Each person must approach the cross one at a time, and find its meaning in the succor Christ gives us. I join millions of others in offering my own words of praise.

Jesus Knows

When affliction sears my soul
And sorrow rends my aching heart,
In my pain the Lord has taken part;
I am assured that Jesus knows.

When temptation-torn I fall and
Seek to hide my fear and shame,
Flows forth from Him the power to heal
In the instant I call His name.

When no defense can stay death's power,
Bent low by a life-shattering loss
For solace in the darkest hour,
I kneel and lean against the cross.

---

79. Jeffrey R. Holland, "None Were with Him," *Ensign*, May 2009.

In peace we each shall overcome
Affliction, sorrow, death and pain.
All these will pass and we shall know
The kind of joy that Jesus knows.

Jesus knows and feels the weight
Of every soul borne down with grief.
He suffered, died and rose again
That we who mourn might find relief.

Jesus knows.

Chapter Thirteen

LIFE AFTER LIFE: THE POWER OF THE RESURRECTION

A few years ago, I suffered several attacks of abdominal pain that eventually landed me in the emergency room. Tests determined that there was, in fact, severe inflammation in my gut, a result of stress. With my tests in hand, I was sent to the Center for Integrative Medicine.

There, a rather gruff doctor showed me the pictures of my angry insides and gave me an ultimatum. "You are living on adrenaline," he said, "and it is eating up your insides. You are on the road to an ulcer, heart problems, and other ailments. You have two choices: you can either wait until the next time you land in the hospital with even worse symptoms, or you can decide to do something about it now." I knew I didn't want to go through another attack like I had just suffered, so at his suggestion I enrolled in something called the "Mindfulness-Based Stress-Reduction Class." It was there that I began to appreciate how little we really know about the connection between our minds, our bodies, and our spirits.

My weeks of study about the mind, body, and spirit gave me a new appreciation for the doctrine of the Resurrection, a principle that is far more comprehensive than just a miraculous rising that will come in the future. What is the Resurrection, and how can its healing power filter into our daily lives right now?

MY BODY: MY FRIEND, OR MY ENEMY?

One of the great functions of the Restoration was to debunk the false doctrine that the body is evil by nature. Joseph Smith taught, "We came to this earth that we might have a body and present it pure before God in the celestial kingdom. The great principle of happiness consists in having a body."[80]

John Tanner, former member of the General Sunday School Presidency, says that we start out loving our bodies, as any new baby will readily demonstrate:

The doctrines of the Restoration . . . suggest that birth liberates the spirit, enabling it to experience the wonder of physical sensation. This is how infants seem to respond to the physical world—grabbing their feet, clutching another's fingers, savoring milk, splashing in the bath—seemingly enthralled with the sheer miracle of themselves and the natural world, every day filled with new wonders. If their eternal spirits could speak, perhaps newborns would salute their bodies as an inestimable treasure.[81]

Melvin J. Ballard agreed that babies are right; our bodies are an inestimable treasure. And without them our spirits are not liberated (as some theologies teach) but are handicapped and unable to fill their full potential.

I grant you that the righteous dead will be at peace, but I tell you that when we go out of this life, leave this body, we will desire to do many things that we cannot do at all without the body. We will be seriously handicapped, and we will long for the body; we then will pray for the early reunion with our bodies. We will know then what advantage it is to have a body.[82]

---

80. *Teachings of the Prophet Joseph Smith*, 181.
81. John S. Tanner, "The Body as a Blessing," *Ensign*, July 1993.
82. Melvin J. Ballard, "The Three Degrees of Glory," in *Melvin J. Ballard . . . Crusader for Righteousness* (Salt Lake City: Bookcraft, 1966), 213.

Our own Doctrine and Covenants affirms that "spirit and element, inseparably connected, receive a fulness of joy. And when separated, man cannot receive a fulness of joy" (D&C 93:33–34).

Somewhere between the happy joy of a baby and the worried adult looking at a wrinkled countenance and graying hair in a mirror, we stop rejoicing in our bodies. In fact for some of us, our relationship with our bodies is more like a cold war. We may vacillate between ignoring it, making insulting comments about it, and actively doing things to damage it. I recently asked my class, "When do you think about your body?" The three most popular answers were: when it hurts, when it's hungry, and when it's time to put on a bathing suit. None of these answers were particularly happy ones.

> And when we are asked why we are such a happy people, our answer is: "Because we have everything—life with all its opportunities, death without fear, eternal life with endless growth and development.
> —Spencer W. Kimball

But the body is so important; it's the key to everything. The only way that God can speak to us, through the Spirit, is by using our bodies. You can't learn anything or feel anything without it having an impact on your body. Synapses fire in your brain. Your heart pounds. Your breath may quicken. Your spirit is housed in your body and that is the medium through which God speaks to you. I've mentioned the word "proprioception," or the sense that you have of your body in space. To have the Spirit speak to you through your mind and heart, you must get a sense of how the Spirit communicates with you, and that involves getting in touch with that troublesome body of yours.

LET'S DO IT RIGHT NOW

Since mindfulness experts teach us that the present is all we have, let's take a moment right now and make connection with our bodies. I'm going to give you a few simple instructions, and then I would like you to put down the book and take just sixty seconds to connect your mind and body.

1. Sit comfortably with your hands relaxed in your lap. Take a few deep, cleansing breaths, and then slow your breathing a bit so that it gently flows in and out.

2. Take a look around you and then draw that attention in as you would pull the string on a laundry bag, gathering your attention to a spot about a foot in front of you. Your eyes are open, but you are not really focusing on anything. Your sight is beginning to go inward. Now, gently close your eyes.

3. Starting at the top of your head, quietly scan down through your body. Relax the muscles of your jaw, your neck, your gut. As your mind travels downward, be aware of where your body is right now. What parts are touching the seat? The floor? What parts are sending you messages of pain, or pleasure, or anything in between? Observe your body as it rests on the earth. Explore the sensations it is feeling right now, the sounds it hears.

4. With the joyful curiosity of the toddler, say hello to this body of yours. Acknowledge the parts that hurt. Observe the way your breath has been going in and out all this time. Your organs are functioning, your blood is flowing. The whole process is miraculous! Thank your body for the service it does you every day. Thank God for that body as well.

5. Open your eyes.

THE TIGER IN THE BUSHES AND THE FOUNTAIN OF YOUTH

Experts tell us that our sympathetic nervous system, or that part of us that leaps into action when we are threatened, is basically under a state of attack in this crazy world. Though there is no real tiger in the bushes, our adrenaline levels are elevated as if there were. When you go on, day after day, at these elevated levels, the system suffers damage from chronic stress. You lie awake, your stomach grinds, you may experience anxiety and panic attacks. Eventually, you may even end up in the emergency room or worse:

> Chronic stress, experiencing stressors over a prolonged period of time, can result in a long-term drain on the body. As the SNS continues to trigger physical reactions, it causes a wear-and-tear on the body. It's not so much what chronic stress does to the nervous system, but what continuous activation of the nervous system does to other bodily systems that become problematic.[83]

DEATH SHALL HAVE NO DOMINION

Now, what does this have to do with the Resurrection? Everything. Jesus had power over death, and He began demonstrating that power early on, by healing people. He had power over everything that could destroy people. He could make food appear for the hungry. He could heal people of disease. And most of all, He could calm the spirit and lower that panicky feeling of impending doom. Even when the threats were real and deadly, Jesus had the power to infuse hope and peace into those who were suffering. He described Himself as "the living bread which came down from heaven." He also said He was "living water," that would make the drinker immortal. He was a "fountain of youth."

> *The reality of the Resurrection of the Savior overwhelms our heartbreak with hope because with it comes the assurance that all the other promises of the gospel are just as real—promises that are no less miraculous than the Resurrection. We know that He can make us whole no matter what is broken in us.*
>
> —Paul V. Johnson

Mark Twain quipped, "Life would be infinitely happier if we could only be born at the age of eighty and gradually approach eighteen." Since time began, people have been fighting time. They

---

83. "Stress Effects on the Body," *American Psychological Association*, http://www.apa.org /helpcenter/stress-body.aspx.

have searched for a magic elixir that would ensure they would live forever, be forever young. A recent article chronicles the search for eternal youth through history:

> For centuries the search for eternal youth or elongated life has been a frequent topic of various myths and legends from around the world. One of the earliest accounts is from the Greek historian Herodotus in the 5th century BC when he wrote of a fountain of youth in the land of Macrobians, which gave the people of the region exceptionally long life spans. Alexander the Great searched for the fountain of youth in the 4th century AD and was said to have come across a healing "river of paradise' and the legendary King Prester John claimed to rule a land that had a fountain of youth during the early Crusades of the 11th and 12th centuries AD. In Japan, stories of hot springs that could heal wounds and restore youth were also common and still are to this day. Similar stories were prominent among the Carribean [sic] people during the early 16th century, who spoke of restorative powers of the water in the mythical land of Bimini. Similar legends have been found in the Canary Islands, Polynesia, and England.[84]

The article goes on to say that part of the reason the Western hemisphere was colonized was the search for the fountain of youth. Though Ponce de Leon was seeking new territory and gold, he was also interested in these legends and the search for a magic spring of water, and his name has long been associated with the search for the fountain of youth.

Our overactive sympathetic nervous systems and our preoccupation with youth both stem from a fear of death and decay. No one wants to get old and die; we want to live and feel good! Jesus had within Him the power over death. Wherever

> *Every one of us has wept at a death, grieved through a funeral, or stood in pain at a graveside. I am surely one who has. We should all praise God for the assured resurrection that makes our mortal separations temporary and gives us the hope and strength to carry on.*
> —Dallin Oaks

---

84. "The Elusive Fountain of Youth," Legends of America, https://www.legendsofamerica.com/fl–fountainyouth.

He went, He infused life into those around Him. If we look at His power over the elements, and His power over illness and demonic possession, we can see how during His mission His power is building toward power over death. First there are healings, and exorcisms, and then the daughter of Jairus and later Lazarus rise from the dead at His command. We see Jesus grow into a being who has the power to resurrect Himself, and then to resurrect everyone who has ever lived. When He says that it is "life eternal" to know Him, we realize that this isn't a figurative statement. We won't just have a better life if we know Jesus. We will have new life, new vitality, infused into us. He said, "I am come that they might have life, and that they might have it more abundantly" (John 10:10, KJV).

MAKING THE RESURRECTION DISAPPEAR

Perhaps no event in scripture is presented in more detail than the Resurrection. It is recorded in every one of the Gospels, and the emphasis is clearly on a bodily resurrection. Jesus is really there; it's very important to realize that His Resurrection is not just a vision. When one of the Apostles doesn't get the opportunity to touch Him, Jesus comes back later and repeats the visit. He shows His hands and feet. He eats with the disciples. He has them thrust their hands right into His flesh. He says, "Handle me, and see" (Luke 24:39 KJV). I can't think of any stronger way that He could have emphasized that His was a corporeal Resurrection. He wasn't just there in spirit!

However, the Resurrection is such a powerful weapon against the adversary that it receives extra attention from him. If Satan can debunk the Resurrection, the hope of Christianity receives a body blow. In a tragic concession to the wrong side, modern scholars scoff at the very idea of a literal Resurrection. Scholar Bart Ehrman offers this rather circuitous explanation of why he believes the Resurrection (probably) didn't happen:

> Many Christians don't want to hear this, but the reality is that there are a lot of other explanations for what happened to Jesus, that are more probable than the explanation that he was raised from the

dead. None of these explanations are very probable, but they are more probable just looking at the matter historically than the explanation of the Resurrection. Historians can only establish what probably happened in the past, and by definition, miracles are the least probable of occurrences.[85]

By contrast, Joseph Smith and his successors have taught that the Resurrection, far from being a hallucination of some overwrought disciples, is a vital part of the future of the planet. Brigham Young viewed the Resurrection as another ordinance of the priesthood, to be carried out by priesthood representatives, as are the healing and blessing ordinances. I love the image this gives me of families rising, as they have lived, loved, and served, together:

[The key of the resurrection] will be given to those . . . who have received their bodies again . . . [and] will be ordained, by those who hold the keys of the resurrection, to go forth and resurrect the Saints just as we receive the ordinance of baptism, then the keys of authority to baptize others.[86]

Similarly, Joseph Smith declared:

The fundamental principles of our religion are the testimony of the Apostles and Prophets, concerning Jesus Christ, that He died, was buried, and rose again the third day, and ascended into heaven; and all other things which pertain to our religion are only appendages to it.[87]

Contrasting these two quotes with the scholar's illustrates the vast difference between the joyful doctrine of the restored gospel and the confusing philosophies that are being taught today.

---

85. William Lane Craig and Bart D. Ehrman, "Is There Historical Evidence for the Resurrection of Jesus? The Craig–Ehrman Debate," Reasonable Faith, March 2006, https://www.reasonablefaith.org/media/debates/is-there-historical-evidence-for-the-resurrection-of-jesus-the-craig-ehrman.
86. Brigham Young, in *Journal of Discourses*, 15:137.
87. *Teachings of the Prophet Joseph Smith,* sel. Joseph Fielding Smith (1938), 121.

WHEN WE MUST FACE DEATH

The Resurrection of Jesus brings power to life and carries a tangible hope that is a lifeline for us as we actually face death. The following are some comments from two women for whom death is part of daily life. Their experiences show how the hope of the Resurrection can ease the burden of grief and loss.

Lise

(Her son lost his life in an accident.)

How does a mother survive the heartbreak of losing a child to death or any other type of devastating loss? As a woman of faith, I knew that my only chance for healing and survival was to apply the miraculous healing balm made up of key elements including my faith in Jesus Christ, His Atonement, the Resurrection, the plan of Salvation, the doctrine of the gospel of eternal lives, as well as my love for and my love from my Savior, my Heavenly Parents, the Holy Ghost, my family and friends. All of these elements and more soothed my soul and brought me strength to move forward.

Jesus Christ said, "I will not leave you comfortless, I will come to you." I believe that my son is mingling with and influencing earthly as well as heavenly friends and family. Understanding that my son is loved and happy as he is fulfilling his eternal mission of bringing souls to Christ, along with my faith in the comforting, saving, loving truth of the Gospel, fills this mother's healed heart with joy even in my sorrow. I will eternally love and praise my Savior for the hope and joy he brings to my life.

As our Bishop spoke at our son's graveside, he said, "It is helpful for me to recognize that we all get out of this life alive. That which is of us eternal, the spirit, never passes through death, it simply moves on." And that is our hope in Christ. Moroni says, "*And what is it that you hope for? Well, the thing that you show hope for is that you'll be raised in the resurrection to life eternal, and we are raised in the resurrection to life eternal because of Jesus Christ.*"

I leave you my testimony that this is not just something to pull out on funeral days. This is not just something to pull out during times of crisis, but this is something during every day of our lives that gives us a perspective about life that is so much better than the one we would normally have. It gives us a sense of where our spirit is in the world. It's on a continuum, and no matter what we face, we can say hello to that pain or that sorrow and say, "Yes, I see you. You are real, but you're not forever," because we will be together again, we will have each other eternally, and that which we fear right now will be defeated through the redemption of Jesus Christ. The things that we're most afraid of will be overcome through Christ's atoning sacrifice.[88]

Jenna

(She is suffering from stage four breast cancer.)

I have two scriptures I want to share. I think I laugh about it because it addresses my situation so exactly.

"The soul shall be restored to the body, and the body to the soul; yea, and every limb and joint shall be restored to its body; yea, even a hair of the head shall not be lost, but all things shall be restored to their proper and perfect frame" (Alma 40:23).

I rejoice in that because I joke that I used to have really great hair! And I miss my old hair. So I rely on this promise, and remind myself, "This is the cancer hair, this is not the hair that I will have forever. I want those big long brown locks again, I want my perfect body back!

And then, Alma says about our Savior: "He breaketh the bands of death, that the grave shall have no victory, and that the sting of death should be swallowed up in the hopes of glory."(Alma 22:14).

My mortal body, as all of ours do, has problems, mine just has a few more than some other people. Some days I joke about them, and some days I pretend that my cancer is not there, but it is. And you get little reminders when you see scars or have a bad blood draw or you're out of medical options. But for me, I rejoice in these two scriptures and knowing that my body, that is not perfect right now, will, because of the gift of my Savior, Jesus Christ, be perfect again. And then my soul will be reunited with my body, and then I will have the opportunity to live on earth, to be able to gain that

---

88. Lise Brown, personal letter to the Del Mar Sisters in Scriptures Class.

exaltation that I so desire to be with my family, with my grandma, with my husband and my children.

Knowing this doesn't make every day easy, but it gives that hope of glory that the scripture talks about. For me, that's what I cling to. My mortal body will be gone, but I know that there's hope that it will be together again and then I will be with my family again. We all have that same hope and I'm grateful for that gift. It's the best gift that any of us have ever been given, and we can look to that for solace and comfort and for joy, here and in the eternities."[89]

BREATHE IN THE BREATH OF LIFE

The Resurrection is working in your life right now. The power of Christ is guarding and guiding you. There are certain things that God would have you do in this life, and fearing death or clinging to youth is not going to make you a more useful servant. Instead, we can draw on the power of the Resurrection, the life that is in Christ. Next time you take the sacrament, use that moment of meditation that we shared to breathe in the breath of life. Feel the presence of your body and sense its vital connection to your mind and spirit. Thank the Lord for the Resurrection and let your heart rest in the hope and joy it brings. Open your heart to accept the flow of life, which includes death, and feel how very close are those that you have loved and lost. That is the power of the Resurrection. It's not just a future event, it's a present source of grace and peace. Dallin Oaks says:

> The "lively hope" we are given by the resurrection is our conviction that death is not the conclusion of our identity but merely a necessary step in the destined transition from mortality to immortality. This hope changes the whole perspective of mortal life. The assurance of resurrection and immortality affects how we look on the physical challenges of mortality, how we live our mortal lives, and how we relate to those around us.[90]

---

89. Jenna McDowell, remarks to Del Mar Sisters in Scriptures Class.
90. Dallin H. Oaks, "Resurrection," *Liahona*. July 2000.

Each of us will have an Easter morning, where the pains and sorrows of this world will be forgotten in a joyful reunion, both with our own bodies and with those we love. C. S. Lewis wrote this epitaph for his wife that seems a fitting summation of this glorious hope.

Here the whole world (stars, water, air,
And field, and forest, as they were
Reflected in a single mind)
Like cast off clothes was left behind
In ashes, yet with hopes that she,
Re-born from holy poverty,
In lenten lands, hereafter may
Resume them on her Easter Day.[91]

> *Christ is my hope. He is my hope on rainy Monday mornings, my hope on dark nights, and my hope in the face of death and despair.*
> —*Chieko Okazaki*

91. C. S. Lewis, *Epitaph for Joy Davidman*.

Chapter Fourteen

HOW TO ACT LIKE AN APOSTLE

The Acts of the Apostles is the second volume of Luke's Gospel, and focuses most of its attention on two of the Apostles, Peter and Paul. Peter, one of the earliest followers of Jesus, was an eye witness to the ministry of Christ, His death, and most important, His Resurrection. This, along with his personal call from Jesus (recorded in every Gospel), placed Peter at the head of the original twelve disciples whom Jesus elevated to an inner circle called the Apostles.

Paul, on the other hand, was known as a sworn enemy of Jesus and His followers, joining the rising cult only after wreaking havoc among its members. His remarkable vision of Christ on the road to Damascus turned his life completely around, but one can certainly imagine that he was viewed with some distrust among the early Church members. Paul, however, claims the apostleship without hesitation and acts under the aegis of that authority for the rest of his life.

A popular Christian dictionary defines an Apostle as "envoy, ambassador, or messenger commissioned to carry out the instructions of the commissioning agent."[92]

Both of these Apostles knew they had been sent. They had received authority, either under the hands of the Savior himself, or through an appointed emissary. It was a calling that would last until death. And from their day until this, the calling of an Apostle is considered a sacred one. In our Church, authority rests in the hands of fifteen ordained Apostles, (twelve in the Quorum of the Twelve Apostles and three in the First Presidency). These men are viewed as "prophets, seers, and revelators," and "special witnesses of Christ" (D&C 107:23).

The calling of an Apostle is an event of note in the Church. After the death of one of the Twelve, speculation arises among members about who might be called next. And often the call comes as a surprise. There seems no particular rhyme or reason to the calls, and this to me is quite inspiring. "No man," says Paul, "taketh this honour unto himself, but he that is called of God, as was Aaron. So also Christ glorified not himself to be made an high priest; but he that said unto him, Thou art my Son, to day have I begotten thee" (Hebrews 5:4–5, KJV). As Christ himself was sent by the Father, so each one of these men steps into the role of Apostle, not as one who has campaigned for the honor, but as one who has been plucked (often from a busy, productive career) and placed in this special role.

I am decidedly in favor of practical religion—of everyday useful life. . . . When eternity comes, I will be prepared to enter on the things of eternity. But I would not be prepared for that sphere of action, unless I could manage the things that are now within my reach.

—*Brigham Young*

---

92. Baker's Evangelical Dictionary of Biblical Theology, s.v. "Apostle," https://www.biblestudytools.com/dictionaries/bakers-evangelical-dictionary/apostle.html.

WHAT DO APOSTLES DO?

We know that Apostles govern the Church, and that they wield authority over the spiritual affairs of a whole people. But I find it interesting that, even before the administrative component to the calling, the first definition of Apostle is simply "one who is sent." It is in this facet of the apostleship that I believe we all may share. We are all sent to perform certain tasks on earth, and in connection with those tasks, we are blessed with unique spiritual gifts that we may use. We are also given spiritual experiences, of which we are commanded to bear witness to others. In the parable of the talents, Jesus made it clear that God holds each one of us accountable for using these gifts and bearing this witness.

While Luke is obviously using the stories of Peter and Paul to establish the authority of the Apostles as the leaders of Christ's Church, he also offers us a unique, personal glimpse into their struggles as they grow into their roles. We see Peter transform from a brash, impulsive man who both defends and betrays Christ, to a tower of strength and a model of egalitarian compassion. He leads the Jews in throwing open the gospel door to the Gentiles. Paul, equally brash, though far more sophisticated and well educated, journeys from city to city, tying the crucial urban centers together to become the scaffolding of the Church through the next centuries. Each man is shown in deeply personal moments: Peter napping on the roof and receiving a life-changing vision, Paul suddenly thrown to the ground on the road to Damascus, rendered blind and nearly senseless by the magnitude of his mistake.

What do these men's lives have to do with us? In reality, most of the things that Apostles are called to do on a daily basis are the same things we are called to do, whatever our personal ministry may be. Perhaps a closer look at how an apostle acts can help us replicate the acts of the Apostles in our own lives.

WHAT DOES AN APOSTLE DO?

Here are four things that we see the Apostles doing in Luke's narrative: Apostles work miracles, they act as special witnesses of Christ, they build the kingdom, and they devote their lives to God.

1. APOSTLES WORK MIRACLES

In Acts chapter 3, Peter and John are walking into the temple through the Gate Beautiful. I can still hear this passage in the deep, melodious voice of President Harold B. Lee, who told it so movingly years ago in a talk titled "Stand Ye in Holy Places." He helped me see how I could emulate the actions of Peter and John.

> I read again and again the experience of Peter and John, as they went through the gate beautiful on the way to the temple. Here was one who had never walked, impotent from his birth, begging alms of all who approached the gate. And as Peter and John approached, he held out his hand expectantly, asking for alms. Peter, speaking for this pair of missionaries—church authorities—said, "Look on us." And, of course, that heightened his expectation. Then Peter said, "Silver and gold have I none; but such as I have give I thee: In the name of Jesus Christ of Nazareth rise up and walk" (Acts 3:4, 6 KJV).
>
> Now in my mind's eye I can picture this man, what was in his mind. "Doesn't this man know that I have never walked? He commands me to walk." But the biblical record doesn't end there. Peter just didn't content himself by commanding the man to walk, but he "took him by the right hand, and lifted him up" (Acts 3:7 KJV).
>
> Will you see that picture now of that noble soul, that chiefest of the Apostles, perhaps with his arms around the shoulders of this man, and saying, "Now, my good man, have courage, I will take a few steps with you. Let's walk together, and I assure you that you can walk, because you have received a blessing by the power and authority that God has given us as men, his servants." Then the man leaped with joy.
>
> You cannot lift another soul until you are standing on higher ground than he is. You must be sure, if you would rescue the man, that you yourself are setting the example of what you would have

him be. You cannot light a fire in another soul unless it is burning in your own soul. You teachers, the testimony that you bear, the spirit with which you teach and with which you lead, is one of the most important assets that you can have, as you help to strengthen those who need so much, wherein you have so much to give. Who of us, in whatever station we may have been in, have not needed strengthening?[93]

We Can Work Miracles

President Lee said:

The greatest miracles I see today are not necessarily the healing of sick bodies, but the greatest miracles I see are the healing of sick souls, those who are sick in soul and spirit and are downhearted and distraught, on the verge of nervous breakdowns. We are reaching out to all such, because they are precious in the sight of the Lord, and we want no one to feel that they are forgotten.[94]

> *How often have you read stories of people that found themselves in a place or situation where they were needed, or where prayers needed to be answered, but who arrived without any premonitions or preparations. . . . All of this is a preparation for me to make this declaration: God often works with us, directs us, or inspires us without our knowledge.*
>
> *—Ted Gibbons*

We work miracles in the lives of others by doing the two things Peter did: calling on the power of Jesus Christ and walking with those who need support. To omit either component is to be either just a preacher or a friend, neither of which is quite enough. When combined, both witnessing to and walking with someone is the essence of ministering. We can heal others with our testimonies and with our touch.

---

93. Harold B. Lee, "Stand Ye in Holy Places," *Ensign*, May 1973.
94. Ibid.

2. APOSTLES ARE SPECIAL WITNESSES

Here is an example of the kind of special witness an Apostle bears; an unforgettable testimony by David B. Haight who, after a serious illness, spoke in general conference about a vision he beheld while in the hospital.

> The terrible pain and commotion of people ceased. I was now in a calm, peaceful setting; all was serene and quiet. I was conscious of two persons in the distance on a hillside, one standing on a higher level than the other. Detailed features were not discernible. The person on the higher level was pointing to something I could not see.
>
> I heard no voices but was conscious of being in a holy presence and atmosphere. During the hours and days that followed, there was impressed again and again upon my mind the eternal mission and exalted position of the Son of Man. I witness to you that He is Jesus the Christ, the Son of God, Savior to all, Redeemer of all mankind, Bestower of infinite love, mercy, and forgiveness, the Light and Life of the world. I knew this truth before—I had never doubted nor wondered. But now I knew, because of the impressions of the Spirit upon my heart and soul, these divine truths in a most unusual way.
>
> I was shown a panoramic view of His earthly ministry: His baptism, His teaching, His healing the sick and lame, the mock trial, His Crucifixion, His resurrection and ascension. There followed scenes of His earthly ministry to my mind in impressive detail, confirming scriptural eyewitness accounts. I was being taught, and the eyes of my understanding were opened by the Holy Spirit of God so as to behold many things.[95]

Elder Haight goes on to relate many experiences from the Savior's life that were shown to him at that time. I think it is important to realize that Elder Haight received this marvelous vision when he had already been an Apostle for thirteen years. Was he a special witness during those years? Of course he was. Sometimes people assume that all Apostles have seen Christ, and that may or may not be the case. They are not called to be "eye witnesses" but "special

---

95. David B. Haight, "The Sacrament—and the Sacrifice," *Ensign*, November 1989.

witnesses." As he said, "I had never doubted nor wondered. But now I knew, because of the impressions of the Spirit upon my heart and soul, these divine truths in a most unusual way."[96]

> "
> *Being humble means recognizing we are not on earth to see how important we can become, but to see how much difference we can make in the lives of others.*
> —*Gordon B. Hinckley*
> "

I have my own witness of Christ, and He expects me to share it. Whatever testimony I have right now is enough to do God's work. I don't need to wait until I'm perfect, or have some kind of vision, or even until I have no doubts or questions. I can witness about what I know right now. I can be a special witness of the discrete units of my testimony. That is my special witness. And as that testimony grows, so will my power to witness of Christ.

All Things Testify of Christ; So Should We

I've been taking a casual survey lately of converts to the Church, asking them if the person who first shared the gospel with them was a great example of it. It seems to come out about half and half! Of

> "
> *It seems as though most of us suffer here from some version of "not being good enough" to one degree or another; some people shape their whole life out of that perception. This darkened view of our self limits our experience of joy and freedom to be and do in this life. We disempower ourselves—but it is all coming from one source; our own thinking. We are the ones who deny ourselves permission to find ourselves worthwhile, loveable, capable creators of a powerful life.*
> —*M. Catherine Thomas*
> "

course, there are those wonderful people who just shine with the gospel and hand out copies of the Book of Mormon. Then there are the doubters, the drinkers, the disenfranchised, who still act as conduits for the Spirit and bring the gospel to others.

At our last stake conference, a lovely woman from Poland spoke about the interesting way that she found the gospel. A single mother, she

---

96. Ibid.

entered into a relationship with an inactive LDS man, who occasionally mentioned his faith to her in relation with his upbringing. Their relationship ended badly, and as she was packing her bags to leave him, she saw a Book of Mormon in the drawer and took it with her! Almost from the moment she began to read it, she felt a feeling of peace and found answers there that she was seeking. Her journey to the gospel was circuitous, but she found it through the gift of the Book of Mormon.

The next time you hesitate to mention aspects of your faith because you are not all you should be, just get over it. God can use your very weakness to help with His kingdom. Then, when you get more righteous, He will use your strength! Your witness is a special one, if you use your real experiences and be honest. Just spouting the "company line" doesn't do anything. But sharing ways in which God has been active in your life will always touch a ready heart.

Ronald Rasband said, "Our personal journey through life provides us with many special experiences that become building blocks of faith and testimony."[97] He goes on to quote Thomas S. Monson:

[The Lord] commands. And to those who obey Him, whether they be wise or simple, He will reveal Himself in the toils, the conflicts, the sufferings which they shall pass through in His fellowship, and . . . they shall learn in their *own experience* Who He is.[98]

If you know from experience that God exists, you need to say so often.

3. AN APOSTLE BUILDS THE KINGDOM

The apostles performed many signs and wonders among the people. And all the believers used to meet together in Solomon's Colonnade. No one else dared join them, even though they were highly regarded by the people. Nevertheless, more and more men and women believed in the Lord and were added to their number. (Acts 5:12–14 NIV)

---

97. Ronald A. Rasband, "Special Experiences," *Ensign*, May 2008.
98. Ibid.

Apostles build the kingdom. It is what they do; it is what they live for. I got a vision of that at the age of seventeen when, as the Laurel class president, I was invited along with four other girls from our stake to join five thousand Laurels at BYU for a special conference. There we were trained to go back to our stakes and put on our own Laurel conference. (I had no idea then how much I would use that training over the course of my life!) The BYU conference ended on Sunday with a special sacrament meeting in the Wilkinson Center ballroom. The First Presidency, led by our Prophet Harold B. Lee, sat on the stand as the speakers. Lined up on the first row were all the members of the Quorum of the Twelve Apostles, who blessed and passed us the sacrament. I'll never forget it.

> *The joyful news for anyone who desires to be rid of the consequences of past poor choices is that the Lord sees weaknesses differently than He does rebellion. Whereas the Lord warns that unrepented rebellion will bring punishment, when the Lord speaks of weaknesses, it is always with mercy.*
> —*Richard G. Scott*

When President Lee spoke, he looked out into a sea of young faces and said something like this, "You may not have a very strong testimony right now, but mine's strong enough to hold every single one of you. So, at times when your testimony is weak, you just lean on mine until yours gets strong again." A few times in my life, when my faith has faltered, I've looked back to President Lee and I've leaned on what he said that day. Though he was only the prophet for eighteen months, they were crucial months in my life, and he became my prophet. I had never felt the spirit as strong up until that time in my life, and the witness I felt then is with me still. Every one of those fifteen men spent every day of their lives building the kingdom.

As Elder Rasband says, these experiences become building blocks for our life. They are precious, and (again to paraphrase President Lee) as fragile as a moonbeam. It's tragic to start discounting such precious gifts. If you start looking back and saying, "Oh, I've had a lot of other experiences since then that have disillusioned me about the Church, so maybe the feeling I felt that day wasn't real," that's a shame. Those experiences are given to us to help us learn to build the kingdom.

Elder Rasband says that it's the conflicts, the toils, and the sufferings through which we pass that become our own unique special witness. I have a couple of other moments in my life that are building blocks of my testimony, where I experienced the power of the Apostles and Prophets as special witnesses and understood at the same time that the source of that power is pure humility. Which leads us to the last great duty of the Apostles, one that we also may share in if we so choose.

4. APOSTLES DEDICATE THEIR LIVES TO THE LORD

Jean Bingham, General Relief Society President, is anxious to let us know that she isn't anyone spectacular.

My story is quite "ordinary." Growing up, although I enjoyed learning, I was not the top student in any class. I cannot boast of any expert skills. I play the piano, but only enough to stumble through a hymn. I love to visit art museums to see the paintings and sculptures by great masters, yet my artistic talents were limited to doodling designs in my notebooks. I learned to sew a wearable skirt, but tailoring a suit was definitely beyond my ability. Although I was blessed with good health and loved to run through the park or swim in the lake, I didn't participate in school sports at any level. I was never asked to the prom, I wasn't the president of anything, I was never one of the popular group, and one strikingly attractive friend said to me after scrutinizing my features, "Well, you'll never be beautiful, but you could be cute." In other words, I was just average.[99]

Yet she goes on to say that as an adult, she was called to lead the Relief Society for the whole Church. "I didn't realize that all of the

99. Jean B. Bingham, "How Vast Is Our Purpose," BYU Women's Conference, May 5, 2017.

time I was looking out, thinking these are the gifts that I want, that Heavenly Father was developing other graces and gifts in me that were what He really needed me to have." Sister Bingham concludes with the challenge that we step up and devote our gifts, whatever they may be, to building the kingdom.

> So, what "extraordinary thing" will you choose to do? Choose something according to your available time and resources. "Do not run faster or labor more than you have strength and means . . . but be diligent" (D&C 10:4). Whether your "work of salvation" is largely in the home at this time in life or your influence extends to a global scale, or somewhere in between, the Lord is pleased with your efforts when you are focused on serving God's children and the eternal goal of returning to Him as a 'new and improved, version of your spiritual self. As President Dieter F. Uchtdorf phrased it so succinctly, "Exaltation is our goal; discipleship is our journey."[100]

Is it possible to emulate the acts of the Apostles? Most certainly. Healing, ministering, building the kingdom, bearing witness, and devoting our lives to God are things every one of us can do. And they are the things that lead to happiness. These are the acts of the Apostles.

---

100. Ibid.

Chapter Fifteen

COGNITIVE DISSONANCE AND THE DAY OF PENTECOST

Cognitive dissonance "occurs when your beliefs, ideas, or behaviors contradict each other."[101] For example, you've grown up believing the world is flat, and suddenly scientists tell you it is a sphere. You believe your parents are in love, yet one day they tell you they are getting a divorce. You believe in a loving God, but then your child dies in a random accident. Suddenly, what you have always believed about yourself or the universe comes into question. If you can't resolve the two conflicting facts, one of them must give way.

All of us experience cognitive dissonance at times, and perhaps more so these days, since so much information is available through our computers, often upending long-cherished beliefs. There was a time when we could enjoy the bliss of ignorance, and also keep unpleasant things from our children! Now, all bets are off. With

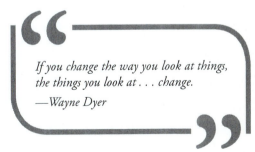

If you change the way you look at things, the things you look at . . . change.
—*Wayne Dyer*

---

101. "Cognitive Dissonance," *Psychology Today*, accessed August 30, 2018, https://www.psychologytoday.com/us/basics/cognitive-dissonance.

this in mind, let's look at the days following the Crucifixion, Resurrection, and Ascension of Christ and try to understand what His followers were experiencing. Perhaps no one in history has faced a greater case of cognitive dissonance than the disciples. There might be something in their experiences to help us in our moments of cognitive confusion.

LOST, AND FOUND, AND LOST

Imagine what it was like to see Jesus die on the cross. Horrible in itself, the event had also been unthinkable to the disciples. This was Jesus, after all, who raised people from the dead, fed thousands, and terrified evil spirits into fleeing their captive hosts. The testimony that Peter bore came as a result of months of observation: "Thou art the Christ, the son of the living God" (Matthew 16:16 KJV). They knew that Jesus had the power to bring the dead back to life. No one could kill Him!

But now the unthinkable had happened, and He was dead. Those that had not fled the scene brought Jesus down from the cross, wrapped Him in linen, and placed Him in the borrowed tomb. We know something of the sorrow and loss they felt, for all of us have laid a loved one to rest. But for them, it must truly have seemed to be the end of everything.

> *Our commitment as members of Christ's true Church stems from the fact that the Lord suffered for every single one of us—the nonmember, the less-active member, even the sinner, and every member in our own family. I believe we can bring thousands to the joy, peace, and sweetness of the gospel, and hundreds of thousands, even millions, in their following generations.*
>
> *—Richard C. Edgely*

And then, it wasn't! Jesus rose from the dead. Talk about cognitive dissonance! Can we blame Thomas for not believing until he saw for himself? For forty days, Jesus walked and talked and even ate with His beloved disciples. Things were still confusing, yet He was there, so now all would be well. Yet once again, the unthinkable happened. At the end of that time, He ascended into heaven with some last instructions to go and be witnesses of Him to all the nations of the earth. Then, He was gone. Lost, and found, and lost again!

> And after He had said these things, He was lifted up while they were looking on, and a cloud received Him out of their sight. And as they were gazing intently into the sky while He was going, behold, two men in white clothing stood beside them. They also said, "Men of Galilee, why do you stand looking into the sky? This Jesus, who has been taken up from you into heaven, will come in just the same way as you have watched Him go into heaven. (Acts 1:9–11 NIV)

I'LL BE RIGHT BACK

Well, what would you have thought then? If it were me, I would have thought, "Surely, Christ is coming again, and soon. Didn't those angels tell us that He would descend in like manner as we saw Him go?" It is evident from the writings of Peter and Paul that they thought the Second Coming was imminent. Why didn't Jesus let the Apostles know that they were now, really, on their own? Why didn't He just tell them, "Listen, I'm going now, and you won't see me again until you die, and even after that it will be a couple of millennia before I come back in an official capacity. So just get over it and move on!"

He didn't tell them because He chose not to. In fact, there must be something very important about not telling us what we think we need to know, because that is the pattern we see over and over again in the scriptures, starting with Adam and Eve! I mean, if you are going to give people conflicting commandments (multiply and replenish the earth but don't eat of the tree of knowledge) couldn't you just give them a heads-up and let them know they are going to have to choose one or the other?

Apparently not. So when we suffer bouts of cognitive dissonance because we believe God has told us one thing and then we seem to get told another, opposite thing, perhaps we should pause and try to understand what we can learn from that experience, rather than just throwing down all our spiritual toys and stomping away. We aren't the first ones in that boat, and we won't be the last.

DOES LOSS OF INNOCENCE EQUAL LOSS OF FAITH?

The coming-of-age novel, or bildungsroman, is one of the most common motifs in literature, from Huck Finn to *The Hobbit*. The young innocent gets thrown into the world of adventure and finds out more than he (or she) wants to know: people are deceitful, life isn't fair, God doesn't answer prayers the way we want Him to, good doesn't always triumph, and so on. What the young person does when faced with these challenges determines whether life defeats him, or she triumphs.

There are many coming-of-age novels that, while brilliantly reflecting the painful experiences of life, can leave us feeling rather hopeless. A great example is the beautiful novel *Jude the Obscure,* by Thomas Hardy. Jude, a young man with a great mind but almost no opportunity to progress, stumbles upon some text books that hold the key to what he most desires: knowledge. He opens a Latin grammar book, which he imagines will teach him a simple formula to translate all the words of his own tongue into any other. Instead, to his dismay, he discovers that to learn Latin, Greek, or any language, he must painstakingly memorize every word. Impossible!

> Jude flung down the books, lay backward along the broad trunk of the elm, and was an utterly miserable boy for the space of a quarter of an hour. This was Latin and Greek then, was it, this grand delusion! The charm he had supposed in store for him was really a labour like that of Israel in Egypt. . . . There were no brains in his head equal to this business; he wished he had never seen a book that he might never see another, that he had never been born.
>
> Somebody might have come along that way who would have asked him his trouble and might have cheered him by saying that his notions were further advanced than those of his grammarian. *But nobody did come, because nobody does*; and under the crushing

recognition of his gigantic error Jude continued to wish himself out of the world.[102]

Many of us reach moments where the personal, loving God in whom we have trusted appears to be an illusion, and instead there looms a stark image of an uncaring universe. The doctrines we have been taught about God and His plan for us suddenly seem like fantasies, as we become aware of faults, inconsistencies, and even outright deception in things we were taught growing up. Like Jude, it is tempting to "throw down the books" that contain our scriptures, laws, and covenants, and simply take off on our own. We understand the meaning of the famous phrase that says, "The truth shall make you free—but first it shall make you miserable."[103] It seems that no one will ever come to make things right with the world again. But, in fact, Someone is there right now.

> The world grows increasingly noisy. This trend to more noise, more excitement, more contention, less restraint, less dignity, less formality is not coincidental nor innocent nor harmless. The first order issued by a commander mounting a military invasion is the jamming of the channels of communication of those he intends to conquer. Irreverence suits the purposes of the adversary by obstructing the delicate channels of revelation in both mind and spirit.
> —Boyd K. Packer

THERE IS AN ALTERNATIVE

Loss of innocence is inevitable and important. Loss of faith isn't. There will come a moment when you question your beliefs, and like the disciples gazing up into an empty sky, wonder what to do next. Let's look at what they did; it's very instructive. Just before Jesus ascended to heaven, the disciples asked Him, point blank, when He would be back.

---

102. Thomas Hardy, *Jude the Obscure* (Osgood, McIlvaine, & Co., 1895), 13.
103. Author unknown, often attributed to Jamie Buckingham or Joe Klaas.

When they therefore were come together, they asked of him, saying, Lord, wilt thou at this time restore again the kingdom to Israel? And he said unto them, It is not for you to know the times or the seasons, which the Father hath put in his own power. But ye shall receive power, after that the Holy Ghost is come upon you: and ye shall be witnesses unto me both in Jerusalem, and in all Judaea, and in Samaria, and unto the uttermost part of the earth. (Acts 1:6–8 KJV).

So, after Jesus was gone, they trusted in the one thing He had told them, that the Holy Spirit would eventually come. They didn't get angry because He didn't explain the big picture; they chose to take the next steps and trust in Him. They went back to Jerusalem and held a prayer meeting with Jesus's mother and brothers.

Then returned they unto Jerusalem from the mount called Olivet, which is from Jerusalem a sabbath day's journey. And when they were come in, they went up into an upper room, where abode both Peter, and James, and John, and Andrew, Philip, and Thomas, Bartholomew, and Matthew, James the son of Alphaeus, and Simon Zelotes, and Judas the brother of James.

These all continued with one accord in prayer and supplication, with the women, and Mary the mother of Jesus, and with his brethren. (Acts 1:12–14 KJV)

After they prayed, they got on with the business of choosing a new Apostle, since they knew that there should be twelve. This might not seem like the most important thing to do in the face of such an existential crisis, but it was the one thing they knew needed to be done, so they did it. And lo and behold, in the process of moving forward and doing the small things, the big answer came. The Holy Spirit was poured out on them.

YOU CAN'T FORCE THE SPIRIT, BUT YOU CAN INVITE IT

When the day of Pentecost came, they were all together in one place. Suddenly a sound like the blowing of a violent wind came from heaven and filled the whole house where they were sitting. They saw what seemed to be tongues of fire that separated and came to rest on each of them. All of them were filled with the Holy Spirit and began to speak in other tongues as the Spirit enabled them. (Acts 2:1–4 NIV)

In every mythological journey, the hero faces a test, and it almost always involves cognitive dissonance. It will appear that everything the hero holds to be true is really false, that the people she trusted are deceiving her, and that the God he worshiped has deserted him. What the heroes do then will determine whether they are really heroes or not.

If you feel your faith slipping away, the day of Pentecost may be just around the corner. An outpouring of Spirit, truth, comfort, and love may be awaiting you. How to bring it on? Do what comes next in your spiritual duty. Don't discard everything that you have believed because you are faced with what appears to be a new set

> *Revelation occurs when a scientist, an inventor, an artist or great leader receives flashes of enlightenment from a loving God for the benefit of His children . . . Revelation in a particular discipline or skill is most likely to come to one who has paid the price of learning all that has previously been revealed on that subject.*
> —Dallin H. Oaks

of facts. Take a step forward, ask God to guide you, and be prepared that a loss of innocence will mean letting go of some of your choicest illusions. God may be different than you thought, but He is still there. The Church may be less perfect than you thought, but it is still God's instrument to bring about miracles. And the people you love may be far more fallible than you ever dreamed, but that only gives us more reason to praise Christ for His grace. Don't give up on faith.

Chapter Sixteen

THE ROOFTOP VIEW: HOW GOD'S CHURCH WORKS

Luke's Gospel is constructed so that we are often in two places at once. It's very cinematic. The tenth chapter of Acts begins with Cornelius, who is described as a "god-fearer." This was a term for a particular brand of believer.

> [God-fearers] were thought to be closely associated with the synagogue in the Book of Acts. Although they did not convert to Judaism, they were an integral part of the synagogue and provided fertile ground for early Christian missionary activity. As pious gentiles, the God-fearers stood somewhere between Greco-Roman piety and Jewish piety in the synagogue.[104]

Cornelius is described both as a Roman centurion, and a pious, devout believer. Thus, he is a perfect example of the difficulty that will be faced by followers of this new Christian sect. Since Jesus and His original disciples were all Orthodox Jews, must Gentile converts fully embrace Judaism in order to become Christian? If not, should Orthodox Jews who accept Jesus give up their Mosaic restrictions?

---

104. Robert S. MacLennan and A. Thomas Kraabel, "The God-Fearers: A Literary and Theological Invention," *Biblical Archaeology Review* 12:5 (September/October 1986), https://members.bib–arch.org/biblical–archaeology–review/12/5/2.

Cornelius receives a visitation from an angel, who instructs him to go to Joppa and meet Peter, the leader of the Christians. This will bring the issue to a head.

After Luke gets Cornelius's entourage safely on the road, he shifts the scene to Joppa, where Peter is staying. Peter goes up on the roof for some private prayer and a nap. It's lunchtime and Peter is hungry, so he dreams about food. He falls into a trance in which he is shown all the unclean animals of which Jews are forbidden to partake. When a voice commands him to eat these forbidden things, Peter is justifiably shocked. He has been raised to avoid these foods like the plague. "Surely not!" he replies. "I have never eaten anything impure or unclean!" (Acts 10:13–14 NIV).

But the voice responds: "Do not call anything impure that God has made clean" (Acts 10:15 NIV). We readers know that Cornelius is on the way, and that God is preparing Peter for the visit. In a beautiful example of dramatic irony, we see with God's eyes as these two men's destinies are about to intersect and change the history of the world.

In order to understand the impact of this experience for Peter, and by extension, for the new members of the Christian faith, we might put ourselves in Peter's sandals for a moment and come up with a modern comparison. Imagine that our new prophet, President Nelson, is praying for guidance, and suddenly he has a vision where a big box opens in front of him that is full of liquor, cigarettes, coffee, and tea. And a voice says, "Russell, have a beer." Our dear prophet would be shocked! Of course, he

> The more we learn about God and feel His love for us, the more we realize that the infinite sacrifice of Jesus Christ is a divine gift of God. This process enables us to have greater love and compassion for those around us. We will learn to see beyond labels. We will resist the temptation to accuse or judge others by their sins, shortcomings, flaws, political leanings, religious convictions, nationalities, or skin color. We will see everyone we meet as a child of our Heavenly Father.
>
> —Dieter F. Uchtdorf

would refuse, saying, "Lord, I have never partaken of these substances in my life! Not only am I a faithful Latter-day Saint, but I'm also a heart surgeon, and I know these things are bad for you!" But what if the voice responded, "What God has made clean, you must not call profane." President Nelson would have to obey, and we would have to adjust our attitudes accordingly. Remember that the voice didn't tell Peter that the forbidden foods had changed in any way. The only thing that had changed was they were no longer a part of religious observance. They were not a measure for worthiness. They were taken off the table (pardon the pun) when it came to what it means to be faithful.

Although these two examples don't exactly match up because alcohol, tobacco, and coffee are dangerous, and the Jewish restrictions were just about types of food, in Peter's day, foods such as pork and shellfish were considered harmful and unclean. To this day the lengths that Orthodox Jews go to avoid non-Kosher foods is extraordinary; the thought of eating pork would be as unsavory to a faithful Jew as smoking a cigarette would be to a faithful Mormon. Our health laws are a fundamental part of our cultural heritage. What is God trying to teach us through Peter's experience?

As Peter attempts to make sense of this change in a sermon, he notes that over the course of Jesus's mission there have been several unexpected developments. For example, he mentions the manner of Jesus's death. "They killed him by hanging him on a cross" (Acts 10:39 NIV). Peter is aware that many of his listeners are Orthodox Jews who know the Torah very well, and he is using some code phrases. The Jews argued that Jesus could not have been the Messiah because He had been hung on a tree to die. And yet He was the Messiah. Peter is saying, *Look, guys, I'm as shocked as you are by this revelation. But there are so many things that have happened that we didn't expect to have happen. This is just the latest one.*

Even though Peter has received a vision, it is hard to imagine how the rank and file members of the new Church are going to feel about welcoming uncircumcised, non-kosher Gentiles into the fold. These are people with whom a faithful Jew would not share a meal. Now they will be expected to co-exist as brothers and sisters in one faith. How will this diverse group come together? As Jesus promised, the great resolution comes through the "helper" that Jesus Christ had talked about at the Last Supper.

> While Peter was still speaking these words, the Holy Spirit fell upon all those who were listening to the message. All the circumcised believers who came with Peter were amazed, because the gift of the Holy Spirit had been poured out on the Gentiles also. (Acts 10:44–45 NIV)

SMOKERS WANTED

Can we find ourselves in this story? Do we, like pre-vision Peter, make assumptions about who is worthy to receive the Spirit? And, like the attendees on the Day of Pentecost, might we be surprised at the people God is willing to choose, even though we aren't? My husband, Craig, was blessed with a wonderful mission president in Glen E. Nielsen. President Nielsen was a self-made millionaire from Cody, Wyoming, who had founded the Husky Oil Corporation. He and his elegant wife, Olive Farr Nielson, presided over the Washington D.C. mission in style, redecorating the former Austrian Embassy as the mission home. President Nielsen was a maverick who taught his missionaries to see past the barriers that we often erect in the Church. One time he was counseling with a bishop who wanted to call a certain man to be the elders quorum president. "I would call him," said the bishop, "but unfortunately he is a smoker."

"You go ahead and call him," said President Nielsen, "and tell him that if he will accept the calling, I'll light his cigarettes for him!" The man was called, and eventually he was able to put aside the habits that had previously kept him from full activity. President Nielson knew how to widen the circle of belief by expanding the definition of faithfulness. Rather than wait for every evidence of worthiness before issuing a call, he trusted the call to bring the Spirit and the Spirit to bring about the worthiness.

HOW DO WE HANDLE CHANGE?

In the history of the Church, there have been a few occasions when the type of shocking change that Peter faced has occurred, causing cognitive dissonance to a degree that was very destructive. Most notably we can cite Joseph Smith's introduction of polygamy, and then the revoking of that practice in 1890. Both revelations caused seismic waves that rocked the faith of some members.

My fifth-great-aunt Lucy Walker Kimball Smith was eighteen years old when the Prophet Joseph Smith told her that it was God's will that she become his polygamous wife. Lucy wasn't having it! With spunk that I deeply admire, she responded that it would take a revelation as great as the one that taught her that the Book of Mormon was true for her to do something that was so reprehensible to her. It went against everything that she had hoped for, wanted, or felt was right in her life, and she told Joseph that she not only would have nothing to do with it, but never wanted him to speak to her about it again.

He smiled at her and said, "You will have the revelation that you desire." He assured her that she would not be required to follow that command without God revealing it to her, as He had revealed it to him. One night, as she lay awake agonizing over this situation, her entire room filled up with light, and she wrote later that she received in her heart an unshakable witness that what the prophet had told her was true, that polygamy was God's will for her, and that she should be at peace about embracing the principle.[105]

Lucy and some of her siblings (her brother was the prophet's body guard) were staying in the Nauvoo Mansion House at the time. In the morning when she came down the stairs, the prophet took one look at her and said, "I see that you have received the revelation you prayed for. I, too, have prayed." She later wrote, "He sat

---

105. Lucy Walker Kimball Smith, Personal History, John Walker Family Record.

me down on the chair, laid his hands on my head and blessed me with every blessing I could ever hope for."[106]

Lucy was sealed to Joseph Smith, who died the next year. Later Lucy testified in Washington, DC, at the Edmunds-Tucker trials that were held to determine whether Utah would continue as a territory and not become a state of the United States because of its practice of polygamy. She was a very courageous defender of "the principle." After Joseph's death she was sealed as a polygamous wife to Heber C. Kimball and went on to have nine children with him that were all sealed to the Prophet Joseph.

Then, in 1890, in response to a revelation received, polygamy was outlawed by the Church. I'm sure that this abrupt change, after all they had suffered for the principle, was as big a shock for those who had received a testimony of polygamy as the revelation about dietary laws was for Peter. There were some people, even at the very heart of the Church, who simply could not take that step with the prophet. They said, in effect, *Look, we had testimonies of this principle. We suffered for it, we believed in it, and now you're telling us it's no longer God's will? We're not buying it!* There were many who left the Church at that point, and some of their descendants still dwell in polygamous settlements, opposing both the government and the mainstream Church.

FATHER KNOWS BEST

It is instructive to watch how Peter progresses in understanding how to lead the Church. First, he gets a vision that he really doesn't understand. In effect, he doesn't know what he knows! However, he does know it's from God. Then when Cornelius arrives he realizes that the vision was to prepare him to welcome the Gentiles into the faith.

After seeing the Gentiles receive the Spirit, Peter said, "So if God gave them the same gift he gave us who believed in the Lord Jesus Christ, who was I to think that I could stand in God's way?"

---

106. Ibid., 31.

He realizes that if God has accepted the baptism of the Gentiles through John the Baptist, they may be eligible for all the blessings. Then the other believers got on board. "When they heard this, they were silenced. And they praised God, saying, 'Then God has given even to the Gentiles the repentance that leads to life'" (Acts 11:17–18 NIV).

We see in this passage how God's prophet gradually receives the guidance, his understanding is opened, and he leads the Church in a new direction. This all happens in a certain time frame. When we get into trouble is when we are either ahead of or behind these developments.

HOW DO WE KNOW IF THE PROPHET IS RIGHT?

The scriptures teach us that occasionally the Lord can make a great sea change in the direction of the vessel of the Church, and that He will reveal that change through the prophet (Amos 3:7). When this happens, it can be confusing, because what had been the will of the Lord the day before has shifted, not because eternal principles are untrue, but because the ways we live and worship may change with time. The Book of Mormon explains, for example, that the principle of polygamy is given to some civilizations at certain times by the Lord and others not. When any change in direction comes, there is always a group of people in the Church who can't make the turn. In addition, there is always a group of people in the Church who want to make the turn before the Church does.

When shifts occur, I like the perspective of Armand Mauss, a sociologist who has spent a lifetime studying the history of the Church regarding these kinds of changes:

> Not everything involved in the rise and development of a religious movement can reasonably be attributed to Deity—not even in the case of the Latter-day Saints. So, in the panorama of LDS history, what can be attributed to the influence and revelation from God and what to human agency? How can we tell? If prophets are fallible and imperfect like other mortals, how can we know when their teachings

might contain error? My research and study in LDS history have convinced me that prophets and other leaders do make mistakes, sometimes serious mistakes, which can affect the flow of Church history. Yet, it is not my job to identify their mistakes, and I am more likely to avoid mistakes of my own if I follow their counsel.[107]

WHAT IF I JUST DON'T AGREE WITH THE POLICY?

President Dieter F. Uchtdorf gave a thoughtful, compassionate sermon about why people leave the Church, in which he said:

> Sometimes we assume it is because they have been offended, or lazy, or sinful. Actually, it is not that simple. In fact, there is not just one reason that applies to the variety of situations. Some of our dear members struggle for years with the question of whether they should separate themselves from the Church. In this Church that honors personal agency so strongly that it was restored by a young man that had questions and sought answers, we respect those who honestly search for truth.[108]

I recently had a conversation with a doctor, a returned missionary who left the Church in his late twenties. He said, "People both inside and outside the Church assumed that I left because it was the easier choice. The Church and its requirements are demanding, but it was not easier to leave; it was much easier to stay and not rock the boat! Leaving the Church was the most difficult and painful decision of my life, but I felt it was the right choice for me." I appreciate President Uchtdorf's sensitivity to those who choose this path.

> *One of the greatest indicators of our own spiritual maturity is revealed in how we respond to the weaknesses, the inexperience, and the potentially offensive actions of others. A thing, an event, or an expression may be offensive, but you and I can choose not to be offended.*
> —David A. Bednar

---

107. "Armand L. Mauss," Fair Mormon, February 2010, https://www.fairmormon.org /testimonies/scholars/armand-l-mauss.
108. Dieter F. Uchtdorf, "Come Join with Us," *Ensign*, November 2013.

When we don't agree with a policy of the Church, we may feel put into a position where to stay would feel hypocritical. I have struggled with this myself, as there have been, and currently are, a couple of policies of the Church with which I disagree. I'd like to suggest that you don't need to agree with everything the Church is saying to be a loyal, faithful Latter-day Saint. The nature of revelation is such that you might be right, and actually be ahead of the Church on the time line. In that case, change is coming, so just hang on. Or, you might be wrong and the Church leaders are receiving inspiration that you don't yet understand. That doesn't mean that you should deny your feelings, or the light that you have received. But it also doesn't mean that you need to turn your back on your faith. And you don't need to speak out against the Church leaders in order to be an honest person. You can concentrate on the positive aspects of your faith and wait on the Lord.

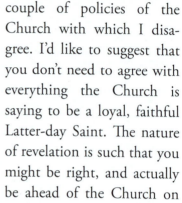

> There will be some things that take patience and faith. You may not like what comes from the authority of the Church. It may contradict your political views. It may contradict your social views. It may interfere with some of your social life.
> —Harold B. Lee

> "You know who I love? LGBT people. How much goodness do they have to add, and how hard does society make it for them? Not right. Also, black people. And Latin Americans. And Mormons. And Hindu and Jews and Muslims and Buddhists and, and, and. . . . Here's to making it easy for good people to contribute and achieve and be happy.
> —David Boyce

Recently, Dallin H. Oaks spoke to this issue in a personal, very candid talk at the "Be One" celebration of the 1978 revelation extending the priesthood to black members of the Church. For many of us, this was an agonizing issue, and at the time, because the Brethren all show a united front, it was easy to think that they weren't nearly as worried about this issue as many of us were. But this was not the case. In his remarks, President Oaks talked about going to the scriptures and doctrinal discourses on the subject and not coming to the same conclusion as the leaders. But, we did not see President Oaks coming out against the policy. We did not see him leave the Church over it. In fact, we were unaware that he was even bothered about it! But he related in his talk that when his son told him about the revelation, he was so happy and relieved that he broke down and wept.

Listening to President Oaks relate this experience was an inspiring moment for me. I felt strengthened in my resolve, both to be true to the inner light that guides me, and true to the Church that has given me the tools with which I receive revelation. Brigham Young said:

> I am more afraid that this people have so much confidence in their leaders that they will not inquire for themselves of God whether they are led by him. I am fearful they settle down in a state of blind self-security, trusting their eternal destiny in the hands of their leaders with a reckless confidence that in itself would thwart the purpose of God in their salvation, and weaken that influence they could give to their leaders did they know for themselves by the revelations of Jesus that they are led in the right way. Let every man and woman know, by the whispering of the Spirit of God to themselves whether their leaders are walking in the path the lord dictates or not.[109]

President Nelson's description of the decision-making process in the highest quorum of the Church reminds us of the humility and dedication to the Lord with which each issue is approached:

> When we convene as a Council of the First Presidency and Quorum of the Twelve, our meeting rooms become rooms of revelation. The Spirit is palpably present. As we wrestle with complex matters, a thrilling process unfolds as each Apostle freely expresses his thoughts and point of view. Though we may differ in our initial perspectives, the love we feel for each other is constant. Our unity helps us to discern the Lord's will for His Church.

---

109. Brigham Young, in *Journal of Discourses*, 9:149–50.

In our meetings, the majority never rules! We listen prayerfully to one another and talk with each other until we are united. Then when we have reached complete accord, the unifying influence of the Holy Ghost is spine-tingling! We experience what the Prophet Joseph Smith knew when he taught, "By union of feeling we obtain power with God." No member of the First Presidency or Quorum of the Twelve would ever leave decisions for the Lord's Church to his own best judgment![110]

We often testify that the Church is led by a prophet, and that when he speaks, we obey. Yet, we need to be sensitive to the fact that, for some of us, this is not a seamless process. When we struggle to "fall into line" with certain policies, we may be comforted to know that the Brethren themselves disagree on many points of policy. But they can reach a position of unity and give total loyalty and support to one another because they have faith that in God's own time, either the policy will change if it should, or their hearts will be opened to understand it in a new way. We can adopt that attitude as well and enjoy all the blessings of worthy faithfulness in the Church while still trusting the guiding light that is the personal gift to every follower of Christ.

---

110. Russell M. Nelson, "Revelation for the Church, Revelation for Our Lives," *Ensign*, May 2018.

Chapter Seventeen

PAUL'S CELESTIAL ROAD TRIP: OUR ROAD TO DAMASCUS

Paul's ministry occupies a lion's share of the New Testament. Because Luke devoted most of the book of Acts to Paul's ministry and because our New Testament contains thirteen of his letters, he comes forward as the most influential Christian leader after Jesus. Though the ministry of Peter may have been just as eventful and just as influential, we don't have as complete a record of him. So, it is through Paul that we learn how the early Christians interpreted the teachings of Jesus and formed a church. And it is helpful to know something about Paul to appreciate what he has to teach us about Jesus.

With a strict orthodox training as a Pharisee and a cosmopolitan upbringing as both a Roman citizen and a Greek intellectual, Paul was uniquely prepared to bridge the gap between Jew and Gentile. Paul was born about the same time as Jesus; he is called a "young man" at the stoning of Stephen (Acts 7:58). Though proud of his Jewish heritage (he referred to himself as "a Hebrew of Hebrews" in Philippians 3:5), Greek, not Hebrew, was his first language. He wrote in Greek and quoted the Septuagint, or Greek version of the scriptures. His father was a tent-maker, and he took some pride in the fact that he earned money with his own hands, though his

Roman citizenship suggests that his family was probably wealthy and influential in Tarsus. So we would imagine that it was study of the Torah, rather than manual labor, that occupied most of Paul's time in his youth.[111]

The Book of Acts covers a period of thirty years, and its structure mimics the structure of the book of Luke, showing how Jesus (in Luke) and then the Apostles (in Acts) offered the gospel first to the Jews, then to the Samaritans, and then to the Gentiles. At the end of the book of Luke as Jesus ascends into heaven, He instructs His Apostles to take the gospel to the "ends of the earth" (Acts 1:8 NIV). At the day of Pentecost (recorded in Acts 2) sixteen nations were represented, so that was a beginning. Yet for the Jews of Jesus's day, the end of the known world was Rome, and that is where Paul ends his ministry. Scholars estimate that Paul died between AD 60 and AD 64, probably martyred under Nero in Rome, shortly before the destruction of the temple and the expulsion of all the Jews from Jerusalem.[112]

THREE KINDS OF JEWS

Up until the time of Jesus, the term "Jew" was basically an ethnic designation. You were either born Jewish, or you weren't. The vibrant, monotheistic faith of the Jews was attractive to many people of other faiths, however, and those who adopted its tenets and came to revere the one God of the Hebrews were called "God-fearers." Some Gentiles opted to take the rather drastic step of being "adopted" into the Jewish clan by going through a period of instruction, observing all the laws, and finally submitting to the rite of circumcision. (Timothy, who had a Gentile father, goes through this process under the tutelage of Paul [see Acts 16:3].) These converts were known as "proselytes."

---

111. Luke Timothy Johnson, *The Writings of the New Testament*, 3rd ed. (Minneapolis: Fortress Press, 2010), 232.
112. Luke Timothy Johnson, *The New Testament: A Very Short Introduction* (Oxford: Oxford University Press, 2010), 65.

What then, were the earliest Christians called? During the lifetime of Paul, they were not called Christians, but "followers of the way." This comes from the Greek word for "way," or *odos,* the root of our word "odometer," referring to Isaiah's injunction to "prepare ye the way of the Lord," and Jesus's description of Himself as "the way, the truth and the life" (Mark 1:3 and John 14:6 KJV). We have reference to this as Paul seeks to root out and persecute these people:

> [Saul who became Paul] asked him for letters to the synagogues in Damascus, so that if he found any there who belonged to the Way, whether men or women, he might take them as prisoners to Jerusalem. (Acts 9:2 NIV)

Each of these groups of believers had certain customs, rituals, and cultural biases. After his conversion, Paul's ministry was devoted to an effort to tie these disparate groups into one believing "body of Christ" (1 Corinthians 12:27 KJV). Though Paul's vision of the resurrected Jesus on the road to Damascus turned him in a completely new direction, he maintained his unique character and personality. Thus he was an example of the kind of person to whom he was ministering. This gave him an unshakeable faith in the possibility of unity in diversity that characterizes all his writings. Luke Timothy Johnson explains that for Paul, Christ diluted the traditional social designations:

> The divisions among humans that in society spell separation are relativized in Christ, so that the markers of male and female, free and slave, Jew and Gentile, lose their absolute character (Gal 3:28) and instead become positions from which humans can contribute to mutual welfare (see Romans 14:1–21).[113]

Paul's name was not changed in the way Abraham's was—Paul is simply the Roman form of Saul—but his spiritual change was absolute. As a first-hand witness of the Resurrection of Christ, he takes his place alongside Peter, James, John, and the other original disciples in proclaiming the Messiahship of the risen Lord. This

---

113. Johnson, *The New Testament: A Very Short Introduction,* 62.

experience defines and directs the rest of his life. He refers to it often in his epistles, and Luke includes three versions of the experience in Acts (see Acts 9, 22, and 26).

> *A religious phenomenon will only be recognized as such if it is grasped at its own level, that is to say, if it is studied as something religious. To try to grasp the essence of such phenomenon by means of physiology, psychology, sociology, economics, linguistics, art or any other study is false; it misses the one unique and irreducible element in it — the element of the sacred.*
> —Mircea Eliade

As a Pharisee and an Orthodox Jew, Paul had a framework in mind as to what constituted "the way." He guided his life by that set of standards. Then, a complete sea change occurred, and he found himself moving another direction. How would he take the first few steps? It is a fitting metaphor that he took the first few steps in complete blindness.

Many converts express a similar feeling in their first experiences with belief: they are simply putting one foot in front of the other, with no clear vision of the road ahead. Al Carraway, a delightful, free spirit who embraced the gospel and has gone on to become a motivational speaker on diversity and faith, described her first forays into her new life in Christ:

> There was so much I didn't know about God and *so* much more I didn't know about the gospel. Every day, it took a lot of experimenting on my part to figure out how He works in my life and what He could do for me at a time when it really counted. What would happen if I prayed this way, or asked something like this, or studied like that, or didn't do this? But those blind experiments brought a full, thick, real, and lasting conversion that would help me in every single trial that followed. . . .
>
> All I had were the simple things of the gospel, freshly taught to me by my elders. Sometimes all you have is Heavenly Father, but

in everything, that's all you really need. The gospel is not our last option: it's our only option.[114]

OUR OWN ROAD TO DAMASCUS

Though it may seem like Paul was moving in exactly the wrong direction, he was, at least, moving in *some* direction, and that is a key toward putting ourselves in a position to be guided by God. Elder Dieter Uchtdorf explains that positive change rarely comes from sitting still:

> There are some who feel that unless they have an experience similar to Saul's or Joseph Smith's, they cannot believe. They stand at the waters of baptism but do not enter. They wait at the threshold of testimony but cannot bring themselves to acknowledge the truth. Instead of taking small steps of faith on the path of discipleship, they want some dramatic event to compel them to believe.
>
> They spend their days waiting on the road to Damascus.
>
> The truth is, those who diligently seek to learn of Christ eventually will come to know Him. They will personally receive a divine

portrait of the Master, although it most often comes in the form of a puzzle—one piece at a time. Each individual piece may not be easily recognizable by itself; it may not be clear how it relates to the whole. Each piece helps us to see the big picture a little more clearly.

Eventually, after enough pieces have been put together, we recognize the grand beauty of it all. Then, looking back on our experience, we see that

And this is the simple truth—that to live is to feel oneself lost. He who accepts it has already begun to find himself, to be on firm ground. Instinctively, as do the shipwrecked, he will look around for something to which to cling, and that tragic, ruthless glance, absolutely sincere, because it is a question of his salvation, will cause him to bring order into the chaos of his life. These are the only genuine ideas; the ideas of the shipwrecked. All the rest is rhetoric, posturing, farce.

—Soren Kierkegaard

---

114. Al Carraway, *More Than the Tattooed Mormon*, 2nd ed. (Springville, UT: Cedar Fort, Inc., 2018), 32.

the Savior had indeed come to be with us—not all at once but quietly, gently, almost unnoticed.

This can be our experience if we move forward with faith and do not wait too long on the road to Damascus.[115]

DIFFERING ACCOUNTS: PAUL'S FIRST VISION AND JOSEPH SMITH'S FIRST VISION

It is easy to become comfortable in our bitterness, or our doubt, or our bad habits, and miss the spiritual manifestations that could be available to us. We wish that Christ would manifest Himself to us, but we are unwilling to get out on the road to Damascus and start walking. I guarantee you that when you do, something will happen, and then another thing, and your spiritual journey will begin to get exciting.

The first thing that will happen is that Satan will try to persuade you to discount the whole experience. Paul offers three versions of his vision, and some details contradict each other. (Most notably in one version his companions see a light but don't hear a voice, and in another they hear a voice but don't see anything.) Some scholars try to discount Paul's entire vision on the premise that, if it really happened, there wouldn't be conflicting reports of it. Bart Ehrmann, a popular New Testament scholar, uses the discrepancies in the three retellings of the Damascus vision to discount their veracity.[116] This makes me wonder if the man has ever been on a fishing trip!

These days many members of the Church are facing a similar challenge, as several different versions of Joseph Smith's First Vision are now available. The first recorded version is from 1832, which he wrote down in an unpublished autobiography that was not found for a long time. In 1835, Joseph related the vision to a man named Robert Matthews, a visitor, and that was written down by his scribe, Warren Parrish. The version with which most of us are familiar (and

115. Dieter F. Uchtdorf, "Waiting on the Road to Damascus," *Ensign*, May 2011.
116. Bart Ehrman, "The Conversion of Paul," The Bart Ehrman Blog, https://ehrmanblog.org/the–conversion–of–paul.

that I painstakingly memorized in Japanese as a missionary) is actually a very late, polished version of the experience, heavily influenced by Joseph's later theological development. It was first written down in 1838 and is the official one that we have in the history of the Church. Joseph recorded it again in 1842 in response to John Wentworth, editor of the *Chicago Democrat*, in the document now knows as the Wentworth letter. In each one of these accounts, Joseph Smith gives a little different version of events. In these days of historical transparency, the Church website has a synoptic version of the First Vision that includes all of the elements from the different available documents.

But there is no question that, for today's literal-minded population, differing versions of an experience tend to call it into question. I've never been very literal-minded, and in fact, have trouble telling the same story twice running. My husband, Craig, who does keep his facts straight, has patiently sat through endless retellings of my missionary experiences in Japan. One day, he quipped, "You know, Marilyn, I've noticed that the longer you've been home from your mission, the harder it was." Well, I just don't like to let the facts get in the way of a good story!

We can get mired in debates over the details of our scriptures and sacred stories and miss their messages. After we took one of our children to the temple, there was some discussion about what seemed to be strange symbolism and the ceremonial clothing that is part of that service. I loved and have since

Reading the scriptures "literally" is a proposition that makes no more sense than trying to read Robert Frost 'literally' since the scriptures contain poetry that are supposed to be read in some fashion other than "literal." On the other hand—much as I value and am interested in scholarship and research—I cannot take seriously the idea of handing the ultimate authority over any spiritual question to a committee of experts, which is about the most optimistic way you can look at the consensus of scholarship on any one particular issue at any particular time. The only person who gets a veto on my testimony is, in the end, me.

—Nathaniel Givens

repeated often the response that my husband made to these objections: "I think it's so interesting how many hours a week I see you kids watch MTV, accepting all of its strange symbols and clothing and even outright lewd acts without objection. For example, you are perfectly willing to accept Madonna dressed in a steel outfit with pointed breasts and blue hair, screaming about immoral things, and you never once stand up and say, 'I just can't handle that. That's just really strange. There can't be anything right about that!'" He went on, "In the temple you are introduced to a new level of symbolism and it is unfamiliar. It's something that you didn't see in sacrament meeting, and you're really put off. That seems a little off base. Why don't we see if maybe we just need to expand our mind a little bit and try to understand it?"

It is true that when gospel questions trip us up, Satan jumps right in and says, *Now, this is the most important thing that's ever happened to you, and the fact that this thought came into your mind means it must be true, and you must quit everything now. All the blessings that have come into your life through the gospel are an illusion. You've been deceived. You need to abandon your covenants, give up on your faith, even if it ruins most of your relationships, breaks the hearts of those you love, and makes you generally miserable. At least you will be honest, and in the long run, (trust me) you'll feel much better.*

DON'T MISS THE MAIN MESSAGE

And we believe it! You see people walk away from a rich faith life over a few facts that make them uncomfortable. This is not to say that we should not be rigorous in our scholarship. But at the same time let's not forget what really happened on the road to Damascus, and what really happened during the First Vision. We know what really happened. Jesus was there and gave a message, and we had better pay attention to it. "Joseph Smith's various accounts of the first vision are a rich resource," says the Church website, "that can help Latter-day Saints better understand this important event. Rather than being cause for suspicion, the differences in his accounts are what historians expect to find in the accounts of events given over time."[117]

This is what we expect and experience in our own lives, right? Over time, when events are remembered and written about, we may emphasize different details but tell a consistent story. Our own recollections are not unlike the different accounts of Jesus's Resurrection in the New Testament, and they are not unlike the accounts of Paul's experience on the road to Damascus. Yet sometimes we can get locked into kind of a stubborn position, where we're almost daring the Lord, in a way, to prove things to us before we are willing to make a change in our lives.

Elder Uchtdorf challenges us to make the first move: "What are you waiting for?" He says, "Let us not wait too long on *our* road to Damascus. Instead, let us courageously move forward in faith, hope, and charity, and we will be blessed with the light we are seeking on the path of true discipleship."[118]

STEP OUT ONTO THE DAMASCUS ROAD

Here's a prayer I think we can pray:

Heavenly Father, first of all, I am going to list for You some of the amazing blessings that You have showered down on me, just even in this last year; I thank You for the miracles that I have witnessed, the things that I've seen, the witnesses that have come to me. Let me just bear my testimony to You about all of the wonderful things that You have done in my life. Now Heavenly Father, there is this one thing that has been bothering me. I'm tripping over it. I have some uneasy feelings about [you fill in the blank]. I feel like if I don't get some peace on this issue, I can't quite get where I need to be. Will You come and meet me on the road to Damascus and help me with this? I'm here. I'm going forward, step-by-step. Will You come and meet me, and shine Your light on me?"

Let me hear Your voice, or see the light, or something, so that I have more clarity. Maybe I'll find out I don't even need this one thing to change. Maybe I'll find out it was me who needed to change. But clearly I need

117. "First Vision Accounts," Gospel Topics, topics.lds.org.
118. Uchtdorf, "Waiting on the Road to Damascus."

You to step into this area of my life before I get lost. Will You please, with Your grace, and Your light, and Your mercy, reach in and help me make that change?

I know if we make our concerns a matter of humble prayer every day, Christ can help us see the light that we have been blind to and hear the voice that we have been unable to hear. He may require that we wait in faith for some answers, but he does not ask us to live without peace of mind. As we pray in faith and step out onto the road of service and love, he can help us exercise influence that we otherwise would not exercise. He can help us be the people we would not otherwise have been and place our feet firmly on the road He means us to walk.

Chapter Eighteen

THE ADJACENT POSSIBLE: HOW DIVERSITY ENRICHES THE CHURCH

In the first century, Corinth was a busy town with two ports that made it a central trade location. It was also a town with a feisty population that gave their Roman conquerors some trouble. In fact, things got so bad that about 150 years before the birth of Christ, the Romans came in and burned the city. The Corinthians started all over again and rebuilt, and by the first century AD there was a large settlement of Jews there, along with a diverse Gentile population. The new Christian sect did not find much success with the Jewish population in Corinth, but a large group of Gentiles joined. This is evident in the two surviving letters to the Corinthians; the subjects range from partaking of food that has been part of a sacrifice to idols, to how strictly the Mosaic restrictions should be enforced for non-Jewish converts.

The Jewish Annotated New Testament notes that after arriving in Corinth around AD 50, "Paul spent over a year organizing several house assemblies." The second letter Paul wrote to this church mentions an earlier correspondence, and Paul will again write to this church in 2 Corinthians, but the factionalism he seeks to mend continued to plague this congregation.[119]

Faced with a diverse and divided group of converts, Paul must help create a spirit of unity in a church that can function out in the "real world," far from the center of the church in Jerusalem. In other words, he is addressing a congregation whose lives are very much like our own.

THE ADJACENT POSSIBLE

The adjacent possible[120] is a term first coined by Stuart Kauffman, a theoretical biologist who has written extensively on the possible origins of life and on the dynamics of biological systems. In his book *At Home in the Universe*, Kauffman acknowledges that the scientific revolution, while advancing the "facts" about the universe in which we live, somehow lost something even more important, the sense of the sacred meaning, or the "truth" about life:

> Once, a scant few centuries ago we of the West believed ourselves the chosen of God, made in his image, keeping his word in a creation wrought by his love for us. Now, only 400 years later, we find ourselves on a tiny planet, on the edge of a humdrum galaxy among billions like it scattered across vast megaparsecs, around the curvature of space-time back to the Big Bang. We are but accidents, we're told. Purpose and value are ours alone to make. Without Satan and God, the universe now appears the neutral home of matter, dark and light and is utterly indifferent. We bustle but are no longer at home in the ancient sense.[121]

Kauffman asserts that in biology, as well as in human civilization, progress is made by incremental shifts toward the nearest

---

119. Amy-Jill Levine and Marc Zvi Brettler, eds., *The Jewish Annotated New Testament*, 2nd ed. (New York: Oxford University Press, 2011), 321.

120. My thanks to our son Kirk Faulkner, who introduced this term to me when he used it in a training course for financial professionals. His creative application of the term spurred my thinking about its relation to spiritual gifts.

121. Stuart Kauffman, *At Home in the Universe: The Search for the Laws of Self-Organization and Complexity* (New York: Oxford University Press, 1995), 4.

possible solution. Dozens, hundreds, or even millions of possible options exist, but as certain ones are selected the options narrow. He sees this trend in human choices as invariably heading toward collective well-being. He argues that in order for civilizations to survive long term, they trend toward democratic solutions, as the best chance for long-term survival as a species lies in choosing options that provide the greatest good for the greatest number of people. For Kauffman, this trend toward the collective good is evidence of the basic goodness of the human species, and, he believes, is the secret of our evolutionary success.

Steven Johnson builds on this theory in his book *Where Good Ideas Come From*. He explains that most of the great "Eureka" moments of history are the result of long, slow movements of scientific thought in a certain direction. (What he calls the "slow hunches.") This is why many of the great inventions have

> *All of us live inside our own private versions of the adjacent possible. . . . We are surrounded by potential new configurations, new ways of breaking out of our standard routines. . . . The trick is to figure out ways to explore the edges of possibility that surround you.*
> —*Steven Johnson*

happened almost simultaneously in different places; the various discoveries in science were creating a narrowing tributary of possible options that led toward a certain result. As an example he cites the creation of eBay, only possible after a certain set of preliminaries were in place:

> eBay could not be created in the 1950s. First, someone had to invent computers, then a way to connect those computers, then a World Wide Web for people to browse and then a platform which supported online payments.[122]

Once that happened, Johnson argues, the creation of an online community of buyers and sellers was inevitable.

---

122. Steven Johnson, *Where Good Ideas Come From* (New York: Riverhead Books, 2010).

PAUL REACHES FOR THE ADJACENT POSSIBLE

What do biological shifts and the creation of eBay have to do with Paul's letter to the Corinthians? In both letters, Paul offers a brilliant example of how to reach for the adjacent possible to move forward in a nearly impossible situation. He reviews the options available to him and, instead of focusing on differences, finds the one common denominator that can unite this disparate group. Paul can act as a role model for us as we face the challenges that confront us today.

Paul states his thesis succinctly in the first few verses of the first letter: Christ has given us a variety of gifts and made us all completely different from each other, and there should be no division among us (see 1 Corinthians 1:1–4). At first glance these two statements do not seem to logically follow each other. If God has made us all so different, wouldn't that naturally cause divisions among us? In fact, He has, and it does. What can Paul do to bring this widely diverse group of individuals together? The theory of the adjacent possible teaches us that there are a variety of possible options that could take place at this juncture. The option Paul chooses takes the history of the church in a new direction, and holds a lesson for us now, at another critical juncture of church history.

Paul knows from his experience as a Pharisee that the intuitive administrative response to diversity is to devise a set of rules to restrict behavior and make members of the group look and act more like each other. This approach had taken the Jewish religion from a dynamic, God-centered faith, to a complicated, burdensome set of restrictions that made it almost impossible even for the willing to be truly compliant. The fact that there was not even a clear route for a believer to convert to the Jewish faith was a sad commentary on how far it had drifted from its vibrant roots.

Instead, Paul opts for the counter-intuitive solution, choosing to celebrate the diversity of individuals and encourage them to become their best and truest selves, and then bring those strengths to the group. This is so brilliant that it seems like common sense! But if you look around at almost every group dynamic—from the office to the Church to the cliques on the quad in high school—order is maintained by encouraging, and sometimes outright coercing, homogeneity. Think how these statements of Paul's must have dismayed the staid, Orthodox Jews who formed the center of the little church at Corinth:

> Just as a body, though one, has many parts, but all its many parts form one body, so it is with Christ. For we were all baptized by one Spirit so as to form one body—whether Jews or Gentiles, slave or free—and we were all given the one Spirit to drink. Even so the body is not made up of one part but of many. Now if the foot should say, "Because I am not a hand, I do not belong to the body," it would not for that reason stop being part of the body. And if the ear should say, "Because I am not an eye, I do not belong to the body," it would not for that reason stop being part of the body. If the whole body were an eye, where would the sense of hearing be? If the whole body were an ear, where would the sense of smell be? But in fact God has placed the parts in the body, every one of them, just as he wanted them to be. If they were all one part, where would the body be? As it is, there are many parts, but one body. (1 Corinthians 12:12–20 NIV)

HOW DO YOU GET UNITY FROM DIVERSITY?

This is all well and good, the Corinthian Church leaders might have responded, but how do we run a meeting around here? The Jews won't eat with the Gentile converts, so everybody is packing their own lunches and sitting in corners, with some feasting and some going hungry! People are divided into factions based on who baptized them and on their cultural identity. How does it help the situation to accentuate the differences between them? How do we get the parts of the body working in harmony? It seems like pure foolishness to say that this is a solvable problem, but Paul contends that foolishness is where we need to look for the solution:

> Jews demand signs and Greeks look for wisdom, but we preach Christ crucified: a stumbling block to Jews and foolishness to Gentiles, but to those whom God has called, both Jews and Greeks, Christ the power of God and the wisdom of God. For the foolishness of God is

wiser than human wisdom, and the weakness of God is stronger than human strength. (1 Corinthians 1:22–25 NIV)

By "God's foolishness" I think Paul means that the solution is simpler than anyone might guess. He reaches out to the adjacent possible; laying hold on the one thing that is shared by all these people of different cultural and theological perspectives: their faith in Christ. With this as their only common denominator they will be one, just as the breath (spirit, "ruach") in the body brings all the disparate parts of the body to life and makes of it a living whole.

THE GEOMETRY OF UNITY

Paul forms a theological triangle with Christ as the head of the Church at the apex, and all His people lined up below Him at the base, with all their various cultural backgrounds and individual concerns. Now, rather than just a random collection of souls, they are a unit, all tied together by Christ.

Christ

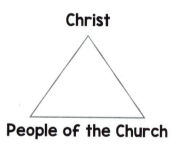

People of the Church

Instead of an infinite number of options for behavior, every problem the new Church faces will now be boundaried within the confines of the triangle: that is, the love of the people for Christ, and the love of Christ for His people. So, do we eat food that has been sacrificed to idols? We look at it, not through the rule book, but through the loving lens of Jesus. Through His eyes, we are more concerned about how our neighbor's faith might be jeopardized than whether it is intrinsically good or bad to eat such food. What is appropriate for the sacramental meal? Well, since everyone has such different dining restrictions, what if we eat dinner at home and simplify the sacrament so that it is something with which we can all feel comfortable? Bread and wine for the sacrament will suffice. Should we take each other to court about our disputes? Of course not; the adversary has won already if we do. We are breaking the triangle of trust.

WANTED: TATTOOS, BLUE JEANS AND THAT SMOKY SMELL

How can we, in our modern setting, apply what Paul is teaching here? We might begin by taking a thoughtful look at our own congregation, and viewing our group as a triangle of trust, with Jesus at the apex, all of us at the base, bound by the rules of conduct we follow as we interact.

Jesus compared the gospel to a net that drew in all kinds of fish. But let's be honest, one look at most of our congregations does not bring to mind a glorious collection of octopi, sharks, crustaceans, and the odd exotic sea creature. No, the average Mormon congregation (even in areas with a lot of cultural diversity) tends to be made up of mostly white, conservative, six-inch trout! In a lovely essay titled "Tattoos and Other Things We Could Use More of At Church," Rob Ghio says of the typical Mormon ward:

> Perhaps the Savior would handpick a far different crowd than we would, and I expect He wouldn't so much as blink at the things that give some of us apoplexy. Tattoos for instance. We need way more tattoos. . . . And we need more people of color. . . . And bring on the gays. We need more LGBT in our LDS. . . . There are many other things I would welcome more of in our Sacrament meetings. The smell of tobacco. Track marks. Breath that carries a hint or more of alcohol. And mustaches. Because mustaches. Most of all, what I think we can use more of is compassion, tolerance, and Christ-like love. His ministry was all about people on the fringes. The physically and mentally ill. The outcast. The adulteress. The possessed. We would do well following that example by embracing whomever

might be lifted, comforted, and enriched through exposure to the gospel. In other words, everyone.[123]

In his affecting memoir, *That They May Be One: A Gay Mormon's Perspective on Faith and Family*, Tom Christofferson says:

> Accepting others does not mean that we condone, agree with, or conform to their beliefs or choices, but simply that we allow the realities of their lives to be different than our own. Whether those different realities mean that they look, act, feel or experience life differently than we do, the unchanging fact is that they are children of loving Heavenly Parents and the same Jesus suffered and died for them as for us. Not just for our LGBTQ sisters and brothers but for many people, the choice to love can literally make the difference between life and death."[124]

BYU professor Eric Hunstman says:

> We have been commanded to love our neighbors as ourselves, and when it comes to neighbors, there are no outsiders . . . Perhaps even more importantly, even when our fellow saints find themselves outside of formal church fellowship or membership, they should never find themselves outside of the fellowship of our friendship and the circle of our love.[125]

WHAT DOES THIS LOOK LIKE IN REAL LIFE?

We all agree with these sentiments, but the Church is a very structured environment, where we are constantly reminded that our actions can undermine the faith of others. Sometimes in an effort to protect the group we may be tempted to shun those who look or act differently. So, how do we balance the need to be inclusive with the need to set a good example? I am going to pose some real-life

---

123. Rob Ghio, "Tattoos and Other Things We Could Use More of at Church," Mormon Hub, October 10, 2017, https://mormonhub.com/blog/life/mormon–culture/tattoos–things–use–church.

124. Tom Christofferson, *That They May Be One: A Gay Mormon's Perspective on Faith and Family* (Salt Lake City: Deseret Book, 2017).

125. Eric Huntsman, "Hard Sayings and Safe Spaces: Making Room for Struggle Instead of Faith" (Brigham Young Universtiy devotional, August 7, 2018), speeches.byu.edu.

situations where diversity comes into play and have you decide what you think Jesus would advise us to do in these situations.

Primary

Recently a mother of four shared a conversation she had with her eleven-year-old son. His father has left the Church on doctrinal grounds and is now attending the Unitarian church. Rather than sweep it all under the rug and confuse the children, they choose instead to have very open conversations about this, so that they will remain close and keep their family ties strong. On a recent Sunday, her son told her that he wanted to start going to Dad's church instead, because his Primary teachers had taught something with which he flatly disagreed. He felt uncomfortable and sad. His mother said, "Your teachers are wonderful people. You can just raise your hand and say how you are feeling and they will talk to you about it." He replied, "No Mom, that isn't what Primary is like. You are supposed to agree and give the right answer. That's what they want. The other kids would look at me funny if I said what I was feeling."

How many of us have sat in Gospel Doctrine class and felt basically the same thing? Is there a way to create a safe space for questions without ruining the inspirational tone?

Mutual

Stake dances have a dress code. Slacks and often a tie are required for the young men and modest dresses or skirts for the girls. Over the years, I have seen many young people turned away from stake youth dances because of what they were wearing. Some stakes choose to make it more fun, having a basket of skirts, ties, etc. for the kids to pull from if they came wearing something

What if you knew that the next person you'd see would be the last person you would ever see? You'd be right there soaking it in, experiencing it. It wouldn't matter what they were saying; you'd just enjoy hearing the words because it would be the last conversation you'd ever have. What if you brought that kind of awareness to every conversation?
—*Michael A. Singer*

that didn't comply with the dress code, but often kids are sensitive to looking funny and refuse to comply. There are inevitably leaders who are more concerned with keeping the rules than keeping the kids in the building, and many times bad feelings result. Dance cards are another issue. One New Year's Eve dance had an hour-long line of kids without a dance card, waiting to be interviewed! Needless to say, many wandered away before they were admitted.

How do we show respect for the dress standards while at the same time opening the blessings of a Church dance to more kids? At what behavioral point do we choose to exclude them?

Adults: Recently a young father I know went to a priesthood leadership meeting where the stake president called out, by name, those who were not wearing a white shirt and tie. He spent several minutes talking about the respect we need to show the priesthood by what we wear and how we are groomed. Colored shirts and open collars were signs of rebellion. This young father was dressed "appropriately" but felt angry rather than inspired. Why, he wondered, did it matter so much what they were wearing? Couldn't the leaders be happy that they were there? A nearly opposite approach was demonstrated sweetly by a Relief Society I visited in Utah, where one member of the presidency wore a lovely pants outfit. I was so touched; she obviously was reaching out to those who might come to church dressed differently. But some were critical that, as a leader, she was not showing proper respect for the standards.

Has the white shirt and tie become a stumbling block rather than a heartfelt show of respect? Can we as leaders show more diversity without sending too many mixed messages?

> *None of us is perfect. I know of no one who would profess to be so. And yet, for some reason, despite our own imperfections, we have a tendency to point out those of others. We make judgments concerning their actions or inactions. There is really no way a person can know the heart, the intentions or the circumstances of another.*
>
> —*Thomas S. Monson*

Callings

Many members of the Church do not live the Word of Wisdom completely, do not attend the temple, pay tithing, etc. Traditionally these members are not extended callings with too much responsibility, or where they might be held up as an example. Yet in many wards the same leadership callings are passed around a fairly small circle of people over the years. One young woman I know juggles three callings and a young family, while many women in her ward do not have a calling. She feels overwhelmed.

What determines worthiness to serve in the Church? Can people who do not qualify for a temple recommend do more to be of service in the Church than is currently the case? Are we practicing a kind of segregation when we narrow the circle of who can labor in the kingdom?

CREATING SAFE, SACRED SPACES

I don't presume to say what should be done in these cases. I'm just throwing the questions out there, because I do not think we will be able to achieve a greater level of diversity in the Church without asking some hard questions about our policies and procedures. Many of our ancestors practiced polygamy, for which they were persecuted, imprisoned, and, at best, viewed as members of a radical cult that needed to be eradicated. It seems to me that people who come from that cultural heritage should be especially sensitive to others who feel ostracized and demand rights that may feel threatening to our current way of life. Once, we were the threat! Whether we agree or not, we cannot take a stance of "us vs. them."

M. Russell Ballard says:

> We need to listen to and understand what our LGBT brothers and sisters are feeling and experiencing. Certainly, we must do better than we have done in the past so that all members feel they have a spiritual home where their brothers and sisters love them and where they have a place to worship and serve the Lord.[126]

126. M. Russel Ballard, "Questions and Answers" (Brigham Young University devotional, November 14, 2017), speeches.byu.edu.

SHAKING UP THE STATUS QUO

Recently I had my temple recommend interview; these happen every two years now, so it had been a while. I've been thinking so much about this problem of diversity, as I have taught a community scripture class for the last several years. I have had many young people share with me the feeling that if they have doubts and questions, they must make a choice: they must either be "all in" or just leave. As a result, I decided to be more forthcoming than I usually am in my interview. And, with some trepidation, I'm going to be forthcoming about it here as well.

Usually, when I am asked if I sympathize or support groups who oppose the Church I simply say no. It's easier and ensures that I won't get on the wrong side of things! I love the Church; I never want to be ungrateful for all the wonderful blessings it has brought me, and I never want to be separated from its safe haven. But a few things bother me. And this time when the question came up I answered, "Yes, though I don't go out marching with groups that oppose the Church, I do sympathize with some of their positions. In fact, on a few points of policy I flatly disagree with the Church's stance, and I hope it changes someday. But until then, whenever I teach or write or do anything that is public facing, I concentrate on all of the wonderful things I feel great about and leave these other issues alone. But to deny that I am troubled by certain things would be to deny the spirit of revelation I've been taught." Both my bishop and the member of the stake presidency who interviewed me paused for a few moments to take that in. My bishop smiled and said, "Well, we will give you a pass on that one I guess!"

Right about the time that interview happened, I turned on my computer one morning to watch the commemoration of the 1978 revelation that extended the priesthood to the black race. I was touched by the candor of President Dallin Oaks, who shared that as he lived in the Eastern states during the late '70s, he was keenly aware of the hardship caused by the ban on the priesthood for black men. He said that as he studied the scriptural and doctrinal arguments that were put forward supporting that ban, he did not feel satisfied with them. But he didn't jump out of the boat. He went on, as a loyal member, praying for and supporting the brethren. As I mentioned in an earlier chapter, he said that when his son told him about the announcement of the revelation, he broke down and wept with joy and relief.

When I heard President Oaks candidly share his struggle to support a policy with which he did not agree, I felt that I was not alone. And if you struggle in the same way, you are not alone either. Over the course of my lifetime, there have been a few issues over which large groups of people have left the Church. In most cases, those issues were resolved with time and further revelation. But those people who left are gone, and their children, and their children's children have lost all the blessings of sealings, the wonderful Book of Mormon, Church service, and on and on and on. That breaks my heart. If you can possibly stay, stay. It will be worth it in the long run.

DEVOTION AND LOYALTY VS. BLIND OBEDIENCE

The great Apostle Hugh B. Brown said:

> More thinking is required, and we [should all] exercise [our] God-given right to think . . . and to be unafraid to express [our] opinions, with proper respect for those to whom [we] talk and proper acknowledgment of [our] own shortcomings. . . . *We must preserve this freedom [of the mind] in the Church . . . and resist all efforts . . . to suppress it.* The church is not so much concerned with whether the thoughts of its members are orthodox or heterodox as it is that they shall have thoughts (italics added).[127]

In Corinth, everybody had an opinion about the best way to take a diverse group of believers and turn them into a fit, functional, and faithful body of Christ. Paul, through inspiration, reached an

---

127. Hugh B. Brown, "An Eternal Quest—Freedom of the Mind" Church College of Hawaii commencement address; italics added.

unlikely but brilliant solution; instead of pushing homogeneity, he encouraged the members to rejoice in their diversity, and trust in the one thing that they all shared: an abiding faith in Christ.

Though it would not seem to be the most effective solution, the choice to focus on faith in Christ rather than our differences narrows the river of possible options. We don't need to make more rules to protect the rules that protect the rules; we just need to focus on Jesus and what He would do. With our eyes facing that direction we may find creative solutions right at our fingertips. For example, we might think to ask a Primary child to prepare a report on the topic that bothered him and share his findings with us. We might find more creative ways to make every young person who comes through the door to a dance feel so welcome they can't wait to come back. We can model as a presidency all the ways people might feel comfortable coming to church, while still showing love and respect for our sacred house of worship. We might even call a smoker to teach elders quorum!

What would Jesus do? He would see the adjacent possible in every individual. He would never worry about the health or well-being of the "church," for He taught us that the Church consists of individual souls. He knew that the hand is as important as the knee, and if you try to make a knee act like a hand, you'll be flat on your face in no time. When motivated by the love of Christ, the priorities will fall into place, the obstacles will seem surmountable, and the adjacent possible, while probably counter-intuitive, will make perfect sense. Then, and only then, can the grace begin to flow.

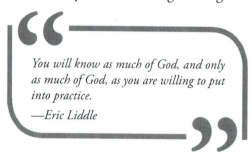

You will know as much of God, and only as much of God, as you are willing to put into practice.

—*Eric Liddle*

Chapter Nineteen

SUPERPOWERS, SPIRITUAL GIFTS, AND THE PARABLE OF THE TALENTS

The discussion of diversity in the Church goes hand in glove with a discussion of the gifts of the Spirit. The gifts of the Spirit are talked about in three of our Standard Works: in 1 Corinthians 12 and 13, in Doctrine and Covenants 46, and in Moroni 10 in the Book of Mormon. These gifts are so important to us as a people that Joseph Smith also mentioned them as one of the thirteen fundamental articles of our faith: "We believe in the gift of tongues, prophecy, revelation, visions, healing, interpretation of tongues, and so forth" (Articles of Faith 1:7).

WHAT IS A GIFT OF THE SPIRIT?

Although this can be one of those familiar phrases that stops meaning anything, a gift of the Spirit is an interesting commodity. My daughter Andrea recently taught a lesson in which she identified three sources of spiritual gifts: natural abilities with which we are born, talents that we develop through desire and personal effort, and special blessings given to us through God's grace, often revealed through our patriarchal blessings or other spiritual means. In Andrea's case, she used the example of her outgoing personality. This is a gift; Andrea just came this way. Since she was a little girl, she has made a best friend of everyone she meets. An example of the second category of gifts is her ability to speak Spanish. Though she does not have a natural gift for languages, Andrea has a great love for the Latin people. She worked hard to learn Spanish and went on several humanitarian trips to South America. She minored in Latin American studies. When she was called on a mission she hoped for a Spanish speaking mission, but was called to Nauvoo, to the visitor's center. While there she used her Spanish whenever she could, and during the six months the center was closed for the winter, she was thrilled when a neighboring mission president requested her to work in a town full of Hispanic workers. She finally got to be Hermana Faulkner! This gift was a product of desire and hard work, but she identifies it as a gift of the Spirit. Finally, Andrea was promised in her patriarchal blessing that she would know the desires of her children's hearts. This phrase touched her; she prayed to understand it. She has a special gift to understand not just her own children's hearts, but to be receptive to those who are near us on the other side of the veil, and that gift has had wider consequences than she expected, some very sacred.

I share all of this to illustrate how gifts of the Spirit can be manifest in our lives in different iterations. With that in mind, here are the statements Paul makes about the different gifts available to us:

> There are different kinds of gifts, but the same Spirit distributes them. There are different kinds of service, but the same Lord. There are different kinds of working, but in all of them and in everyone it is the same God at work. Now to each one the manifestation of the Spirit is given for the common good. To one there is given through the Spirit a message of wisdom, to another a message of knowledge by means of the same Spirit, to another faith by the same Spirit, to another gifts of healing by that one Spirit, to another miraculous powers, to another prophecy, to another distinguishing between spirits, to another speaking in different kinds of tongues, and to still another the interpretation of tongues. All these are the work of one

and the same Spirit, and he distributes them to each one, just as he determines. (1 Corinthians 12:4–11 NIV)

Rather than go through all the types of gifts, and what they might include, I just want to pause and notice this one phrase: "the same Spirit." As Paul says, "There are different kinds of working, but in all of them and in everyone it is the same God at work." What does this mean to you and me? It means that if you have a gift, you need to use it, because it isn't really yours; it came from God.

GOD'S VERSION OF A TALENT SHOW

Which brings us to the parable of the talents, or as it is called in the NIV, the parable of the bags of gold. (Since a talent was worth about twenty years' wages, the bag of gold works even better to illustrate what a great gift was left to the servants.) This is one of three parables that comprise the twenty-fifth chapter of Matthew. It challenges us to think seriously about spiritual gifts and how to use them.

Take a moment and, following Andrea's definition of spiritual gifts, jot down something you were born with; something at which you naturally excel. Let's call that your superpower. My children used to get discouraged because they were not stellar athletes, nor were they talented musicians, nor were they incredibly gifted at anything that would, for example, be featured in a talent show. So what was their superpower? I used to tell them that their personalities were their superpower, and I was right. Each of our children has a big personality; we don't have any shy people in our family. Everybody is competing for attention! I think it is great fun to be in

One of the great tragedies of life, it seems to me, is when a person classifies himself as someone who has no talents or gifts. For us to conclude that we have no gifts when we judge ourselves by stature, intelligence, grade-point average, wealth, power, position, or external appearance is not only unfair but unreasonable.
—*Marvin J. Ashton*

a family with them (though it is often loud and chaotic as well) and it is wonderful to see God use them, just the way they are. Their fearlessness is fabulous.

On the other hand, it is wonderful to see God use shy, retiring, people as well. During my last pregnancy I developed kidney stones that sent me into early labor. I was in the hospital for about a week while they tried to stop the labor and get my pain under control. They couldn't remove the stones though, so along with the fear for my unborn baby I was facing many weeks of pain. Meanwhile, there were four little ones who needed me at home! It was definitely a low moment in my life.

A woman from our ward, Becky Higginson, was a nurse on the maternity ward. One night as she was going off shift, she came in and sat with me for some time. I don't remember what she said, only that her quiet, unassuming manner calmed my fears and made the pain easier to bear. She was like a visiting angel strengthening me in my own Gethsemane. God needed Becky's gift that night: the gift of a quiet soul who does not need to be the center of attention. No Faulkner could have filled that role; we suck all the air out of any room we enter! But Becky was the perfect person for the job, and she followed the prompting to come and share her gift with me.

> So, what "extraordinary thing" will you choose to do? Choose something according to your available time and resources. Whether your "work of salvation" is largely in the home at this time in life or your influence extends to a global scale, or somewhere in between, the Lord is pleased with your efforts when you are focused on serving God's children and the eternal goal of returning to Him as a "new and improved" version of your spiritual self. As President Dieter F. Uchtdorf phrased it so succinctly, "Exaltation is our goal; discipleship is our journey."
> —Jean B. Bingham

Whatever your gift is, it is needed. Marvin J. Ashton gave a beautiful talk about this many years ago; I have never forgotten how inspired I was by his gentle assurance that the range of spiritual gifts was great, and all of us had something to contribute:

> Let us review some of these less-conspicuous gifts: the gift of asking; the gift of listening; the gift of hearing and using a still, small voice; the gift of being able to weep; the gift of avoiding contention; the gift of being agreeable; the gift of avoiding vain repetition; the gift of seeking that which is righteous; the gift of not passing judgment; the gift of looking to God for guidance; the gift of being a disciple; the gift of caring for others; the gift of being able to ponder; the gift of offering prayer; the gift of bearing a mighty testimony; and the gift of receiving the Holy Ghost.[128]

FINDING YOUR SUPERPOWER

Recently my grandson Walker and I were looking online for a gift for his upcoming fifth birthday. He wanted a Lego set with Pokémon figures. This is important stuff to a five-year-old, so we reviewed a few of the videos that show the features of the different sets we were considering. (I

> *Our family motto, while our children grew up, was "Try something new!" Whether it was encouraging a toddler to be adventuresome and try something new at dinnertime, or a middle-schooler to be brave and join a club, that motto served us all well.*
>
> *—Carolyn Allen*

think it would make an interesting scientific study to try to understand why these little sample videos are so fascinating to children. If you are a parent or a grandparent, you know what I am talking about; they are strangely addicting.) I was interested to see that each Pokémon character is defined by his or her superpowers, strengths, and weaknesses. I began to wonder what my little sample video would look like:

Marilyn, a.k.a. Motomouth:
Superpower: Can talk forever, about nearly anything, with or without actual facts.

128. Marvin J. Ashton, "There are Many Gifts," *Ensign*, November 1987.

Strength: Is relentlessly optimistic, regardless of evidence to the contrary.

Weakness: Has trouble stopping talking to listen, ignores warnings and past experience.

The interesting thing about these types of summaries, is that gamers will invest in characters with weaknesses to get a balance of the types of superpowers and strengths they need to defeat an enemy. One consultant recommends a study of the Avengers, with their various superpowers, as a key to building a successful business team:

> The reason the Avengers story is such a fascinating one for business leaders, is because it's about a group of exceptional people using their extraordinary skills to achieve a common goal. Power alone isn't enough. No matter how many superheroes you assemble, their powers are worthless to you if they're not the right ones for the task or if your heroes are at odds with one another. Great teams need smart leaders.
>
> Which superpowers will we need? When you've got a project in mind—a villain to defeat or an innocent to save—you need to decide which skills and strengths are the most important. You may need the vision that Iron Man brings with his ability to fly at 30,000 feet and as an operator that can drive things to completion. You may not need Thor's hammer, but you may well need a financial modelling ninja, who can keep track of the business case and make sure it stays together.[129]

HOW GOD USES YOUR SUPERPOWERS, STRENGTHS, AND (YES) WEAKNESSES

In building a family, youth group, or ward organization, each person has superpowers, strengths, and even weaknesses that can all be used by God. These are like bags of gold; they are valuable and should not be hidden or buried.

---

129. Scott Propp, "What Marvel's Avengers Teach Us about Leading Great Teams," Scott Propp, April 25, 2012, http://scottpropp.com/avengers-leading-great-teams.

You may think, *I'm just not talented. I'm not one of those people who is a great Church leader or is a great speaker; in fact, whenever they ask me to speak, I nearly die!* Although I don't fear speaking in public, there are other things I might be asked to do that take me right out of my comfort zone. For example, I tried to be a receptionist in the temple, but I talked so much that my supervisor actually put me in "time out" one day. I'm not kidding! She said "Sister Faulkner, please go and sit on the bench for a while and let's just think about reverence." And after that, she had me fold towels in the laundry, where there wasn't anyone to talk to. It was torture! Somehow, the Church does find a way to bring us out of our comfort zones and do things that are very difficult for us. But in doing so, we may be useful to God in a way we didn't expect.

It has taken me forty years to share this experience, but it illustrates how God uses everything about us for His good. When I served a mission in Japan, we were sometimes really out in the middle of nowhere; in one city where I served it took seven hours by train to get to the city where our mission president lived. He was a wonderful Hawaiian-Japanese man; he loved his missionaries and we loved him, but he was not a person who wanted to talk about uncomfortable things. He just liked to hear that all was well, and we didn't like to worry him. Sometimes as a result there were serious problems that went overlooked. One snowy winter day after a district meeting, I was chatting with one of the elders. Our companions were both Japanese, and so they did not understand our conversation. While they were talking to each other, this elder confided to me that he was thinking of going home. He felt discouraged, unworthy, and useless. In that moment,

> *The untrained Human mind tends to run in negative channels, gravitating toward feelings of fear, despair jealousy, hatred contempt vengeance, grudges, self-blame, self-doubt—just to name a few. These negative mind-states are false, a deception, and they have a poisonous effect on our soul. They create toxins in our being.*
>
> —M. Catherine Thomas

I had a very strong impression to ask him some direct, specific questions that identified exactly what was wrong. We were both quite surprised, so much so that he shed tears and so did I. Just having a chance to speak freely about things that were troubling him gave him enough hope and courage to keep going. It was a strange and yet sacred moment neither of us ever forgot. He completed his mission (which I'm sure he would have done anyway), and I know that we both felt God's love for him in that faraway place that day.

I share that because this was a moment when all three of my defining characteristics were used by God. My superpower: I talk. I'm always getting in big conversations with people, and this day was no exception. My strength: I'm very optimistic. Even if there is a lot of evidence to the contrary, I usually feel like things are going to work out. My weakness: I don't know when to stop talking; and I don't have a good filter that stops me from talking about inappropriate things. It's a weakness I struggle with all the time.

I can just see some guardian angels in heaven, reporting on this elder, alone and discouraged in an outpost in Northern Japan. Angel #1 says, "I'm worried about Elder X. He needs to talk to someone, but he won't go see the mission president. And even if he does, the president is too reticent to bring up the difficult subjects." Angel #2 replies, "Hey, I know, we could send Marilyn over there. She'll talk about anything, she has no filter, so maybe we can nudge her to bring up some sensitive subjects with him. And she's pretty cheerful, so maybe she can help him feel how much we love him and how much we know he can be a great missionary." They agree to send me and are actually relieved that for once they might do some good with me, since I usually just require lots of damage control. Do you see how, without my weakness, I might not have been just the right person for the job?

I'm not using this story to excuse my weaknesses. (I really am trying to learn to talk less, and not to laugh at all the wrong jokes.) But, in the meantime, it comforts me to know that Heavenly Father is so great that He can use everything about us to build His kingdom.

214

His grace is sufficient for all our weaknesses and strengths to be used for His good. We don't need to wait until we are perfect to use our talents. Whenever we are asked to pray, speak, serve, cook, clean, go to camp, sing, or do anything for the kingdom, we should just try to do it, even if it is not one of our strengths. We may feel like we offer very little, but God compares any talent He gives us to a bag of gold, and if you read the end of the parable, He's not very happy with people who hide the gold because it doesn't seem like enough (Matthew 25:14–30 NIV).

I often pray that God will use what is wrong with me as well as what is right with me to help build the kingdom, and this prayer has been answered many times. That weakness that you consider to be a bag of lead that weighs you down, might turn to something valuable for God. Your gift is not just your superpower, or your strength; even your weaknesses can be useful to Christ. In His alchemy of grace, He can turn even a bag of lead into gold.

Chapter Twenty

LESSONS FROM THE MASTER MINISTER: CHRIST AMONG THE NEPHITES

We've had a rather thrilling ride recently in the Church as we have sustained a new prophet. Let's be frank: Knowing that our new prophet was ninety-three years old, most of us were expecting a benign, smiling patriarch who would basically maintain the status quo. But in President Russell Nelson we have something entirely different. This energetic leader has invited us to start thinking outside the box, and we are all stumbling to catch up! In one fell swoop, he did away with a system of visiting each other that has been in place for more than a century, and challenged us to become "ministers," guided by the Holy Spirit rather than assignment sheets. What is the difference between "visiting" and "ministering?" It might be interesting to look at the Book of Mormon narrative to see what happens when the Master Minister comes to visit.

LESSONS FROM THE MASTER MINISTER

Christ is the ultimate minister. His visit to the Nephites is instructive, in part, because it is rather brief; He must accomplish in just a few days what He had three years to accomplish in His earthly ministry. As I examine the record of that visit, I notice four characteristics of His ministering style that I can try to emulate. (Of course, there are many more, but four is a good starting place.) And this account also serves to illustrate how the temple is our best training ground for our new calling as ministers.

1. Jesus goes where He is sent (and wherever He is is where He was sent).
2. Jesus ministers to one individual at a time, using His wounds as a witness.
3. Jesus uses the scriptures and ordinances as a source of power.
4. Jesus empowers His followers to become leaders as well.

We don't know exactly when Christ visited the Nephites. The scripture seems to indicate that several months had gone by since His Resurrection, so we can imagine that a period of rebuilding had ensued after the massive destruction that occurred at the time of the Crucifixion (see 3 Nephi 8). The account of His visit begins in 3 Nephi 11:

> There were a great multitude gathered together of the people of Nephi, round about the temple, which was in the land Bountiful. . . . While they were thus conversing one with another, they heard a voice as if it came out of heaven; and they cast their eyes round about, for they understood not the voice which they heard; and it was not a harsh voice, neither was it a loud voice; nevertheless, and notwithstanding it being a small voice it did pierce them that did hear to the center, insomuch that there was no part of their frame that it did not cause to quake; yea, it did pierce them to the very soul, and did cause their hearts to burn." (3 Nephi 11:1, 3)

Since Jesus chooses the temple as the setting for His visitation, we might look at this scene through a temple lens, and notice all the elements of temple worship that are included in this episode. The first is the ritual repetition of messages, three times, one of the most common motifs in scripture. (By the way, as a parent it always makes me feel better to know God has to repeat most things three times before anyone even starts to pay attention.)

It takes a while, but the frightened people finally recognize that the disembodied voice they hear is coming from heaven:

> They cast their eyes up again towards heaven; and behold, they saw a Man descending out of heaven; and he was clothed in a white robe; and he came down and stood in the midst of them; and the eyes of the whole multitude were turned upon him, and they durst not open their mouths, even one to another, and wist not what it meant, for they thought it was an angel that had appeared to them.
>
> And it came to pass that he stretched forth his hand and spake unto the people, saying: Behold, I am Jesus Christ, whom the prophets testified shall come into the world. And behold, I am the light and life of the world; [*"Light and life" must have been wonderful words to hear after the traumatic experience of darkness and death that they had experienced.*] and I have drunk out of the bitter cup which the Father has given me, and have glorified the Father in taking upon me the sins of the world, in the which I have suffered the will of the Father in all things from the beginning." (3 Nephi 11:8–11)

I. Jesus Goes Where He Is Sent

This brings to mind the first point of Jesus as a minister: He is sent. Christ came to earth because the Father sent Him, and He continually referred to that fact, intertwining His will with the Father's. One commentator notes:

> In John's Gospel, Jesus uses the Greek verb "pempein" to refer to "the Father who sent me" no fewer than 24 times. These references put the focus on the Father, who through this action of sending authorizes and empowers the Son in his mission. In another seventeen passages, however, some form of the verb "apostellein" is used to focus instead on Jesus, as the one who is sent. This verb invests Jesus' acts with the full authority of the Father because he seems to do only what the Father wills. Indeed, for John, the Father is present, speaking and acting in Jesus (John 5:17, John 5:19–20).[130]

---

130. John Painter, "God as Sender, Jesus as Sent," *Bible Odyssey*, accessed August 30, 2018, https://www.bibleodyssey.org/en/passages/related–articles/god–as–sender–jesus–as–sent.

WHEREVER YOU GO, THERE YOU ARE

This is a major ministering lesson, but most of us miss it. Think how much time we spend being upset about our plans being interrupted, our agendas not working out, or our expectations going unfulfilled. My husband, Craig, used to say, as he taught our children to drive, "Always remember when you are on the road, that basically everybody is angry."

And why are we angry? Because we are in a hurry to get to where we are going. We have an agenda to meet! But even though He had the most important mission in the history of the world to perform, we never hear Jesus complain about His agenda being interrupted. At the end of His great sermon to the 5,000, when the crowd looks at Him hungrily, He doesn't say, *Wait a minute, this is not what I expected! Why didn't you five thousand people pack a lunch if you were coming out into the desert all day? I give the sermons—I don't serve a meal—this isn't an all-inclusive resort! What do you expect Me to do about it?* Instead, when His disciples make exactly those kinds of comments, Jesus simply says, *Well, what are you going to do about it, send them away hungry? Find them something to eat!*

In business, and in sports, we call this "pivoting." Jesus can stop and change direction in an instant, while keeping the ultimate goal in sight; He does not see an obstacle as a setback, but just as a part of the drive toward His objective. The ministry to the Nephites is particularly instructive in this area. Notice how many times in the narrative Jesus changes direction based on the reactions of the people to whom He is ministering. He sends them home to rest and think when they look exhausted, He has them come forward and touch him one by one to build their testimonies, and He even stays an extra day or two, all in response to their needs.

Perhaps we could take a lesson from Christ's ministry to the Nephites and see how we might loosen up our ministering to be more sensitive to the needs we see along the road. On that ever-present "to-do" list, we might even pencil in a spot for "pivoting," and assign ourselves the task of listening for the Spirit to tell us to change direction and do a task that is on the Lord's list rather than our own.

2. Jesus Ministers to One Individual at a Time, Using His Wounds as a Witness

Here is the first thing that Jesus does after He descends from heaven into the midst of the Nephites:

> And it came to pass that the Lord spoke unto them saying: Arise and come forth unto me, that ye may thrust your hands into my side, and also that ye may feel the prints of the nails in my hands and in my feet, that ye may know that I am the God of Israel, and the God of the whole earth, and have been slain for the sins of the world. And it came to pass that the multitude went forth, and thrust their hands into his side, and did feel the prints of the nails in his hands and in his feet; and this they did do, going forth one by one until they had all gone forth, and did see with their eyes and did feel with their hands, and did know of a surety and did bear record, that it was he, of whom it was written by the prophets, that should come" (3 Nephi 11:13–15).

Hugh Nibley says this:

> You notice that Christ comes to every individual; it's all on an individual basis. He takes them by the hand, he gives each one the signs and tokens, and blesses them one by one. Everyone gets this private, individual attention here, the private treatment.

> *In serving others, are we giving what we want to give—or what is needed? True generosity requires . . . imagination—the capacity to see people in all their perplexities and needs, and to know how to expend ourselves effectively for them.*
> —A. R. Wylie

An average temple session is about two hours long, which means I'm usually hungry by the end. Sometimes I have caught myself thinking: "Couldn't we shorten this a bit? Why can't we all just get up and go on in to the Celestial room together? Why take all this time to go one by one?" This beautiful episode in Third Nephi reminds us that every important step taken in the gospel is taken one person at a time. We don't have group baptisms, or mass confirmations. We take the sacrament one person at a time. We enter through the veil into the celestial room one person at a time. Every ordinance emphasizes the value of one soul, and our ministering should reflect that. Time after time in the scriptures, we are reminded that the actions of one person can change the course of history. Each of us represents the beginning of a new world. Each of us is that important to God.

One commentator said, "[Jesus's] power is in His weakness and His vulnerability." This is truly a miracle; Jesus uses His vulnerability as a redemptive tool. Have you ever thought about the fact that the official proof of Jesus's divinity is His set of wounds? It is not His power to change water to wine or cast out a devil. It is the way He was willing to "take one for the team" and suffer immeasurable pain for all of us, when He himself was innocent. Whenever we rely on our strengths and accomplishments to impress others, or to push events our way, we should remember the wounded Christ.

When my father was called to be a bishop, he told me that the biggest surprise for him was that God expected him to be vulnerable and show his weakness. My dad was a very strong man; one of the bravest men I've ever met. Once when a street thief stole my mother's purse in Rome, my dad took off running after him, chased him down and got it back! Dad would try anything: he was a jeweler and traveled the world on buying trips. Once he went down in a kind of crate on a rope into an emerald mine in South America. ("Nobody else wanted to do it," he marveled.) He regularly led caravans of families down to the southern tip of Baja California to go camping, with his revolver and a stack of cash for emergencies stowed in the glove compartment of our Winnebago. I relate all these little anecdotes to say that there is only one thing I knew my dad feared, and that was revealing his weaknesses, fears, and failings.

For Dad, strength was strength. His outward facing manner was either resolutely positive or closed up and intimidating; it was difficult to get past that outer shell and have a heart-to-heart discussion with him. That is, until he became a bishop in his fifties. He once shared with me how shocking it was when, in one of his first interviews, a troubled member shared some struggles he was facing. The Spirit whispered to Dad, "Tell him he is not alone and that you have had similar struggles." Dad staunchly resisted the impression, but it came again and again until he was forced to relent. It was truly a revelation to Dad that the vulnerability to show his weaknesses was really a source of strength. Jesus, the suffering servant, is the model of this paradoxical truth.

Jeffrey R. Holland wrote:

> The wounds in Christ's hands, feet, and side are signs that in mortality painful things happen even to the pure and the perfect, signs that tribulation is not evidence that God does not love us. It is a wounded Christ that comes to our rescue. The evidence of His pain in mortality is undoubtedly intended to give courage to others who are also hurt and wounded by life, perhaps even in the house of their friends.[131]

All of us have wounds, all of us have illnesses, all of us have terrible things that have happened to us, many times undeserved. Jesus wears His wounds so that we know that we're not alone. When we minister, what do we have to offer to other people? We may think that if we are not a talented speaker or a brilliant scriptorian, we are not prepared to minister. Perhaps our weakness counts more than our strengths at times. Jesus later poses a compelling question:

> Behold I have given unto you my gospel, and this is the gospel which I have given unto you—that I came into the world to do the will of my Father, because my Father sent me. And my Father sent me that I might be lifted up upon the cross; and after that I had been lifted up upon the cross, that I might *draw all men unto me*, (3 Nephi 27:13–14, italics added).

---

131. Jeffrey R. Holland, *Christ and the New Covenant: The Messianic Message of the Book of Mormon* (1997), 259.

It is instructive to notice how many words to describe Christ are "pulling" words. When we talk about the ministering of Jesus, the words *invite, beckon, pull, tug,* and *draw* come to mind; they're all compelling words. None of them are forcing-pushing words. Everything about His ministering is an opening, not a closing. His "curtains [perhaps the veil?] are stretched out still" (Moses 7:30). "Draw all men unto me" doesn't mean He's going to force us into belief (John 12:32 KJV). It doesn't mean He's going to make us feel so guilty about everything we're not doing that we finally start doing it. It means that He reaches out to us with what Orson F. Whitney called "the tentacles of divine providence."[132] G. K. Chesterton's wonderful priest/detective Father Brown described this bond between Savior and saved in an extension of the metaphor "fishers of men."

> "Yes," he said, "I caught him, with an unseen hook and an invisible line which is long enough to let him wander to the ends of the world, and still to bring him back with a twitch upon the thread."[133]

3. Jesus Uses the Scriptures, Ordinances, Blessings, and Healing as Sources of Power

It is marvelous how Jesus institutes the major ordinances of the gospel to the Nephites, one at a time, interweaving them with His teachings. "And the Lord said unto him: I give unto you power that ye shall baptize this people when I am again ascended into heaven" (3 Nephi 11:21). Then He goes on to teach the meaning behind the ordinance, and concludes:

> And again I say unto you, ye must repent, and be baptized in my name, and become as a little child, or ye can in nowise inherit the kingdom of God. Verily, verily, I say unto you, that this is my doctrine, and whoso buildeth upon this buildeth upon my rock, and the gates of hell shall not prevail against them. (3 Nephi 11:38–39)

---

132. Orson F. Whitney, in Conference Report, April 1929, 110.
133. G. K. Chesterton, *The Innocence of Father Brown* (1911).

Hugh Nibley explains what that means:

> It is the proper function of a gate to shut creatures in or out of a place; when a gate "prevails," it succeeds in this purpose; when it does not "prevail," someone succeeds in getting past it. But prevail is a rather free English rendering of the far more specific Greek katischyo, meaning to overpower in the sense of holding back, holding down, detaining, suppressing, etc. Since all have fallen, all are confined in death which it is the Savior's mission to overcome; their release is to be accomplished through the work of the church, to which the Lord promises at some future time he will give the apostles the keys."[134]

True doctrine, combined with priesthood ordinances and Christ's redeeming grace, opens the gates of death for everyone who has ever lived. The Atonement consists of this triumverate of saving power: grace, doctrine, and ordinances. As each ordinance is introduced to the Nephites, it is accompanied by doctrinal discussion and episodes of healing and blessing.

> And it came to pass that Jesus commanded his disciples that they should bring forth some bread and wine unto him. . . . And when the multitude had eaten and were filled, he said unto the disciples: Behold there shall be one ordained among you, and to him will I give power that he shall break bread and bless it and give it to the people of my church, unto all those who shall believe and be baptized in my name. And this shall ye always observe to do, even as I have done, even as I have broken bread and blessed it and given it unto you. And this shall ye do in remembrance of my body, which I have shown unto you. And it shall be a testimony unto the Father that ye do always remember me. And if ye do always remember me ye shall have my Spirit to be with you. (3 Nephi 18:1, 5–7)

Jesus focuses on the power of the ordinances in His teaching. This made me think about my role as a covenant Christian. Do I witness to others about the power of the ordinances in my life? That power is very great. I think often about my baptismal covenant as I

---

134. Hugh Nibley, *Mormonism and Early Christianity* (Salt Lake City: Deseret Book, 1987).

try to mourn with those who mourn and comfort those who stand in need of comfort on a daily basis. I use the gift of the Holy Ghost in my life every day. I take the sacrament every week; my covenant there is the framework upon which my worship life is built. And my temple covenants mean everything to me. My washing and anointing as a daughter of God, my sealing to my husband and my children, and my special endowment of power to bless them through my covenants comprise the temple of faith I have constructed on the framework of baptism and confirmation. But do I talk about that with my children and with those whom I am called to serve? I really don't do that very often. Why would people think that ordinances are important if we don't help them make the connection between those ordinances and the daily joy, peace, and power we receive as members of the Church? Jesus shows us how to do that here.

Along with ordinances, Jesus quotes scripture. He instructs His new Apostles to make sure that the scriptures are complete, and that several chapters of scripture are included in the record of His visit.

As He did with the disciples on the road to Emmaus, He opens new vistas of understanding as He relates the scriptures to His mission. No effort at ministering is complete without including the scriptures. Otherwise, you are just offering your own wisdom. Anyone can do that. Once again, ordinances plus doctrine plus grace—or the blessing and healing power of Christ—equal the full gospel message.

>
>
> *If you don't have some vision of what god is doing, it finally beats you down. Mary sits at Jesus feet and listens to his word, listens to that Vision, and without that word we cannot go on like Martha pairing meals of hospitality for the world. It will finally worry us, distract us, anger us, exhaust us and beat us down. With that word, though we can prepare meals for the hungry, care tenderly for the sick, show hospitality to the stranger and keep on loving and living in the name of Christ.*
>
> —*Rev Thomas Long*

SUFFER THE LITTLE CHILDREN, NO MATTER HOW MUCH THEY MAKE YOU SUFFER

My daughter Alison and her husband, Eric, have a popular podcast with a variety of interesting segments.[135] My personal favorite is the segment titled, "Nobody Cares About Your Kids," in which they tell a funny story about their three children, with the caveat that they understand that this is interesting only to them: nobody really wants to hear stories about other people's kids; they just want to talk about their own! Alison is on to something here: everyone is endlessly interested in their own children. Jesus understood this perfectly and always showed interest in other people's children. He loved every child as if that child were His own, because in fact, they were. The episode in which He blesses the children of the Nephites is transcendently beautiful because of the way He elevates these oft-ignored little beings to the forefront of His ministry. Are we doing the same?

The greatest experience of my mission was the opportunity I had to teach a woman named Sister Hayakawa in Fukushima, Japan. Her husband was the elders quorum president in the small, struggling Fukushima Branch. Our mission president wanted to call him as the branch president, but his wife was so hostile to the Church that it was impossible. He called me on the phone one time, explained all of this to me, and then told me that he was going to send me and a new Japanese sister to Fukushima (where sisters had not previously served) just to convert this woman! A marvelous spiritual journey ensued that lasted over a year, involved many people, and eventually resulted in the baptism of Sister Hayakawa. Thirty-five years later I was able to travel back to Fukushima with Craig, and we stayed with the Hayakawa's. (This was before the tsunami and nuclear accident of 2011 that left Fukushima an uninhabitable

---

135. *Awesome with Alison*, https://itunes.apple.com/us/podcast/awesome-with-alison/id1191721368.

226

wasteland. It was a beautiful city before then.) Our reunion felt like a little taste of heaven.

It was a joy to reconnect with the Hayakawa's, who have been a mainstay in the Church for decades, and also a joy to become reacquainted with their son, who was just three at the time we taught Sister Hayakawa the discussions. I was thrilled to learn that he was now serving as the bishop of the Fukushima Ward! I have to admit that at this point I was feeling pretty proud of myself for the impact I had had on this future Church leader. But just as I was framing up an outline in my mind for an *Ensign* article about how I (like Alma) had converted one soul who turned out to be crucial in the kingdom, Sister Hayakawa turned to her son and said, "Do you remember the time that Sister Green got so annoyed with you she picked you up and put you in the futon cupboard?" Everyone laughed as I turned bright red with embarrassment and apologized to him. The future *Ensign* article dissolved as I got a glimpse of the amount of damage control God has to do every time I show up!

I admit I was not born with a huge maternal urge, like many girls are. I was never a great babysitter, you know, one of those girls who have a kit with finger puppets and stories to read. I was much more interested in what was in the fridge and on TV than I was in the kids I was supposed to watch. And even though I fiercely loved my own children, I was not the type that would *ever* be called to the Primary. I used to sit in the noisy chapel (with my own little ones leading the charge in disturbing the peace) and think to myself, "For Pete's sake, little kids don't understand what goes on in church, and they make it impossible to feel the Spirit. Why don't we just put them in the back somewhere and give them a movie to watch?" Obviously I had a long way to go before I would reach Jesus's perspective. The Savior takes a significant amount of the precious time He has on this visit to minister to each child, one by one. We know from the record that those children remembered and followed His teachings (see 4 Nephi).

4. Jesus Empowers His Followers to Become Leaders as Well

Jesus is the Master Minister, but He won't be satisfied until He turns His disciples into ministers too. He shows us how to pass the baton, and help those we love and serve to become the full measure of what they can become as leaders and ministers in their own right.

> And behold, the multitude was so great that they did cause that they should be separated into twelve bodies. And the twelve did teach the multitude; and behold, they did cause that the multitude should kneel down upon the face of the earth, and should pray unto the Father in the name of Jesus. And the disciples did pray unto the Father also in the name of Jesus. And it came to pass that they arose and ministered unto the people. And when they had ministered those same words which Jesus had spoken—nothing varying from the words which Jesus had spoken—behold, they knelt again and prayed to the Father in the name of Jesus. And they did pray for that which they most desired; and they desired that the Holy Ghost should be given unto them.
>
> And when they had thus prayed they went down unto the water's edge, and the multitude followed them. And it came to pass that Nephi went down into the water and was baptized. And he came up out of the water and began to baptize. And he baptized all those whom Jesus had chosen. And it came to pass when they were all baptized and had come up out of the water, the Holy Ghost did fall upon them, and they were filled with the Holy Ghost and with fire. And behold, they were encircled about as if it were by fire; and it came down from heaven, and the multitude did witness it, and did bear record; and angels did come down out of heaven and did minister unto them. And it came to pass that while the angels were ministering unto the disciples, behold, Jesus came and stood in the midst and ministered unto them. (3 Nephi 19:5–15)

WE ARE ALL IN TRAINING NOW

Our new prophet is so tech savvy that when he announced in general conference that we were expected to become ministers, he already had secured the domain name and had the website up and running! Here is a quote from that website about what it means to minister:

> The Savior showed by example what it means to minister as He served out of love for His Father and for each person. He loved, taught, prayed for, comforted, and blessed those around Him. As Church members minister, they prayerfully seek to serve as He would—to "comfort those that stand in need of comfort," "watch over the church always, to be with and strengthen them," "visit the house of each member," and help each become a true disciple of Christ (Mosiah 18:9; D&C 20:51, 53; see also John 13:35).[136]

When you heard this statement read in general conference you might have been thinking what I was thinking, something like, "Oh shoot. It's not just those three people on my list anymore! It could be anyone! I might actually have to be prayerful and have Heavenly Father guide me. This is going to be hard." Yet, like many of you, I woke up the very next morning with a little thought in my mind of somebody that I should call. It was that simple. That morning I had this mental image of little light bulbs going off all over the world, where members of the Church were waking up and asking, "Lord, where do you want me to go? Who am I supposed to text? Who needs my help?" And the answers begin to flow. So we are all in training to be ministers now.

MINISTERING: THE SUM IS GREATER THAN ITS PARTS

The culmination of this experience—and in fact the culmination of the Book of Mormon—is recorded in 3 Nephi 17, one of the most beautiful passages of scripture on record. We can see here how all the elements of ministering come together:

> Behold, now it came to pass, that when Jesus had spoken these words he looked round about again on the multitude, and he said unto them: Behold, my time is at hand. I perceive that ye are weak,

---

136. First Presidency Letter, April 2, 2018.

and ye cannot understand all my words which I am commanded
of the Father to speak unto you at this time. Therefore, go ye unto
your homes, and ponder upon the things which I have said, and ask
the Father, in my name, that ye may understand, and prepare your
minds for the morrow, and I come unto you again. But now I go
unto the Father, and also to show myself unto the lost tribes of Israel,
for they are not lost unto the Father, for he knoweth whither he hath
taken them. (3 Nephi 17:1–4)

Like all of us, Jesus has His agenda, He needs to leave, because
another group of His children is waiting for Him. Yet though it is
time to go, this is a vulnerable Savior, one who can be moved to
change the schedule, which is just what He does. The result is too
beautiful and profound to abridge, we must simply quote it straight
through:

> And it came to pass that when Jesus had thus spoken, he cast his eyes
> round about again on the multitude, and beheld they were in tears,
> and they did look steadfastly upon him as if they would ask him to
> tarry a little longer with them. And he said unto them: Behold, my
> bowels [*The bowels are His gut, the pit of His stomach, where we feel guilt,
> sorrow, etc.*] are filled with compassion towards you. Have ye any that
> are sick among you? Bring them hither. Have ye any that are lame,
> or blind, or halt, or maimed, or leprous, or that are withered, or that
> are deaf? (3 Nephi 17:5–7) [*Think of how He had just experienced every
> single thing that can go wrong with us, and how that would impact this
> moment.*]

> They did all, both they who had been healed and they who were
> whole, bow down at his feet, and did worship him; and as many as
> could come for the multitude did kiss his feet, insomuch that they
> did bathe his feet with their tears. [*And now we get to the part where
> you think nobody cares about your kids but you, and find out there has
> been someone all along who cares about them even more than you do.*] And
> it came to pass that he commanded that their little children should
> be brought.

> So they brought their little children and set them down upon
> the ground round about him, and Jesus stood in the midst; and
> the multitude gave way till they had all been brought unto him.

And it came to pass that when they had all been brought, and Jesus stood in the midst, he commanded the multitude that they should kneel down upon the ground. And it came to pass that when they had knelt upon the ground, Jesus groaned within himself, and said: Father, I am troubled because of the wickedness of the people of the house of Israel. (3 Nephi 17:10–14)

Seeing the beautiful righteousness and love He felt here, Jesus may have been reminded of the terrible experiences He had had in Israel with the rejection. I imagine it just made His heart ache that those people couldn't experience what these people were experiencing.

When he had said these words, he himself knelt upon the earth; and behold he prayed unto the Father, and the things which he prayed cannot be written, and the multitude did bear record who heard him. And after this manner do they bear record: The eye hath never seen, neither hath the ear heard, before, so great and marvelous things as we saw and heard Jesus speak unto the Father." [*I always wonder here "What exactly was He saying?"*]

And no tongue can speak, neither can there be written by any man, neither can the hearts of men conceive so great and marvelous things as we both saw and heard Jesus speak; and no one can conceive of the joy which filled our souls at the time we heard him pray for us unto the Father. And it came to pass that when Jesus had made an end of praying unto the Father, he arose; but so great was the joy of the multitude that they were overcome. And it came to pass that Jesus spake unto them, and bade them arise. And they arose from the earth, and he said unto them: Blessed are ye because of your faith. And now behold, my joy is full."

And when he had said these words, he wept, and the multitude bare record of it, and he took their little children, one by one, and blessed them, and prayed unto the Father for them. And when he had done this he wept again; And he spake unto the multitude, and said: Behold your little ones. And as they looked to behold they cast their eyes towards heaven, and they saw the heavens open, and they saw angels descending out of heaven as it were in the midst of fire; and they came down and encircled those little ones about, and they were encircled about with fire; and the angels did minister unto them. And the multitude did see and bear record. (3 Nephi 17:15–25)

WITH JESUS'S HELP WE CAN BE MINISTERS

We all have people that we love. What do we have to give them? We have a hope in Christ. We know He lives. We know He saves. We know that no matter what mistake they make or hardship they must endure, He can lighten that burden, share it, teach them wisdom about it, and turn it into something that will exalt them. Life is given new meaning because of the Savior, and if we share His love, His teachings, and His truth, then we are ministers; more than just friends. More than just visitors. We have something substantive to give.

> *A man that advances in spiritual and in temporal matters at the same time, minding to keep the spiritual first, will not let the temporal lead him; he will not place his heart upon his farm, his horses, or any possession that he has. He will place his desires in heaven, and will anchor his hope in that eternal soil; and his temporal affairs will come up as he advances in the knowledge of God.*
> —Jedediah M. Grant

Through the power of the Holy Spirit, we can combine the elements we have discussed here into ministering moments that will change lives. Simply following a checklist will not be adequate; our ministering must, like the Savior's, become a unique experience that models what He would do in that particular instance. And thus we become His designated helpers: what Obadiah called Saviors on Mt. Zion (see Obadiah 1:21), or what C. S. Lewis referred to as "little Christs":

And now we begin to see what it is the New Testament is always talking about. It's talking about being born again, it talks about putting on Christ, about Christ being formed in us or having the mind of Christ. Put right out of your head the idea that these are only fancy ways of saying that Christians are supposed to read what Christ said, and then try to do it all. As a man may read what Plato or Marx said and try to carry that out. They mean something much more than that. They mean that a real person, Christ, here and now, in this very room where you are sitting, where you are saying your prayers, is doing things to you. It's not a question of a good man who died 2,000 years ago. It's a living man, still as much a man as you, and yet as much a God as God, really coming and interfering with your very self, killing that old natural self and replacing it with the kind of self he has. At first, only for moments, then for longer periods, and finally, if all goes well, turning you permanently into a different sort of thing, into a new little Christ, a being which in its own small way has the same kind of life as God and shares in his power, joy, knowledge and eternity.[137]

If we only share friendship, we are just like everybody else, and not enough like Jesus. If we take the Master Minister as our guide, we can strive to be "little Christs" for Him. We can have an intention that whenever we interact with anyone, we will bless, teach, love, share, witness, feed, or do at least one or two of the life-changing things that He did, so that we can be easily identified as ministers of Christ.

137. C. S. Lewis, *Mere Christianity*, book 4 (San Francisco: Harper Publishing, 2001).

Chapter Twenty-One

A SACRED SPACE: FINDING JESUS IN THE TEMPLE

I once heard a story about two men who were called into an interview with an illustrious ecclesiastical personage. The first man came in and (perhaps suspecting that he was being considered for an important position) was eager to make a good impression. The interviewer said, "Tell me what you know about Jesus Christ," and so he told about His life, how He was born in a stable and lived a humble life, suffered for our sins, died an ignominious death, and was resurrected. The interviewer thanked him, and he was excused from the room. The next man came in to be interviewed and simply fell to his knees and said, "My Lord and my God."

> The temple, as the very name proclaims, is a place where one takes one's bearings on the universe. . . . We live in Vanity Fair today, and the temple represents the one sober spot in the world where we can really be serious and consider these things.
> —Hugh Nibley

That story had an impact on me because it challenged me, at a fairly young age, to focus my spiritual study life. And throughout the years I have occasionally asked myself, "Am I learning facts about Christ, or am I actually getting to know Him?" It almost seems presumptuous to think that we could know Jesus, but He invites us to. He says, "And this is life eternal, that they might know thee, the only true God, and Jesus Christ, whom thou hast sent" (John 17:3 KJV). Rather than a distant, king/subject relationship, He is saying, *I invite you to know Me. I want you to get close to Me. I want you to interact with Me. Getting to know Me is a key to finding your own eternal self.* One of the ways we can do that is to attend the temple.

HOW MUCH SHOULD WE TALK ABOUT THE TEMPLE?

We don't talk about the temple very much because certain symbolic parts of the ceremony are not discussed outside its walls; this tends to make us reticent about talking about any of the worship services that go on there. These days, the line that divides private and public information has gone rather blurry; the advent of the internet means that privacy is essentially a thing of the past. When it comes to the sacred temple ordinances, everything that goes on in the temple is now available on the internet. In one way it is good, because it proves what we have always asserted, that the temple ordinances are uplifting and sweet, and not some sinister secret. But it also means that if we don't take the initiative to have meaningful conversations about the temple with our children, they will go to the internet for information. After all, when it's time for them to go to a movie, our kids Google it and read the reviews. When it's time for them to buy a phone, they Google it and read the reviews. Don't kid yourself that when it's time for them to go to the temple they won't Google it and read the reviews!

Since conversations that we used to be able to keep far more private are now a part of the public domain, we need to decide who is going to direct our conversations about the temple. We need to step into the role of being the main influence on the people we love and help them get the spirit of what the temple is about. The bulk of what goes on in the temple is not only open for discussion, it needs to be talked about more frequently. Armand Mauss, an LDS sociologist, says this:

There is no real reason that even devout Church members could not talk more about the temple, could not talk more about the temple ceremonies than they do, with appropriate discretion about time and place, since the oaths of secrecy attach only to new names, signs, tokens. Indeed, more open talk about the temple would not only facilitate understanding among both Mormons and non-Mormons in certain historical and scholarly respects, but would also infinitely improve the preparedness of initiates, almost all of whom now enter the temple with only the vaguest idea of what to expect or of the obligations they will be asked to assume.[138]

Information is power. When we go to the temple, we go with high hopes for a spiritual feast, but unfortunately sometimes we are not armed with the information we need to properly appreciate it. Perhaps you or someone you love has had an experience of being rather disillusioned or a little taken back by their first temple experience. David O. McKay gave a beautiful address about the temple to a group of outgoing missionaries that began with this very candid reflection:

So many young people have been disappointed after they have gone through the House of the Lord. They have been honest in that disappointment. Some of them have shed tears with me as they have opened their hearts and expressed heart-felt sorrow that they did not see and hear and feel what they had hoped to see and hear and feel.[139]

When I was in college, I rented a room in the home of a lovely family. The husband had been a member in name only for most of their married years. He had finally decided to become active in the Church, and they went through the temple preparation course together. At that time, most of the course was devoted to discussions of worthiness; there was very little discussion of what goes on in the actual temple session. I remember that there was so much happiness and joy when the day finally arrived, and they all got dressed up and

---

138. Armand L. Mauss, "Culture, Charisma, and Change: Reflections on Mormon Temple Worship," *Dialogue: A Journal of Mormon Thought* 20.4 (Winter 1987): 77–78.
139. David O. McKay, Salt Lake Temple Annex address on September 25, 1941.

went to the temple to be sealed together. I also remember that when they came home, that excitement had been replaced by a troubled expression on the father's face, and his answer was somewhat vague when I asked him how it was. As far as I know, he never went back. Perhaps he was expecting his temple experience to be like a sacrament meeting, only with everybody dressed in white. Whatever the case, he was disappointed.

President Ezra Taft Benson expressed concern about this lack of communication:

> Because of [the temple's] sacredness we are sometimes reluctant to say anything about the temple to our children and grandchildren. As a consequence, many do not develop a real desire to go to the temple, or when they go there, they do so without much background to prepare them for the obligations and covenants they enter into.[140]

The temple endowment is a highly symbolic worship experience, and it is quite different from our Church meetings. If we focus more on getting everyone dressed up and having a nice lunch afterward than we do on the experience itself, we may not adequately give our young people the opportunity to feel what they are hoping to feel. I remember one of our children saying as we drove away from his first temple visit, "Okay. I'm waiting for someone to explain to me why that wasn't weird." I realized that, as his mother, that "somebody" should have been me, and I had failed to prepare him properly. If we look at the temple as a house of learning, a house of meditation, and a house of prayer, we can see why it is not, in fact, weird, but is actually a powerhouse of strength for the covenant Christian, a place where we find Jesus manifested in every aspect of the ordinances and other activities.

---

140. Ezra Taft Benson, "What I Hope You Will Teach Your Children about the Temple," *Ensign*, August 1985.

JESUS AND THE TEMPLE

We can get a little confused about the temple when we set it off in a category by itself and say, "These are the things that go on in the temple, and they don't go on anywhere else." If we expand our vision a bit, we can see that the scriptures contain many, many "temple moments." The life of the Savior is filled with them.

For example, Jesus created the earth, and a narrative about the Creation opens our learning experience at the temple. Jesus spent many hours in prayer and in teaching and blessing others. We have records of several formal prayers He offered on behalf of others. All those things are part of our temple experience. Washing and anointing were important as Jesus assumed His role as King and Priest, and these are a beautiful part of the temple experience. Jesus was baptized, and one of the most important functions of the temple is to ensure that everyone has that opportunity, along with the receipt of the gift of the Holy Ghost. Jesus modeled the connection between healing and the forgiveness of sins, and that connection is beautifully made in the temple, as we achieve a new level of spiritual wholeness through our covenant relationship. As we read about Jesus in the scriptures, we see that He is doing nearly all the things that we do in the temple.

In the Garden story, good and evil are found on the same tree, not in separate orchards. Good and evil give meaning and definition to each other. If God, like us, is susceptible to immense pain, He is, like us, the greater in His capacity for happiness. The presence of such pain serves the larger purpose of God's master plan, which is to maximize the capacity for joy, or in other words, "to bring to pass the immortality and eternal life of man."
—*Terryl Givens*

Other moments from the life of Christ could be called temple moments. When Jesus appeared after His Resurrection, He retained the stigmata, or signs of His Crucifixion, so that His covenant children could recognize Him as the Savior. In fact, when He appeared to the Nephites, He took that time to make sure every person felt those marks in His hands.

Another temple moment occurred on the Mount of Transfiguration. On that occasion, Moses, Elijah, and perhaps other figures from the past who were very important in the spiritual history of the world were shown to the disciples. The dramatic narrative in the temple includes participation by great spiritual figures from the past. On another occasion, Satan appeared in person and tempted the Savior. It is fitting that the very disciples who stood on the Mount with Jesus assume a roll in a presentation that also includes Satan. These are all temple moments. And why? Because each of these moments pulls us up and out of our earthly perspectives and offers instead a long-range view of our place in the eternal scheme of things. We experience the "condescension of God" as Jesus literally reaches through the veil to bring us to Him. In all the great myths, the hero must enter the realm of death and escape back into the world of the living. This happens in the temple. Jesus rends the veil of death just as He did when He gave His life for us.

Another temple behavior that helps us connect to Christ is the time given to us to meditate and pray. Jesus took a great deal of time in His life to meditate, contemplate, and pray. The temple invites us to be still, to enter a meditative state. That is actually one of the hardest things to adjust to in the temple. It is quiet. Things move slowly. The session takes almost two hours, and there is a lot of repetition. This is difficult for our digitally scattered brains, but it is actually very important. Hugh Nibley said, "We live in Vanity Fair today, and the temple represents the one sober spot in the world where we can really be serious and consider these things."[141] So let's walk through the progression of ordinances together and look for Jesus as we go.

ORDINANCES OF PREPARATION

Hugh Nibley says this:

---

141. Hugh Nibley, "The Meaning of the Temple," in *Temple and Cosmos: Beyond This Ignorant Present* (Salt Lake City: Deseret Book and FARMS, 1992), 38.

Why do we call the temple a school? The initiatory ordinances make that clear. We begin there with the first requirement, that our brain and our intellect should be clear and active—we are there to learn and understand. Bring your brain with you and prepare to stay awake, to be alert and pay attention; also come often for frequent review, repeating the lessons to refresh our memory, for you cannot leave without an examination—you have to show you have learned some things in the temple.[142]

Before we attend the temple, we have been baptized and confirmed. These ordinances are performed in the temple for those who have died in what is known as baptism for the dead. The ordinances of preparation, or initiatory ordinances, come next, where we are washed and anointed symbolically and receive our temple garment. This is followed by the endowment ceremony and then marriages and sealing of families. (As the ordinances progress, we rise in the temple; baptisms, a symbol of death and Resurrection, take place on the lowest level, and the marriages and sealings take place on upper floors.) Since all the temple ordinances are performed by patrons for people who have died, we have the opportunity to come back and hear them again and again. John Widstoe, an educator, saw its brilliance as a teaching tool:

The wonderful pedagogy of the temple service, especially appealing to me as a professional teacher, carries with it evidence of the truth of temple work. We go to the temple to be informed and directed, to be built up and to be blessed. . . . Altogether our temple worship follows a most excellent pedagogical system. I wish instruction were given so well in every school throughout the land, for we would then teach with more effect than we now do. For these reasons, among many others, I have always felt that temple work is a direct evidence of the truth of the word reestablished by the Prophet Joseph Smith. It may be that the temple Endowment and the other temple

---

142. Ibid.

ordinances form the strongest available evidence of the divine inspiration of the Prophet Joseph Smith.[143]

The ordinances of initiation are solemn and beautiful. Fragments and shadows of these can be found in almost every faith, and even in the coronation ceremonies of monarchs.[144] The purpose of these ordinances is to change your view of who you are. You receive a new identity; you are no longer just an average person, you are destined to become a king and a priest or a queen and a priestess. Of this transformative power David O. McKay says:

> Let your spiritual eyes see the significance of that anointing, and then you will realize what it means to be initiated into the House of God and all its mysteries, and to have in your heart the realization that anything which any other man or any other woman has accomplished, you may, through the help of God, also accomplish. You know what that means to the human soul![145]

When we go into the temple, we receive a blessed break from the negative messages we take in every day. One of my friends observed, "Have you noticed that when we dress in those simple white clothes, all the social barriers that divide us go down? No one's rich, no one's poor, no one's even really fat or thin. We all just sort of look the same." For a few hours, we discard the outward trappings and focus on the inner person. You don't wear a designer temple dress; it would be ridiculous! You put on the temple clothing, and for once you get to stop worrying about your surface. We are directed into a chapel where we sit quietly and are given scriptures to read. Hopefully we move into a contemplative state. Now, what is it that we will be taught to think about in the temple? Interestingly enough, we will begin with the idea that we are not who we think we are; we're taught that we have a divine identity.

---

143. John A. Widtsoe, "Temple Worship," *Utah Genealogical and Historical Magazine*, April 1921, 59.
144. The Netflix series *The Crown* has a lovely episode about the coronation of Queen Elizabeth II that both explains and demonstrates her anointing (series 1, episode 5). Every temple goer will find it fascinating.
145. David O. McKay, Salt Lake Temple Annex address on September 25, 1941.

WHAT'S IN A NAME?

As is done through all the scriptures, the concept of the power of names is taught to us in the temple. In the Old and the New Testaments, when people receive a spiritual rebirth, they are often renamed. Adam had dominion over the animals of the earth because he named them. Whenever you are involved in a naming it is a very impactful process.

Truman Madsen reminds us that divine power is concentrated in divine names. At the burning bush, Moses asks God, *Who shall I tell them you are?* Jesus replies, "I am that I am" (Exodus 3:14 KJV). That Hebrew verb "I am" actually means "I am becoming who I am." In other words, "I am the source of all eternal life, I am the center of things, and I am also the source of eternal progress, of becoming. I exist more fully than anyone else. I am *that* I am."[146]

It is interesting to note that nearly every ordinance has a naming component: baby blessings, baptism, the sacrament, the endowment, and marriage all involve renaming in some way. There is real power in taking the divine name upon oneself. When I am baptized, I now have an internal "name tag" that identifies me as a Christian; I am a member of Jesus Christ's family. That is something that we can talk about in our families. Children love to talk about how they came to be named, and we can teach them how names are a source of power. That is why taking upon ourselves the name of Christ has such great significance.

> In Hebrew culture, names are more than labels. To "call one's name" or to know one's name signals power. Given mastery over the woman, Adam "calls her name Eve" (Gen. 3:20). A name change signals a change in one's fate and the fate of one's descendants.
>
> —Amy Jill Levine

---

146. See *By Study and Also By Faith: Essays in Honor of Hugh W. Nibley on the Occasion of His Eightieth Birthday* (Salt Lake City: Deseret Book and FARMS, 1990), 1:458–81.

ENDOWMENT: THE GIFT

Part One: Taught by Angels

There are two distinct parts to the endowment ceremony. The first is passive. We witness a presentation in the form of a drama, various iterations of which have been a part of most cultures. If you look at Greek drama, or even at the ancient dramas that were represented on the walls of caves, you will notice that they all share certain elements. There is usually a storyteller, or a chorus, that both narrates and comments on what's going on. There are at times voices offstage that speak about what needs to happen next, and even direct the action. The drama is figurative; we know it never actually happened in the exact way it is presented, because the participants all come from different places and times in history. So we are aware that it represents a spiritual snapshot of our life's journey. What we are receiving is a microcosm of the history of the world, and the point of it is to teach us once again who we are and who we are in relation to the Savior.

In the temple we are asked to view ourselves as if we were (respectively) Adam or Eve and consider their dilemmas as if we were the first inhabitants of the new world. What would we do in their place? What forces would be working against us and for us? How would we discern between good and evil? How would we decide what to do when faced with two worthy, yet conflicting choices? Would we be loyal to each other even if we did not totally agree with the choice the other made? These deceptively simple things turn out to be what life is all about. Nothing could be more like

> *I believe there are few, even temple workers, who comprehend the full meaning and power of the temple endowment. Seen for what it is, it is the step-by-step ascent into the eternal presence. If our young people could only glimpse it, it would be the most powerful spiritual motivation of their lives.*
>
> —*David O. McKay*

the daily challenges of life than the drama that is portrayed in the endowment.

The most important thing to contemplate as we watch the drama in the endowment room is how this drama is being played out in our own lives. What does this have to do with the choices I am making right now? Just as we've talked about placing ourselves in the stories of Jesus, we might ask ourselves, "How can I recognize the messages that God is sending to me? How good am I at clinging to the things I absolutely know to be true and not wandering off and getting mired in the stuff that I don't quite yet understand? How loyal am I to my spouse? How diligent am I in seeking God's will for my life?"

One of the things I think is most inspiring about the temple drama is the way it teaches how the two people in a marriage can complement each other through their unique strengths. Adam has a truly obedient heart: *Listen, this is what we've been given to do, and we're going to do it,* he says. Eve is a little more nuanced and points out the long-range picture: *Look, we want to have children, we need to know good from evil, and we have to make some difficult choices that are not always the letter of the law. We've got to figure out what the spirit of the law is.* This is important, because at certain points in life we're going to have to choose between two good things. We're going to have to choose between conflicting commandments. We do this all the time, and it can be very confusing. We are taught in the temple that it can be done, that God will guide you, and that even if you make a few bad decisions you should be loyal to each other, and God will continue to bless you and send you messages from on high.

Here are two very personal responses I have to the temple drama. As a woman, I can't help but rejoice in Eve's intelligence and understanding. If I ever doubt myself as a woman, the temple encourages me to trust my instincts and my inspiration. I see also the equality between Adam and Eve in the garden and how, in the fallen world, Eve's position seems to be somewhat downgraded. (Notice that she never speaks after they leave the garden.) This encourages me that the closer we get to our Heavenly home, the more these inequities will disappear.

The temple uses a variety of dramatic motifs to convey a powerful message. A dramatic motif is a theme or a pattern that is used in drama. For example, dramatic irony is used in the temple drama; we all know what's going to happen before they do. Adam and Eve are making choices in the garden, and we all know what the consequences will be. Mentally we may shout out, "Adam! Don't listen to Satan! Trust Jesus! This is going to work out all right," and "Eve, watch out for that guy. He just wants to deceive you. Childbirth is going to hurt if you make this decision!" We see it coming, and they're just kind of blithely walking, holding their baskets! That's dramatic irony.

> "
> *A religious symbol conveys its message even if it is no longer consciously understood in every part. For a symbol speaks to the whole human being and not only to the intelligence.*
> —Mircea Eliade
> "

In the temple drama we learn that one of the challenges that Adam and Eve have is to recognize this: who are the divine messengers? Who's telling you the truth? There are all kinds of messages coming at us every day. How do we recognize the divine messages? The temple gives us some keys for recognizing those messengers and how to be aware that those messengers will also share our same commitment to Jesus Christ and His gospel. We will be able to recognize that shared commitment.

Every time we view this drama, it invites us to the whole experience of life in microcosm. Hopefully we come to the end of the drama (as we do from any great literary or artistic experience) having a bigger view of our own life.

The dramatic motifs of the temple and its ordinances are found throughout the world from the very earliest times, but there are two parts of the temple ceremony, the dramatic and the pragmatic. The play is ended by the appearance of heavenly messengers who now bid farewell to the artifice of theater, and they engage us in a new type of learning."[147]

John Widtsoe said:

The philosophical completeness of the endowment is one of the great arguments for the veracity of temple ordinances. Moreover, this completeness of survey and expounding of the gospel plan makes temple worship one of the most effective methods of refreshing the memory concerning the whole structure of the gospel.[148]

You can wander into the temple thinking about the messy details of your life, and if you really just sit down and take it in, your mind quiets down and your vision opens up. You see the greatness of creation and how little we are in relation to it. Yet it's all about us, each individual is precious. There's something really, really marvelous about that.

Part Two: Interacting with Angels

Now we move from a dramatic presentation to an interactive session; we learn by doing. Whenever I read a book or watch a play I think, "What would I do if I wrote this?" If I wrote the temple endowment, this is where I'd insert a nice lecture to explain everything that has happened so far in the drama. It is a good thing that I didn't write it, because what the temple does is completely different, and it is brilliant. The tone switches, and we move from being passive listeners to active participants. As a participant you are asked to make commitments about your behavior, and how you should center your life. As disciples of Jesus Christ we're going to be asked to step up now and make some covenants that tie us to Him.

Nibley says:

Recall that in the time when you move from room to room, you leave the Creation Room, you move into the Telestial Room, and then things really begin to happen. The whole temple represents *teliotes,* or the telestial world, a word that nobody but Joseph Smith

---

147. Nibley, in *Temple and Cosmos: Beyond This Ignorant Present.*
148. John Widtsoe, *Utah Genealogical and Historical Magazine,* April 1921, 58.

was using at the time. It meant the very thing, the lowest world, the world in which we now live, the world that is placed between the other two. The ordinances bridge the two worlds between the telestial and the celestial. The events of the temple are thought to take place in the terrestrial and the telestial spheres, the world of the mysteries or ordinance, but the Coptic text called the in-between world, the world of transition.[149]

WHERE DID JOSEPH SMITH GET THE TEMPLE CEREMONY?

Joseph Smith created the endowment ceremony through inspiration, but (just as he used Biblical language in his translations) he used materials with which he was familiar. Much has been said about the similarities between the endowment ceremony and certain parts of the Masonic rituals. When I was in college and someone brought this to my attention I thought, "Well, that's interesting, and maybe that's something to be disturbed about." But then I took a Japanese literature class from a former Zen Buddhist monk, and one day he took us through the process of worship in the Shinto tradition. The Shinto faith is so old that there are no written records of it. In Japan, they combine Buddhism and Shintoism. Japanese people say, you're born into the Shinto faith, and you have your funeral in the Buddhist faith.

Our teacher explained that when you approach the altar, you kneel or bow and you clap two times. You approach God through prayer in a very measured and step-by-step way. Prayers are written on little slips of paper that are left at the altar. You go through a series of oaths that are connected to promises and punishments. The ancient ritual of *hara-kiri* (or what Americans call harikari) is connected to this, in which the person who has betrayed those who trusted him cuts out (kiri) the bowel (hara), or the place in the pit of the stomach where we feel guilt. This is only one of three ritual punishments. The great importance of oaths, integrity, and honor

---

149. Nibley, in *Temple and Cosmos: Beyond This Ignorant Present.*

that are so familiar to us in the Japanese culture have their root in the ancient rituals of Shinto.

Recently, a member of our ward returned home to Turkey to oversee the burial of his father, a Muslim. As the eldest son, he participated in the washing, anointing, and preparation for burial of his father by the Amim, or priests. It was a sacred experience, and he was struck by many similarities of these ancient rites to our temple worship. He came home with his faith strengthened in the echoes that resound in every culture of these very ancient forms of worship. When I traveled to Israel recently, I joined faithful women at the Western Wall to put a slip of paper into the sacred stones with the name of a loved one for whom I am praying.

Experiences like that have led me to believe that we often look at the temple in a spiritually short-sighted fashion. Rather than be disturbed by similarities with other practices, we should expect to see bits and pieces of the temple ceremony in many religious rituals. Aprons, robes, sashes, and the various trappings of the clergy all are resonant of temple robing. The use of clothing to remind us of our priorities is deeply rooted in our natures. If you casually observe people out in public, you can tell a great deal about how they perceive themselves from their clothing. Temple clothing invites us to see ourselves in a new way. The temple teachings and covenants build on that symbolic framework.

The Masonic rituals only date back to about the 1400s, which is fairly recent when you compare it with something as ancient as Shintoism or the rituals of the Tibetan Buddhists, but undoubtedly Joseph Smith saw things there that resonated with the impressions that he was receiving. We may think that Joseph Smith, or other inspired prophets, must not show influences from other sources to qualify as true prophets. This seems, once again, spiritually short-sighted to me. When I left for Japan on my mission, a friend said to me, "You will use everything worthwhile that you have ever learned on your mission." And that was true. In various settings I found that all my life experiences, linguistic training, literary study, and anything else that was knocking around in my head could be used by the Spirit to teach a principle. This, on a higher level, is what I feel happened with the prophet. He used the things with which he was familiar as a springboard for his revelations, then far surpassed them through inspiration.

The endowment originated from Adam and Eve, so we will see bits of it everywhere. If we find a piece of the ritual in Shintoism, or Catholicism, or in the Muslim tradition, do we say then that it is all just fabrication, that they are all copies of each other? No. Where there are copies, there is an original somewhere. I would tend to think that they all come from one root. To paraphrase Hamlet, there are more things in heaven and earth than we dream of in our particular philosophy. They are all part of one great truth.

Hugh Nibley again:

Did Joseph Smith reinvent the temple by putting all the fragments—Jewish, Orthodox, Masonic, Gnostic, Hindu, Egyptian, and so forth—together again? No, that is not how it is done. Very few of the fragments were available in his day, and the job of putting them together was begun, as we have seen, only in the latter half of the nineteenth century. Even when they are available, those poor fragments do not come together of themselves to make a whole; to this day the scholars who collect them do not know what to make of them. The temple is not to be derived from them, but the other way around. . . . That anything of such fulness, consistency, ingenuity, and perfection could have been brought forth at a single time and place—overnight, as it were—is quite adequate proof of a special dispensation.[150]

John Widtsoe says:

Let me suggest that the reason why temple building and temple worship are in every age on every hand among every people is because the gospel in its fullness was revealed to Adam and all religions and religious practices are therefore derived from the remnants of

---

150. Hugh Nibley, "What Is a Temple," in *The Collected Works of Hugh Nibley: Volume 4—Mormonism and Early Christianity,* ed. Todd M. Compton and Stephen D. Ricks (1987), 366–67, 383.

the truth given to Adam and transmitted by him to the patriarchs. The ordinances of the temple in so far as then necessary were given in those early days. Very naturally corruptions of them have been handed down through the ages, but those who understand the eternal nature of the gospel planned before the foundations of the earth understand clearly why all history seems to revolve around the building and use of temples.

PROMISES, PROMISES: BECOMING A COVENANT CHRISTIAN

In the second half of the endowment, we learn what it means to be a covenant Christian. This is like the difference between being in love and getting married. We go from feeling a love and gratitude toward Jesus to being tied to Him by covenants. Let's examine these covenants more closely.

Says Hugh Nibley:

> Like the Ten Commandments the promises and covenants of the temple seem strangely negative to the vanity and arrogance of men. The first is obedience, the restraint on the individual's power. The second is restraint on possession of things; the eternal spirit cannot be attached to them—one must be willing to sacrifice. The third puts restraints on personal behavior, it mandates deportment, self-control to make oneself agreeable to all. The fourth is restraint on uncontrolled appetites, desires, and passions, for what could be more crippling on the path of eternal progression than those carnal obsessions which completely take over the mind and body? Finally, the fifth covenant is a limitation on the innate selfishness of the other four—everything you have must be set apart to the everlasting benefit of all.[151]

I remember being nineteen years old and visiting with my bishop. I was upset and crying about something that seemed huge to a nineteen-year-old. I remember saying, "I'm sorry to take up

---

151. Hugh Nibley, "Abraham's Temple Drama," 1999, https://publications.mi.byu.edu/fullscreen/?pub=995.

your time." He replied, "No, no, no. You don't get it. I gave my time to the Lord. So I'm happy to have you take up my time with the Lord's work. My other time is kind of wasted." That was his world view, and it made a big impression on me. Boyd K. Packer used to say that the real strength of the Church is in the covenants made by individual members in the temple, to turn their lives over to God.

Year after year as we continually promise that we will consecrate our time, our talents, all the good things that come to us to God's service, we become different people. We get to a point where we really don't think about our possessions, even our talents, as ours. We are stewards, we take care of these things, but we think about them as belonging to God. This is something that we can start talking about very early on in our families, so that these covenants don't seem surprising. We can articulate the attitude of consecration, not just model it.

Truman Madsen said:

> The earlier you can give your whole heart to covenant-making, the greater can be your expectations of the Lord's blessings. I believe that as long as we say, sometimes dishonestly, "Well, I don't want to make a promise like that; I'm afraid I couldn't keep it," that's only beginning to get ready to think about anticipating, and it does not bring any strength. It's when you make a covenant in the presence of witnesses and even in the sense of the presence of God that the heavens begin to shake for your good when you mean it, and then he promises with absolute conviction and trust in you, "I make the same covenant with you, and I will never break it." Ultimately he asks us to give our all in covenant-making, with the promise that then and only then, he will give his all in our behalf. Every blessing that is possible to receive will remain with us and down the road in greater and greater fulfillment as we live.[152]

---

152. Truman G. Madsen, "Foundations of Temple Worship" (Brigham Young University–Idaho devotional, October 26, 2004), http://www.trumanmadsen.com/media/FoundationsofTempleWorship.pdf.

CHOOSING HOLINESS EVERY DAY

When I received my endowment, I was struck by the covenant which has to do with general deportment, or how we conduct ourselves as Christians. I was really taken back. I thought, "Well, that doesn't even sound like me. It sounds like a much finer person than I am." I turned to my mother and said, "Can I say no?" (I wasn't sure if I said no what might happen! Would I be escorted off the premises?) God bless my mother, because her reply has been a guideline for the rest of my life. She simply said, "Marilyn, say yes and think, 'I'll try.'" I shared this with my children as well. As you covenant with the Lord think, "I'll try. I'll just try. I may not look like that person you seem to be describing, but I'm all in. I want to try."

POWERFUL PRAYER

The fundamental virtue of Christianity is love, or helping others who need help. Once we have taken upon ourselves the name of Christ, we are ready to fulfill the baptismal covenants articulated in Mosiah 18. And we take it a step further as we invoke the power of those covenants in a formal prayer for others. Note is taken of the names of those we love (or even people we don't know) who are in special need, and those names are placed right on the altar of the temple. Then, with a systematic reminder of everything that we have just promised to do and who our center is, even Jesus, we plead with him on behalf of others. My family has been the recipient of those beautiful prayers and have felt the strength of them so that there's no denying that the power of those prayers is real.

We know that among its other functions, the ancient Israelite temple was a place of prayer. When Solomon dedicated the first temple in Jerusalem nearly three millennia ago, he devoted a large portion of his prayer to asking the Lord to harken to the prayers of those who would pray in or toward His holy house: "And hearken thou to the supplication of thy servant, and of thy people Israel, when they shall pray toward this place: and hear thou in heaven thy dwelling place: and when thou hearest, forgive" (1 Kings 8:30 KJV). For this reason, Jews throughout the world still pray facing Jerusalem while those living in Jerusalem face the temple mount or go to the Western or Wailing Wall, one of the few remnants of the temple built by Herod on the site of Solomon's earlier structure.

When we see the Jews rocking in prayer at the Western Wall, they are expressing the same faith that we have when we are in the temple and we approach the Lord in prayer. It's a very holy moment. We approach in the knowledge that however weak we are, we're promised to Him. We're all in, and we know He is too.

Another BYU scholar said, "There is symbolism in raising the hands in prayer. The gesture exposes to God both the breast and the palms of the petitioner."[153] I remember the first time I went to the Episcopalian Church; it was with my girlfriend across the street when she had her first communion. I felt a little nervous about what to do, and her mother said, "Don't worry, it's easy. We kneel to pray, we stand to sing, we sit to listen."

Some religions stand to pray, some religions sit to pray, and others kneel. In our faith we do all three at various times. In reference to this Donald Parry, a BYU scholar, quotes Psalm 24:

> "Who shall ascend into the hill of the Lord? or who shall stand in his holy place? He that hath clean hands, and a pure heart." We expose our hands and our heart to God. "Who hath not lifted up his soul unto vanity nor sworn deceitfully." We show God that our hands and heart are clean. The message of the psalm is clear. To enter the temple, the hill of the Lord, one must have clean hands and a pure heart. In other words, both acts, that are represented by the hands, and thoughts, represented by the heart, must reflect righteousness, along with our lips that utter the prayer. This is probably what the author of Job had in mind when he wrote, "Prepare thine heart and stretch out thine hands toward him." Also in Lamentations it says, "Let us lift up our heart with our hands unto God in the heavens." We have the opportunity to look up as well as look down. We have

---

153. John A. Tvedtnes, in Donald W. Parry and Stephen D. Ricks, eds., *The Temple in Time and Eternity* (Salt Lake City: FARMS, 1999).

the opportunity to pray with our hearts and our hands open to God.[154]

"Endowment" means gift. What is the gift of the endowment? It is power. The temple covenants of obedience, sacrifice, righteous living, chastity, and consecration lay the foundation for a very different kind of life. As a result of living in this sacred space, we are promised power; not the power that politicians seek, but the kind of power than Jesus had. What kind of power are we talking about? Among other things, we are blessed with power to conquer our own weaknesses, power in our marriages and family life, power in our secular activities, and power in the lives of those who come after us.

Power comes from authority, and the endowed person has entered the ranks of those who live, not for themselves, but for God. Like members of the military, their commitment to lay everything on the line for God gives them the power to act in His name. In a very real way, the endowed person has the power to call upon God and have Him respond.

I'm often struck by how little we seem to rely on this great power we have been given. Our temple covenants are there to make our lives richer and more spiritually successful. When we pray or bless someone, we are perfectly justified in calling upon the power of our covenants. We can invoke God's blessing in a special way because we are covenant people.

We sometimes get so caught up in the details that we think there is something "magical" about the symbols and sayings that go with our temple worship. This is not the case. The power of the temple is miraculous, but it is not magic. Everything we do in the temple is meant to lead us to the meaning behind the symbols, sayings, and sacred vestments. What matters is not that we adhere perfectly to every detail, but that we absorb the power of the experience.

> Thus, what matters in such tests for knowledge is not only the name, but also the meanings that stand behind it. Likewise, in our time,

---

154. Ibid.

Elder Dallin H. Oaks has emphasized that in the day of final judgment it will not be enough to merely go through the motions—the essential question is what we have ourselves become during our period of probation. Hugh Nibley further elaborates, explaining that, for the same reason, the saving ordinances, as necessary as they are, in and of themselves are mere forms. They do not exalt us; they merely prepare us to be ready in case we ever become eligible. [155]

SAFE IN GOD'S HANDS

Once we are endowed our lives are in God's hands; we are promised that God will protect us through the power of our covenants until we have finished our work on the earth. It is a remarkable thing to feel that your life is not governed by random chance, but that God's protecting hand is on you. You may not live as long as you hoped, but you will live as long as it is part of God's plan. And you will have peace that those you leave behind are tied to you by the sacred sealing power.

THROUGH THE VEIL

Joseph Campbell cites the Mount of Transfiguration as an example of the great mythological theme of connecting with the divine. A Christian might call it transfiguration, and a Buddhist would call enlightenment, but the aim is the same. We are seeking a state in which we're still on Earth but we are being transfigured into something higher, more refined.

> The freedom to pass back and forth across the world division . . . is only the talent of the Master. He has the power to do that. Jesus is the guide, the way, the vision, and the companion of the return. The disciples are his initiates, not themselves masters of the mystery, yet being introduced to the full experience of the paradox of two worlds in one [a perfect description of the temple. Peter was so frightened by this that he babbled, says Campbell.] Flesh had dissolved before

---

155. Jeffrey M. Bradshaw, "The False and the True 'Keeper of the Gate,'" *Meridian Magazine*, February 4, 2010.

their eyes to reveal the Word as God. They fell upon their faces and when they arose, the door again had closed.[156]

The Mount of Transfiguration is the ultimate temple experience. For a brief period the Apostles had a God's eye view of the world and their place in it. At the end of that "session," it was time to return to regular life. Jesus was back to that person that they dwelt with, lived with, and ate with every day. But their lives were changed; they had been to the top of the mountain and seen Him transfigured, and they were witnesses of it. That transfiguration happened because Jesus touched them. Joseph Smith believed that this was when they were endowed with power.

In Jesus's time, there is evidence that sacred ceremonies were part of the temple worship in Egyptian and Hellenistic temples, but those sacred ceremonies that center on individual salvation were not a part of the Jewish temple. Those truths had been lost. There were only a few things that could be identified as sacred ceremonies—for example, the Day of Atonement where the priest enters the Holy of Holies in atonement for the sins of the people. But the temple of Jesus's day offered only a shadow of the truth that had been given to Adam and Eve.

Members of the New Testament church did not receive sacred ordinances in Herod's temple. As Jesus lamented, that holy house had been defiled by money changers and corruption, but Heber C. Kimball affirmed that the early Apostles received their temple blessings at the hand of the Savior Himself. Joseph Fielding Smith believed that Peter, James, and John received the endowment on the Mount of Transfiguration. The New Testament confirms that some sacred truths taught to the faithful disciples were not appropriate for the world to have. Jesus specifically charged the three Apostles to speak to no one concerning the events on the Mount of Transfiguration. The vision they received there changed everything for the disciples, and it can do the same for us.

---

156. Joseph Campbell and Bill Moyers, *The Power of Myth* (New York: Anchor Books, 1991).

FINDING JESUS IN THE TEMPLE

This is what David O. McKay says about approaching the veil of the temple.

> When you and I can stand at a certain place in the House of God and say conscientiously and truly, I will consecrate my life, my time, my talents to the advancement of the Kingdom of God, then you are prepared through inspiration to enter into God's presence. And that is what you do at the veil, symbolically, the veil is drawn asunder and you enter into God's presence in Celestial Room.[157]

Now, who is the keeper of the gate? As we approach the veil, how will we recognize our Savior? As He appeared to His disciples in the upper room and as He appeared to the Nephites, He made it completely clear how we recognize Him. "Handle me, and see," He says, "for a spirit hath not flesh and bones, as ye see me have" (Luke 24:39, KJV). The keeper of the gate is Jesus Christ. There's no servant there. Elder Neal A. Maxwell wrote:

> God's is a loving and redeeming hand which we are to acknowledge, for "eye hath not seen, nor ear heard." Even His children in the telestial kingdom receive "the glory of the telestial, which surpasses all understanding." He is an exceedingly generous God! One later day, Jesus' *hand* will not give the faithful merely a quick, approving pat on the shoulder. Instead, both Nephi and Mormon tell of the special reunion and welcome at the entrance to His kingdom. There, we are assured, He is "the keeper of the gate and He employeth no servant there." Those who reject Him will miss out on a special personal moment, because, as He laments, He has "stood with *open arms* to receive you." The unfaithful—along with the faithful—might have been "clasped in the arms of Jesus." The imagery of the holy temples and holy scriptures thus blend so beautifully, including things pertaining to sacred moments. This is the grand moment toward which we point and from which we should not be deflected. Hence, those

---

157. David O. McKay, Salt Lake Temple Annex address on September 25, 1941.

who pass through their fiery trials and still acknowledge but trust His hand now will feel the clasp of His arms later![158]

The temple gives us an opportunity to get in touch with our divine center. We commit; we raise our hands and say, "Yes, I will do this," we clothe ourselves symbolically so that we think of ourselves as something different, something higher. The temple opens our minds to rethink who we are, that maybe we're not who the world tells us we are; maybe we're something higher after all.

David A. Bednar says:

The gospel is so much more than a routine checklist of discrete tasks to be performed; Rather, it is a magnificent tapestry of truth, fitly framed and woven together, designed to help us become like our Heavenly Father and the Lord Jesus Christ, even partakers of the divine nature. Truly, we are blinded by looking beyond the mark when this overarching spiritual reality is overshadowed by the cares, concerns, and casualness of the world.[159]

In relation to that, Truman Madsen said:

We say that we go through the temple. I wish that verb could be improved. I wish we could somehow speak of the temple going through us. It's a kind of Mormon activism to talk about temple work. There is a sense, of course, in which it is work: but too rarely do we speak of the temple worship, which can send us back to our work changed.[160]

How shall we bring the power of the temple into our everyday interactions? We can simply lower the barrier and let it come into our kitchens and living rooms and bedrooms. Let it seep into our conversations with our children. For example, you might be having a conversation with a child who's being baptized and take that opportunity to say, "This is just the beginning of the promises you're going to be making to your Heavenly Father. This is the

---

158. Neal A. Maxwell, *Wherefore, Ye Must Press Forward* (Salt Lake City: Deseret Book, 1977).
159. David A. Bednar, "Exceeding Great and Precious Promises," *Ensign*, November 2017.
160. Madsen, "Foundations of Temple Worship."

beginning of a covenant relationship with Him, and He's going to give you your whole life to practice keeping these promises." Help that child develop a sense of the ordinances as the scaffolding of our spiritual lives. By the time the day of endowment comes, a young, covenant Christian will enter the temple ready to take the next step in a relationship that has been building for years.

The Spirit of God comes through the Holy Ghost through the ordinances. As we are reminded in the Book of Mormon, "My beloved brethren, come unto the Lord, the Holy One . . . the keeper of the gate is the Holy One of Israel; and he employeth no servant there" (2 Nephi 9:41). The keeper of the gate of the temple is Jesus Christ Himself. That's where we're headed. That's where every single step in the endowment and the initiatory work is headed. Everything is headed to meeting our Savior.

David O. McKay concludes:

> Do not shut your eyes to the glories of the temple and open them to the mechanics. The mechanics may seem simple and may be performed awkwardly, but the glory is what you need to see.[161]

---

161. McKay, Salt Lake Temple Annex address on September 25, 1941.

Chapter Twenty-Two

CONCLUSION: WHAT WOULD JESUS REALLY DO?

I have a book that's very precious to me, my Franklin Planner, which was a faithful companion that helped me keep my schedule (and my sanity) while raising five children. In 1996, we started a family tradition of beginning the new year by setting individual and family goals, and I have twelve years of those goal-setting sessions recorded in the back of that old leather planner. The year we started, our youngest son, Blake, was just five years old. We all had very ambitious goals, but Blake kept it simple. While the rest of us were going to lose thirty pounds, read the scriptures every day, and go to the temple twice a month, Blake only had one goal: "Go Somewhere." Interestingly, Blake was the only one of us who actually accomplished his goal that year! In fact, after several years of goal setting, one of our sons-in-law voiced what many of us were feeling when he said, "I don't want to do this anymore. I'm tired of reading out loud everything I didn't do last year."

This experience caused me to rethink how I feel about goals. We often set lofty objectives for ourselves. Are they helpful or harmful for us? In this context I would like to talk about the common phrase, "What would Jesus do?" It would seem reasonable that if we could simply model what Jesus would do in any given situation, goal setting would be unnecessary. We would live our best life, simply by modeling His. Yet "What would Jesus do?" is such a common question that I think we've lost the meaning of it a little bit. Can we really know what Jesus would do in any given situation?

For example, on my regular errands, there's a man who begs on the same corner every day. What would Jesus do about that man? I'm not asking what is the smart thing to do, nor am I asking for a statistical estimate of how many beggars are actually in need. I'm not asking any of those questions. I'm just asking what Jesus would do about that particular man. If Jesus were going by that man every day, would He stop? Every day? What would Jesus do in a situation where He saw someone hurting another person? Would He intervene personally? What would Jesus do about the internet: would He post on Facebook? And if He posted, would He talk about politics? (I ran into trouble on that one). He was definitely a social radical in a time when it was life-threatening to be one, yet at other times, He was very neutral on political topics.

For example, in Matthew 25, Jesus is quoted as saying, "When the Son of Man comes in his glory . . . all the nations will be gathered before him, and he will separate the people one from another, as a shepherd separates the sheep from the goats" (Matthew 25:31–32 NIV). He goes on to say that the basis on which He will welcome some nations into His kingdom, and reject others, is the way they treated the needy, marginalized members of society.

> Then the King will say to those on his right, "Come, you who are blessed by my Father; take your inheritance, the kingdom prepared for you since the creation of the world. For I was hungry and you gave me something to eat, I was thirsty and you gave me something to drink, I was a stranger and you invited me in, I needed clothes and you clothed me, I was sick and you looked after me, I was in prison and you came to visit me." (Matthew 25:34–36 NIV)

Even though Jesus gives a very personal response to a political situation, this still could have easily been construed as a criticism of the ruling government. These statements certainly sounded like a threat to the Jewish leaders and were enough to get Him arrested if they had been posted on whatever public forum existed in His day. Yet, when challenged by Pilate and others, He said, "My kingdom is not of this world" (John 18:36 NIV). Jesus was obedient to Rome, He was obedient to the Jewish leaders, but His first loyalty was to His heavenly calling. It is easy to take Him out of the historical setting and expect Him to act in accordance with our modern ideas of correct behavior, but Jesus was unique. He was the first, and best, Christian. The perfect Christian. So as developing Christians we need to look to Him and say, "How can I get a better idea of what Jesus would do?"

My Facebook experience shows me that if I try to pull Jesus into my world and ask if He would choose A or B in a given situation, I'm going to get off track pretty quickly, because we all tend to recreate God in our own image.

For example, during every presidential campaign, people of faith are convinced that God is backing their candidate. Even though our Church leaders send out a letter that says, in effect, that there are good candidates from each political party and we should vote according to our best lights, each of us thinks that God is on our side, and if everybody understood the principles of the gospel properly they would agree with us! But, since I would venture a guess that you have never succeeded in changing anyone's political stance with your Facebook posts, the chance of any of us trying to sway Jesus toward our way of thinking may not be very productive. Instead, it might be more useful to step into Jesus's world and identify some behaviors that He repeatedly displayed in response to His daily challenges. By placing His actions in context, we might get a better sense of

> *Christ's victory over death ended the human predicament. Now there are only personal predicaments, and from these too we may be rescued by following the teachings of him who rescued us from general extinction.*
>
> —Neal A. Maxwell

what He was like. I may not be able to categorically state what Jesus would do in my world, but I can clearly identify things He did every day in His world, and then try to bring more of those behaviors into my life.

WHAT JESUS ACTUALLY DID EVERY DAY

Here are five behaviors that I can state with certainty that Jesus manifested in His life every day when He walked the earth. While He may not have set goals, certain priorities clearly guided His daily actions, and these are some that stand out for me.

1. Focus on the individual first.
2. Bring sacred meaning into daily tasks.
3. Respond to specific needs as they arise.
4. Heal, bless, and teach in any setting.
5. Seek and surrender to God's will.

I. Focus on the Individual

Whether Jesus was talking to a group (as in the Sermon on the Mount) or to one follower (such as Nicodemus), He always spoke directly, person to person. "You are the salt of the earth." "You are the light of the world." "Verily I say unto you." (Matthew 5:13, 14, 18 NIV, KJV) "Ye must be born again." (John 3:7 KJV). He didn't speak in the third person. (If we change the phrase to "People are the light of the world," it stops sounding like Jesus and sounds more like a Broadway tune.) This very personal address is more than a rhetorical style. He really is speaking to each of us, one person at a time, and that is why His words are at once both startling and inspiring.

When we find ourselves speaking "group-speak" we are moving away from Jesus's voice. It's hard to imagine Him saying, *This isn't personal, it's just policy,* or *The organization needs to make a change.* He knew that every policy is personal when it affects lives. Any time we stop thinking about one person at a time and start thinking about advancing the group, or protecting the organization, whatever it is, we are moving in a dangerous direction. When faced with choices that affect people, we can generally assume that Jesus would focus on the individual. That is a good guideline; it helps us lean the right direction.

Recently I heard a dad tell about going over to the church late in the evening to play a little basketball with his fourteen-year-old son. Around ten o'clock a meeting of the stake leaders adjourned, and one of the council members came into the gym and found them still playing ball. He spoke to them pretty sharply, telling them to shut down the game because they needed to close the building. They apologized and began to pack up, but just a minute later the stake president came into the gym, greeted them, and asked if he could join in the game for a few minutes. He took off his suit coat and played ball with them for about twenty minutes. Then they all said goodnight and left. This dad described the impact this brief interaction with the stake president had on his son, and how, four years later, when the stake president came to set him apart for his mission, they still had this connection that had been formed that night. That is what happens when a Christian is striving to put the individual before the policy; personal connections are made that can change lives.

2. Bring Sacred Meaning into Daily Tasks

One of the things we have record of Jesus doing a lot is eating; it's actually one of the few areas where I can really relate to Him! We follow Him going to meals, people inviting Him to dinner, and (in the case of Zaccheus) Jesus inviting Himself to dinner. We even see Him prepare food for others. His very first miracle was performed at a wedding reception, providing the refreshments, and in His very last recorded experiences with His disciples they were eating together, just before His death and then after His Resurrection. Jesus worked with His hands, first with His father who was in construction, and then later with His disciples. He went fishing with them and had some record catches. (My father would be happy about that.) He did everyday kinds of things and seemed to take great relish in them, and He did them better than anyone.

Jesus brought a balance to everyday tasks. He was not an ascetic, nor did He over-indulge; He modeled the perfect balance. Though He fasted, He also feasted. Though He withdrew in prayer and contemplation, He also prepared lunch for thousands of people. He didn't delegate the mundane tasks to others, He engaged in them and brought them into the realm of the sacred, as in the day when He turned the simple task of drawing water from a well into a life changing experience for a lost and lonely woman.

How can we bring sacred meaning into our daily tasks? I remember a time when my mother let me skip a day of high school and help her make jam. We had a few flats of strawberries, and together we worked until we had turned them into several gleaming jars of rich red jam (one of the most satisfying sights in the life of any cook.) And because this was my mom, there was more than just the task at hand, because Mom was always thinking. The conversations we had that day were deep and wide ranging, from favorite books, to spiritual theories, to whatever came into her bright, open mind.

At one point, I caught her gazing thoughtfully at me, in her characteristic cooking pose, with one hand on her hip and the wooden spoon stirring mechanically. As her gray-blue eyes looked deep into mine, she said, "You know, Marilyn, we haven't always been mother and daughter. At one point, before we came to this earth, we were friends, and I feel that we've known and loved each other a long time." I can go back to that moment, nearly fifty years ago, and feel what I felt then, how time slipped away and we were just two spirits with an eternal bond, looking across the cooking island and the vast expanse of eternity at each other. I knew what she said was true, and I felt honored and loved and special in a way I had never felt before. As is often said, "We are not human beings on a spiritual journey. We are spiritual beings on a human journey."[162] My mother created a moment when I understood that, and in that way she was doing just what Jesus would have done. If you went fishing, ate dinner,

---

162. Origin unknown, often attributed to Pierre Teilhard de Chardin.

went for a walk, or made jam with Jesus, something miraculous and sweet would happen.

3. Respond to Specific Needs as They Arise

In life it can be hard to respond to what is happening in the moment rather than responding to what has happened in the past or what might happen in the future. Jesus had an uncanny ability to zone in on the present moment and respond to what was really needed. One of the great examples is the exchange He had with the rich young ruler in Matthew 19, where He did not allow the clever conversation to cover what was really going on. He heard what the young man said, but more importantly, He saw what the young man needed, and spoke to that need. (It was more than a little painful for that young man, who went away sorrowing because he wasn't ready to hear truth instead of flattery.) Another day, on the way to perform a great miracle, He was literally stopped in His tracks by the touch of a suffering woman, and stayed long enough to meet her need, answering a prayer of twelve years. Then, He moved on toward His destination.

> *Come to him. He turns no penitent one away. Would you, if you had paid so much in suffering? Would you ever give up? All the doors that are locked against the Lord are locked by us.*
> —*Truman G. Madsen*

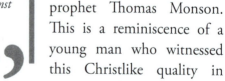

Some people have a gift for responding to the needs of others, right when the need is greatest, and one of the foremost examples was our late prophet Thomas Monson. This is a reminiscence of a young man who witnessed this Christlike quality in action. While serving in Zimbabwe in the 1970s, this young elder seldom saw any leaders, as Africa was only one mission, and the distance from their town to the mission home was as far as traveling from Tijuana, Mexico, to Calgary, Canada! So when this little district of elders, who could go months without seeing the mission president, heard that an Apostle was coming to visit them, they were elated. And they were in for a surprise.

> Our small district of 8 missionaries was sitting in a semi-circle when Elder Thomas Monson entered the room, accompanied by our beloved Mission President, Robert P. Thorn. . . .
>
> After a song, prayer and some pleasantries, Elder Monson, then just 48 years old, started at one end of the line of missionaries and began asking some very pointed questions, customized by inspiration to fit the needs of each individual recipient. I was amazed to note that each question was precisely what each respective missionary was struggling with in his own personal ministry. . . .
>
> The questions went something like this. "Elder, have you told your companion that you love him?" This was the only missionary in the room struggling with his relationship with his companion. I was impressed. As the District Leader of this isolated district of elders serving in the middle of Africa, I was privy to some confidential information due to my private interviews and exchanges with the elders.
>
> A different question would then be asked to the next missionary: "Elder, are you memorizing the lessons?" This was the only elder in the room who refused to try to memorize the lessons, which was standard procedure in those days. "Elder, are you exercising daily?" Then, "Elder, are you reading the scriptures every day?" Followed by, "Elder are you saying your personal prayers every day?" This went on and on, with a little sermon and some loving advice shared by Elder Monson with each missionary after their honest and sincere answers to his queries. No two questions were the same. Each question was tailor fit for the recipient, and to the best of my recollection, each question dealt with the single most important issue that the particular missionary was struggling to overcome or master.
>
> It was an electrifying experience to observe first hand an Apostle of the Lord walk into a room filled with missionaries he did not know, look them each in the eye, and then know exactly, through the Holy Ghost, with no hesitation whatsoever, the particular challenge that each respective missionary was struggling with and how to best encourage them to overcome their unique challenges. It was

an inspiring meeting never to be forgotten. I still recall it as if it was yesterday.[163]

4. Meeting Both Physical and Spiritual Needs

Because I like to feed people, I love that Jesus also liked to feed people. He understood that it is hard to respond to the Spirit when your belly is empty. After a long session teaching a group of several thousand, Jesus was upset that the Apostles weren't worried about the people being hungry. He created a miracle to meet an urgent need, just as He did in His very first miracle where the wedding guests ran out of wine. (We know Jesus wasn't Mormon, but He shared at least one cultural trait with us; He was worried about the refreshments!) It was important to Him that people were fed, not just spiritually but also physically. The wine He made was the best wine, and I'll bet the fish and loaves luncheon was delicious.

> *If you want to be happy, you have to let go of the part of you that wants to create melodrama. This is the part that thinks there's a reason not to be happy. You have to transcend the personal, and as you do, you will naturally awaken to the higher aspects of your being. In the end, enjoying life's experiences is the only rational thing to do.*
>
> —*Michael Singer*

We should never, ever think that any task is too mundane for us as followers of Jesus. He was willing to get His hands dirty, and we should be too. I've told elsewhere the story of going back to the church alone with Craig one night after an evening session of stake conference. As a high council member, his responsibility was to have the building ready for the meetings, and there had been hundreds of people there that night. As we were having dinner after the session, he began to worry, so we went back together, opened the building, and found the restrooms in less than pristine condition! We got to work cleaning

---

163. Mark Albright, "An Unforgettable Meeting in Africa with a Young Elder Thomas S. Monson," *Meridian Magazine,* January 7, 2018, https://ldsmag.com/an-unforgettable-meeting-in-africa-with-a-young-elder-thomas-s-monson.

them. At one point I wandered into the men's room (something I don't usually do, let me hasten to say) and there was my husband, on his knees in his suit, scrubbing the toilets. I don't remember when I have felt such a rush of love for him, and at the same time an overwhelming sense of gratitude for a Church that teaches us that we are never above cleaning the toilets that our brothers and sisters have used. Jesus would have done it, and done it well.

5. Heal, Bless, and Teach

Thomas Monson said:

> There are many out there who plead and pray for help. There are those who are discouraged, those who are beset by poor health and challenges of life which leave them in despair. I've always believed in the truth of the words, "God's sweetest blessings always go by hands that serve him here below." Let us have ready hands, clean hands, and willing hands, that we may participate in providing what our Heavenly Father would have others receive from Him.[164]

The question "What would Jesus do?" has special relevance to our busy lives, because He was constantly forced to prioritize, just as we are. Jesus couldn't be everywhere, and He couldn't do everything, so He had to use every moment wisely, just as we do. Walking in the light of the Spirit, under the direction of His Heavenly Father, He was very aware of what needed to be done and when. When was it time to heal someone, feed someone, or bless someone? When was it time to just teach truth, no matter how hard it was to hear? Jesus walked in a flow of spiritual power that helped Him squeeze the most out of every moment. We all want that.

That takes me back to my original, rather flippant question (and I apologize if it is irreverent): Would Jesus be political? What would He post on Facebook? I think that we get lost on that kind of debate because the question is wrong. Jesus couldn't be described as "political." Whether it was on the internet or in person, Jesus would simply speak truth wherever He was. We may think we are doing

---

164. Thomas S. Monson, "Priesthood Power," *Ensign*, November 1999.

the same thing when we make blanket statements that cause division, but we are not. Let's be honest, we all have our opinions, and in contrast, we have the things that we *know are true*. If we set our opinions and prejudices aside, and instead concentrate on the things that we know are true—gospel truths, eternal truths—we will not become embroiled in the kind of acrimonious wrangling that passes for social discourse these days. The good news of the gospel, the message of love and of Christ's grace, is not offensive to other believers; those truths don't cause division among good people. These kinds of statements cause joy when they are shared. Jesus was very aware in each situation of what He was called upon to do. We are not called upon to pronounce judgement on our fellow believers because they don't think like we do. We are called upon to love and uplift.

During high school I worked a summer in a gift shop. One day a woman came into the shop, obviously upset and, since we were alone, I engaged her in conversation. It turned out that she was a pediatric nurse and had just finished a shift at the hospital where a little child in her care had died. She questioned how God could allow this to happen. Why did this little child have to suffer? I certainly didn't have the whole answer, but I shared with her what I had been taught. I told her that in my faith, we believe that all children who die before the age of accountability, or around eight years old, went directly back into God's arms in the celestial world. There was nothing but joy and happiness ahead for that little spirit, she had nothing to prove on earth and her test was over. She just needed a body, and she could go home to God.

Well, it was a long time ago, and I don't remember the exact words, but I do remember how much I hoped that this one nugget of truth would comfort her. And it did. She was visibly more peaceful after our little talk. I can't even remember if I told her what faith I believed in. I just taught her something true, and it brought peace to her. That experience has guided me many times, giving me the courage to just say a true thing, even if it seems out of context. The truth just sounds true, and it resonates with a struggling spirit, even if we are sharing just a little bit of a greater picture. I've never had anyone be offended by that kind of sharing, and I have been the recipient of similar gifts, as people of other faiths have shared great spiritual truths with me as well. It is something I believe Jesus is asking us to do for each other.

As our family has faced a life-threatening disease over the last few years, we have learned the great power of simply praying for and blessing others. Craig has received blessings that have sustained us through the worst days and built our faith as they have proven to be prophetic. There are some things that can't be fixed, but they can certainly be borne more easily when others are praying with us. That is a beautiful thing that I think we can learn from Jesus as He interacts with others. He prays with people, and He lets them hear Him pray for them. As the Nephites testified, "No one can conceive of the joy which filled our souls at the time we heard him pray for us unto the Father" (3 Nephi 17:17).

We can all take more opportunities to heal, bless, and teach. We can turn small moments into bigger ones as we stop to say a prayer for someone, then share that prayer with them via text or email. Or as we quietly teach a truth that can be a comfort to another person, no matter what their faith might be. And of course, as we lay our loving hands on others and serve them.

One missionary told how embarrassed she was when they invited a bright, sophisticated investigator to church for the first time. It was a particularly noisy meeting, with crying babies and the usual commotion in a ward full of young families. Later, when she asked (with some trepidation) if the visitor had enjoyed the meeting the woman responded, "I loved it. I was so moved by all the expressions of affection between family members during the meeting." Instead of being distracted by crying children, this woman was moved while watching a father rubbing a son's back, a daughter with her arm around her mother, and grandparents rocking grandchildren on their laps: these may seem commonplace moments to us, but they are a vital part of a healing, blessing, teaching environment.

Jesus modeled all those behaviors and more. He touched everyone He met in some way, physically as well as spiritually. We can try to do more of this.

6. Seek and Surrender to God's Will

Jesus's life was bookended and filled with seeking and following His Father's will. The first recorded words of Jesus are spoken to His parents: "Wist ye not that I must be about my Father's business?" (Luke 2:49 KJV). One of the last things He ever said was, "Father, not my will, but thine be done," and then, "Into thy hands I commend my spirit" (Luke 22:42 and 23:46 KJV). Learning to seek and surrender to the will of God is maybe one of the greatest lessons He modeled in His short life.

A dear friend shared a life-changing experience that taught her more about this facet of the life of Christ:

> On a trip to Vermont to see the colors, I had a little brush with asphalt, blew up my bicycle going down a hill, and broke seven ribs (five in two places) punctured a lung, injured my rotator cuff, and my hip. I was in the ICU for five days, and the hospital for eight. After all of that, I couldn't go home, because I couldn't fly. So my husband drove me to my daughter's house, and for another month I was totally dependent on someone else. I could not get out of the chair alone, I couldn't do anything for myself. I couldn't get a shirt off or on. It was shocking for me, because my whole life, I have been so independent. I have made a list every day of what I was to do the next day, almost by the hour, and the next day, I just got up and did it! Now, all I could do was just lay there and think.
>
> And as I lay there, I began to wonder if Jesus made lists, and if He pushed Himself as hard as I had always pushed myself. I finally decided that He just worried about doing the will

The joyful news for anyone who desires to be rid of the consequences of past poor choices is that the Lord sees weaknesses differently than He does rebellion. Whereas the Lord warns that unrepented rebellion will bring punishment, when the Lord speaks of weaknesses, it is always with mercy.

—*Richard G. Scott*

of His father. Mosiah 3:19 is a now favorite scripture of mine: "For the natural man is an enemy to God, and has been from the fall of Adam, and will be, forever and ever, unless he yields to the enticings of the Holy Spirit, and putteth off the natural man and becometh a saint through the atonement of Christ the Lord, and becometh as a child, submissive, meek, humble, patient, full of love, willing to submit to all things which the Lord seeth fit to inflict upon him, even as a child doth submit to his father."

In light of that experience, I just decided that for this year, rather than setting a lot of goals, I was just going to concentrate on becoming as a little child spiritually in character. Of course, I don't want to go back to being so dependent physically, but I have really thought a lot about this and thinking about how to yield to the enticing of the Spirit as you make a to-do list. And being dependent on Christ and His inspiration for everything. I know that I have to be full of love, because if you're full of love, no matter how hard you're squeezed or pushed or hurt, only love comes out. I know that this is only possible through the Atonement of Jesus Christ, His enabling power. And so that is my new goal.[165]

Boyd K. Packer said:

I cannot with composure tell you how I feel about the Atonement. It touches the deepest emotion of gratitude and obligation. My soul reaches after Him who wrought it, this Christ, our Savior of whom I am a witness. I testify of Him. He is our Lord, our Redeemer, our advocate with the Father. He ransomed us with His blood. Humbly I lay claim upon the atonement of Christ. I find no shame in kneeling down in worship of our Father and His son. For agency is mine and this I choose to do.[166]

Each year as we set our goals and our objectives, we have a choice of what to make the year like. And looking back on all those goal-setting sessions, I realize that we were putting the cart before the horse, as it were, and that is why at the end of each year the cart hadn't moved! If we put Jesus first and let goals and objectives follow,

---

165. Sherry Weeks, Rancho Santa Fe, California. Personal recollection.
166. Boyd K. Packer, "Atonement, Agency, Accountability," *Ensign*, May 2013.

there will be a power that propels our actions and makes them truly meaningful. We can open our hearts and ask Jesus, "What would You do, and if I can't do exactly that, can you help me get pretty close?" Our lives will be different if we "lay claim on the Atonement of Christ" rather than just strive after our own objectives.

> *When the Savior knows you truly want to reach up to Him—when He can feel that the greatest desire of your heart is to draw His power into your life—you will be led by the Holy Ghost to know exactly what you should do.*
> —*Russell M. Nelson*

As we reverently ask what Jesus might do, the things that are fleeting and unimportant will be seen in their perspective. We'll understand that there's no problem or policy more important than the person it involves. We'll see that there's no situation so sorrowful that some joy and hope cannot be part of it. We'll see that there's no relationship that can't be improved and made less painful by His healing grace and power. As Tennyson says, "the larger heart, the kindlier hand" emerges as we look toward Jesus.[167] Though we may not always know what He would do in our setting, we can, for a moment, place ourselves in His, and imitate one of the behaviors He modeled for us. That, I believe, is a safe place to start, and the best reason in the world for becoming a passionate student of the New Testament.

---

167. Alfred, Lord Tennyson, "Ring Out, Wild Bells," from *In Memoriam*, 1850.

Index

A

adjacent possible 194–98, 206
Alma 20, 101, 112, 151, 227
angels 18, 26, 28, 62, 65, 70, 76, 86–87,
     101–4, 110–11, 126, 133–34,
     137–38, 167, 173, 210, 214, 218,
     228, 231, 243, 246
Anointed One 9
anointing 2, 9–10, 119, 123–24, 225,
     238, 240–41, 248
Atonement 16–17, 21, 39, 70–71, 95,
     111, 121, 132, 135, 140, 150, 224,
     256, 273–74

B

baptism 44, 65, 106–16, 149, 159, 178,
     187, 221, 226, 240, 242
baptismal covenant 112, 114, 224
bar mitzvah 2, 22
birth 13–24, 28, 44, 65, 93, 106, 109–11,
     116, 132–33, 143, 157, 193
born again 18, 107, 109, 114–17, 232,
     263
branding 41–42, 45, 51
breath of life 110, 152

C

chiasmus 45–47, 62
cognitive dissonance 165–67, 171, 176
covenant 60, 86–87, 94, 97, 101–2,
     108, 111–16, 127–30, 169, 190,
     224–25, 237–38, 246, 248,
     250–55, 259
Crucifixion 106, 119, 120, 132, 134,
     138, 159, 166, 217, 238

D

death 1, 6, 8, 11, 16, 20, 22, 24, 27,
     42–43, 50, 62–63, 70, 96–98,
     109, 112, 119, 125, 128, 132, 135,
     137–41, 144–55, 174, 177, 200,
     218, 224, 234, 239–40, 262, 264
diaspora 62
diversity 185–86, 196, 199, 201–7
dramatic irony 173, 245

E

endowment 225, 237, 240, 242–56, 259
exorcism 46, 148

F

Fall of Adam 23–24
fountain of youth 146–47

G

Gabriel 25–26, 65
Gentiles 15, 46–48, 62–63, 156, 172,
     175, 177–78, 183–85, 193, 197
Gethsemane 70, 132–36, 210
God-fearers 172, 184
good Samaritan 63, 72–73
grace 19, 36, 48, 60, 65, 81, 112, 116,
     124, 152, 164, 171, 192, 206–7,
     215, 224–25, 270, 274
guardian angels 214

H

holiness 53–54, 58, 60, 81, 136
Holy Spirit 11–12, 65, 67, 124, 159,
     170–71, 175, 216, 232, 273

I

immaculate conception 22–23
initiatory ordinances 240
intercalation 44
Isis and Horus 15

J

Jairus 7, 45–47, 50, 148
John the Baptist 11, 178
Joseph Smith 11, 24, 87, 94–95, 101, 109,
     143, 149, 176–77, 182, 187–90,
     207, 240–41, 246–49, 256

L

Last Supper 118–30, 175
lawful 4, 55–60
law of Moses 4, 7
Lazarus 119, 148
Lord's Prayer 84, 91

M

manna 9, 66, 82
Markan sandwich 44, 50
Mary and Martha 119, 123, 225
Mary, mother of Jesus 14–15, 20,
 22–30, 65, 110, 170
meditation 85, 89, 91, 130, 152, 237
Messiah 2, 9–11, 25, 94, 98, 108, 174
midrashim 3
ministering 59, 104, 158, 164, 185,
 216–32
miracle 2, 6–7, 9, 22–23, 50, 80, 95–97,
 100–104, 110, 117, 143, 221,
 264, 266, 268, 274
motif 48, 63, 168, 217, 245

N

nativity 16
Nephi 16–19, 29, 110, 228, 257
Nephites 87, 216–17, 219–20, 223–24,
 226, 238, 257, 271

O

oil 73, 121–22

P

parable of the talents 156, 209
Passover 108, 119
peace 19, 46–47, 80, 82, 101, 124–26,
 139, 141, 143, 146, 152, 161, 166,
 176, 191–92, 225, 227, 255, 270
pericope 45
Pharisees 55–56, 58, 109, 183, 186, 196
polygamy 176–78, 203
prayer 49, 66–67, 71, 76, 78–92, 98–99,
 126–30, 170, 173, 191–92, 211,

215, 237–38, 247, 252–53,
 265–67, 271
proprioception 38, 144
proselytes 184

R

rabbi 2–5, 9, 36, 54–56, 88, 104
Resurrection 22, 29, 62, 70, 77, 109,
 112, 142–43, 146–54, 159, 166,
 185, 191, 217, 238, 240, 264

S

Sabbath 4, 52–60, 85, 93, 119
sacrament 67, 113, 116, 122, 124,
 129–30, 152, 162, 190, 199, 221,
 225, 237, 242
sealing 205, 225, 240, 255
Sermon on the Mount 31–34, 38–40,
 263
special witness 155, 157, 159–60, 163
spiritual gifts 156, 194, 207, 209, 211
symbolism 7, 16, 20, 28–29, 47, 62–63,
 106–10, 124, 189–90, 235, 237,
 240, 245, 248, 253–54, 257–58
synagogue 5, 45–48, 55–56, 59, 93, 107,
 172
synapses 106–7, 110, 144

T

Talmud 2–3
temple 8, 22, 62, 86, 123–24, 127–28,
 189–90, 203–4, 217, 225, 234–60
Torah 4, 55, 93, 104, 174, 184
tree of life 4, 16–17, 19, 29, 110, 125

W

washing of feet 119–24
way, the 185–86, 255
weakness 136, 161, 198, 214–15,
 221–22
weaknesses 39, 162, 179, 211–12,
 214–15, 221–22, 254, 272
wedding in Cana 22, 27, 94

About the Author

Marilyn Green Faulkner likes to read and talk about books. She earned a BA in humanities and an MA in literature and sneaks away to Cambridge or Oxford University every summer for further study. For seven years, she wrote a monthly column on the classics for *Meridian Magazine*. Her first book, *Back to the Best Books: How the Classics Can Change Your Life*, was a finalist for nonfiction indie book of the year in 2010. As senior content creator for FMG Suite (a digital marketing company), she wrote articles and videos on financial marketing.

Marilyn served an LDS mission in Japan, has taught Seminary classes, and has been a presenter at the BYU Women's Conference and at BYU Education Week. For the last five years, Marilyn has taught a scripture course in the Del Mar California Stake. The outgrowth of that experience has been this series of scripture study guides: *The User-Friendly Book of Mormon*, *The User-Friendly Old Testament*, and now *The User-Friendly New Testament*.

Marilyn and her husband, Craig, are the parents of five children and a growing group of grandchildren. They live in Rancho Santa Fe, California, with their dogs, Frankie and Jonny.

Videos and recordings of class lessons, along with other information, are available on Marilyn's website: marilyngreenfaulkner.com.

Scan to visit

www.marilyngreenfaulkner.com